e · Det røde · 大姨妈 · La regla · Эти дни · Chico

Ketchup · Il marchese · Tante Rad... ...es (e

eles dias · 女の子の日 · 例... e A

ivati i parent · Damedage · 來... ...spues

e · Les équerres · E'arrivato Giorgio · Det Røde Hav

мия · 小紅 · Time of the month · Rote Welle · C'es

个 · Cosas de Niñas · Красный день календар

te Woche · Le Beaujolais nouveau est arrivé · Son

el Bistec · Красный день календаря · 血祭...

Les anglais ont débarqué dans ma culotte · Semafor

сти (из Краснодара) · Vermelho · ブルーデイ

periodo del mese · Rødbedeskede · m到 · La Color...

Auf der roten Welle surfen · Les carottes sont cuite

Tus diablos · Красные Жигули · De Visita · 血...

Le petit clown qui saigne du nez · Settimana rossa

Coisas de mulher · ペリー来航 · Having the painte...

大姨妈 · La luna · Месики · Sinal vermelho · ...

travaux · Ho le inondazioni · 倒霉 · Semaforo Rojo

e Meer stechen · Faire du boudin · Le mie cose · D...

алендаря · Estar de bode · お客さん · Tomatensa...

PERIODS
GONE PUBLIC

PERIODS

GONE PUBLIC

TAKING A STAND FOR
MENSTRUAL EQUITY

JENNIFER WEISS-WOLF

Arcade Publishing • New York

First Edition

Arcade Publishing books may be purchased in bulk at special discounts for sales promotion, corporate gifts, fund-raising, or educational purposes. Special editions can also be created to specifications. For details, contact the Special Sales Department, Arcade Publishing, 307 West 36th Street, 11th Floor, New York, NY 10018 or arcade@skyhorsepublishing.com.

Arcade Publishing® is a registered trademark of Skyhorse Publishing, Inc.®, a Delaware corporation.

Visit our website at www.arcadepub.com.

10 9 8 7 6 5 4 3 2

Library of Congress Cataloging-in-Publication Data is available on file.

Cover design by Erin Seaward-Hiatt

Print ISBN: 978-1-62872-797-5
Ebook ISBN: 978-1-62872-798-2

Printed in the United States of America

For
Annie
my intuition

Nathaniel, Rebecca, and Sarah
my inspiration

Alan
my everything

CONTENTS

iNTRODUCTiON

IF YOU'RE PICKING UP A book called *Periods Gone Public*, perhaps you're among those who don't find the topic of menstruation to be awkward, uncomfortable, or a source of total embarrassment. Welcome to the club. Clearly, I'm not one who shies away from it either. And given how this particular bodily function has been relegated to millennia of stigma and shame, mockery and marginalization, it turns out there's a whole lot that many of us have been waiting and wanting to say out loud about it.

I'm actually a bit of a latecomer to the conversation myself. It wasn't that I previously avoided the subject or had any particular aversion to it. As a mom of three teens, I'm open and pragmatic about everything they need to know. With friends, I am quick to share a laugh or commiserate over a menstrual mishap. I can be counted on to gladly lend or borrow a tampon when the moment calls for it. I'm fine with using anatomically correct terminology, not so easy to embarrass, and rarely resort to cutesy code like "My friend is in town. . . ." (Though, since writing this book, I've learned that there are around five thousand such euphemisms for menstruation used around the world, many quite clever.[1] I rather enjoyed tapping them as chapter titles.)

But periods as a matter of political discourse? The driver of a policy agenda? Period feminism? Quite honestly, these were not ideas I'd ever seriously entertained or even imagined.

That changed on January 1, 2015. As the New Year dawned, I felt in need of extra momentum, aiming for as much potential and purpose as I could muster. It's an annual rite for me to ring in the year in Brooklyn with a cohort of friends (and hundreds of others) crazy enough to take a dip in the icy Atlantic Ocean. The Coney Island Polar Bear Club New Year's Day swim is one of New York City's finest traditions—a raucous scene and freezing cold mishmash of quirkily costumed, skin-baring revelers. When asked by a local reporter about why one would participate in such a thing, my friend Peggy's answer hit the nail on the head: "The camaraderie is almost inexplicable. Our group runs into the ocean holding hands. People think it's crazy. And maybe it is. But it's actually a very proactive, symbolic way to set an intention and direction for the remaining 364 days of the year. Like grabbing the year by the hand and saying, 'This is how we're gonna do this.'"

We took the plunge that year doing our very best Wonder Woman impersonations, four middle-aged women decked out in matching star-spangled swimsuits, wrist cuffs, and capes. I've always secretly revered Wonder Woman. (True fact: I hyphenated my last name when I got married so I could claim the initials "WW.") The superhero theme was absolutely part of the adrenaline-driven sprint into the sea that Peggy described. We shivered, even shimmered after a full body dousing with golden glitter, courtesy of a pack of urban mermaids in drag whose towels were parked next to ours on the beach.

Later in the day, once I thawed out and shook off all the sand and glitter—though the sparkle never completely dissipates—I logged on to Facebook to share my glorious photos. (Giving away my age here, I realize; not Snapchat, not Instagram. Facebook.) And that was when I saw the post in my newsfeed. An acquaintance, a local mom of two teenage girls, announced her family's drive to collect donations of tampons and pads for the low-income patrons of our community food pantry. Their project was aptly, simply named, "Girls Helping Girls. Period."

I was immediately captivated and curious—and honestly, even mildly ashamed that I'd never, ever considered this before. A self-aware, self-professed feminist, I've marched on Washington over the decades for women's rights, volunteered as a rape crisis advocate and an abortion clinic escort, and worked professionally as a lawyer and writer for social justice organizations all of my adult life. How had I managed to completely overlook this most basic issue? If periods could be a hassle for me, someone with the means to have a fully stocked supply of tampons, it was nakedly, painfully obvious that for those who are poor, or young, or otherwise vulnerable, menstruation could easily pose a real obstacle and problem.

I had to know more. I spent the rest of New Year's Day and well into the night obsessively scouring the Internet to see what more I could find. Here's what my Google search on the first day of 2015 turned up:

It took some digging, but there was indeed reporting about the lack of access to menstrual products and adequate hygiene facilities in countries like India, Nepal, Kenya, Uganda, Bangladesh, and other places—enough so that it had been recognized as a public health and human rights issue by the United Nations and the World Health Organization.[2] The key culprits named included a combination of extreme poverty, lack of health education and sanitation, and an enduring culture of taboo and shame. Stories of creative enterprise and innovation to tackle this problem were prevalent, too.

Coverage of menstrual access issues for the poor in the United States was minimal, though there was one story that stood out. A few months prior, in August 2014, the *Guardian* published one of the first mainstream articles to explore the feasibility of subsidized or tax-exempt menstrual products, "The Case for Free Tampons," by Brooklyn-based author and columnist Jessica Valenti. She wrote: "Menstrual care is health care, and should be treated as such. But much in the same way insurance coverage or subsidies for birth control are mocked or met with outrage, the idea of women even getting small tax breaks for menstrual products provokes incredulousness because some people lack an incredible amount of empathy . . . and because it has something to do with vaginas. Affordable access to sanitary products is rarely talked about outside of [nonprofit organizations]—and when it is, it's with shame or derision."[3] That sounded right along the lines of what I was starting to think, too.

A few more clicks revealed that her ideas had triggered a barrage of vitriol. And, yes, it clearly had something to do with vaginas. Outraged conservatives fired back across the Internet. Among them, former *Breitbart* editor Milo Yiannopoulos (the same right-wing provocateur who was later permanently banned from Twitter in 2016 for unleashing an abusive tweet-storm at actress Leslie Jones, lost a major book deal in early 2017 for prattling approvingly about pedophilia, and proudly sports T-shirts with phrases like *Feminism is Cancer*) derided Valenti's column as, "[a] volley of provocation, misandry, and attention-seeking from the far-left in a political atmosphere that rewards women . . . for demanding MORE FREE THINGS."[4] Valenti captured some of the many hundreds of crude responses on Storify, perhaps most neatly summarized by this tweet: "If you're so worried abt tampon availability, maybe U need 2 stick a few fingers in UR you-know-what to stem the bleeding." (Yeah, we-know-what. I guess that's kind of the point.)

As for any systematic attention to the scope of this issue as a domestic matter? None at all. What I unearthed amounted only to an occasional, singular blog post or lone call for donations by a local shelter or food pantry. Nothing that attempted to narrate, quantify, or formally document the potential problem, or—more disappointingly—even sought to identify or acknowledge it as one.

All of this was enough to consume my every waking thought for several more days. I kept furiously researching and reading. I met with the family who created "Girls Helping Girls. Period." to learn more about the project and signed on to host a donation drive. And as the thoughts continued to churn through my head, I channeled them into an essay detailing my initial response along with some ideas and inspiration. I shared it, cold, with a *New York Times* columnist whom I read regularly and admired from afar, Nicholas Kristof. He writes frequently about the global plight of women and had even briefly covered menstruation in his books, *Half the Sky: Turning Oppression into Opportunity for Women Worldwide* and *A Path Appears: Transforming Lives, Creating Opportunity*. Much to my surprise, I heard back quickly, and he offered to publish my piece.

During the months that followed, my enthusiasm swelled to the point of minor obsession. Truly, this issue struck me as one of the most vital outlets for my energy and skills—as a writer, lawyer, policy wonk, feminist, even as a mother. By day, my job at the Brennan Center for Justice, a think tank affiliated with New York University School of Law, had me contemplating the mechanics of achieving legal and democratic change in America. After hours, I kept reflecting on menstruation, placing it squarely in the context of social justice, civic participation, and gender equity. Before long, I began to connect with journalists, lawmakers, activists, and entrepreneurs, and found myself entrenched in a growing global network of people who were equally intrigued and motivated by the power of periods.

And so began the journey—from a freezing cold Wonder Woman on the beach, to the inauguration of what NPR came to call "The Year of the Period." (One year later, almost to the minute, NPR made this declaration on New Year's Eve, December 31, 2015.)

Today the landscape looks remarkably different. We've gone from zero to sixty, periods as a whisper or insult to the initiation of a full-blown, ready-for-prime-time menstrual movement—the story of which is detailed throughout this book. And thus unlocking a radical secret: half the population menstruates! There really are ways to address periods that are practical, proactive, and even political. In so doing, somehow we have achieved a level of discourse that has otherwise eluded society for nearly all of time. Periods have indeed gone public.

And with that, so too has my own story crystallized. I now believe unequivocally in the sheer sway of menstruation as a mobilizing force, so much so it has turned my world upside down. I have spent the last few years juggling my responsibilities at work and home with crisscrossing the globe to discuss menstruation with lawmakers and innovators, testify before legislatures, brief reporters and editors, speak at universities, and shout into megaphones at rallies. I've written dozens more op-eds and essays on the topic, drafted model bills, and launched a menstrual policy nonprofit called Period Equity. I've met and joined forces with a diverse array of inspiring activists from Mumbai to Nairobi, London to Kathmandu, and New York City to Los Angeles.

Wonder Woman herself even came home to roost. Since that fateful New Year's Day, I've managed to score my own, admittedly oddball, alter ego and fighting persona. According to *New York* magazine, I morphed into the nation's "tampon crusader."[5] *Bustle* went with "badass menstrual activist."[6] Tweeted at by the editors at *Cosmo*: "slayer of the tampon tax." Slayer! Damn. Even my kids were impressed.

While I never would have envisioned that there would come a time when thinking and talking and writing about periods would become what I do—*all the time*—well, here I am. As this menstrual movement has taken hold, I've been eager to relay my firsthand vision of this potent era, a.k.a. "The Year of the Period," and how it came to be. Among the cast of characters I've encountered and whose contributions are featured in these pages: a "free bleeding" marathon runner; entrepreneurs who have shaken up the multibillion-dollar menstrual hygiene industry; innovators forging social enterprise models in the most impoverished corners of the world, as well as the women and girls whom they serve; politicians willing to break taboos; homeless and formerly incarcerated women; transgender and gender nonconforming people who menstruate; and a diverse array of organizers, artists, poets, athletes, and actors. And, of course, the everyday people whose everyday period stories are truly the lifeblood of the movement. Their testimonies run the gamut from funny to poignant to cringe-worthy to devastating.

I also offer my own deeply personal account of what the fight for "menstrual equity" is about. It's a phrase and a frame I first offered in an interview with the *Chicago Sun Times* in March 2016. The reporter was impatient, skeptical: "Menstrual equity, that's not a *thing*! What does that even mean?" Here's what was published: "Pressed to define 'menstrual equity,' [Weiss-Wolf] said, 'Fairness for how women are treated in society because they menstruate. They shouldn't have to pay more for the simple biological fact and for needing a medically-necessary item.'"[7] Had I been given a chance to self-edit, I'd have aimed for a bit more eloquence and clarity. For what I mean by the phrase is this: In order to have a fully equitable and participatory society, we must have laws and policies that ensure menstrual products are safe and affordable and available for those who need them. The ability to access these items affects a person's freedom to work and study, to be healthy, and to participate in daily life with basic dignity. And if access is compromised, whether by poverty or stigma or lack of education and resources, it is in *all* of our interests to ensure those needs are met.

Menstrual equity is still an evolving concept and goal. And why I've come to write *Periods Gone Public*. A caveat: I'm not an academic, historian, theologian, or medical expert. Mine is the view of a newly ignited advocate and activist, one committed to generating and harnessing the momentum needed to keep up the fight to eradicate menstrual stigma and advance a period-focused public policy platform.

The inaugural political fights for menstrual equity in the United States thus far have been the push to eliminate sales tax on menstrual products (the "tampon tax") and to ensure they are freely accessible to those most in need—low-income students, the homeless, the incarcerated. These campaigns have seen early success with surprisingly robust bipartisan support and interest. But that is only the beginning. A truly comprehensive menstrual equity agenda would eventually drive or help reframe policies that foster full participation and engagement in civic society—and that accept, even elevate, the reality of how menstruating bodies function.

The need for such perspective is even more urgent today given the treacherous political environment in which we must fight for our health and dignity. "The Year of the Period" is now saddled with the misogyny of and daily danger unleashed in the era of Trump. This American president, who has a history of openly bragging about sexual dominance—caught on tape boasting crassly how he'd grab women "by the pussy"—singled out menstruation for a special dose of derision early in the 2016 campaign when he taunted then FOX News correspondent Megyn Kelly for having "blood coming out of her wherever."[8] The Trump administration and current Congress are hell-bent on rolling back civil rights gains and trampling hard-won protections for social justice and reproductive freedom. Many statehouses, too, are emboldened to advance laws that profoundly compromise women's bodily autonomy. Six-week abortion bans. Threats to eviscerate health care and contraceptive coverage, and to defund Planned Parenthood. The fact that we've begun to coalesce a successful movement around menstruation may be but one bit of hope—new blood (literally!) and momentum in the greater fight for our lives. Even at the historic global Women's March that took place post–Inauguration Day 2017, period activism was nearly as visible a theme as the sea of crocheted pink "pussy" hats. (My favorite placard of the day: "Watch out . . . our cycles are synced up!")

The pace with which all this activity has unfolded has been nothing short of breathtaking. In this book, I trace my personal path of exploration since January 2015, and, in so doing, weave together the stories and experiences of many others I've met along the way. It is not often a person gets to at once narrate, participate in, collaborate on, and help coalesce a social movement in real time. It makes for an unusual outlook. And it also enables me to pose a healthy dose of critique. Have we made any missteps along the way? What might we learn from one another right now, while much of the energy is relatively new, the activism still emerging?

All of these interactions have also opened my eyes to two particular issues that I hadn't fully appreciated previously. First, the impact of menstruation on those who are transgender or gender nonconforming, and the default culture of their exclusion from the conversation. It is a challenge, given that the vast majority of people who have periods are cisgender women and girls, as well as that so much of menstrual taboo is rooted in ages-old misogyny. Ultimately, though, everyone and anyone who menstruates needs to be included in discussions *and* decisions about their own health. In my activism I have met with and listened to individuals from across the gender spectrum and do my best to acknowledge and address those perspectives in the forward-looking menstrual equity policies I propose in part three.

The other is environmental—in particular, balancing the dangers of our nation's throwaway culture and reliance on disposable products with helping the most vulnerable populations manage menstruation. The convenience of conventional tampons and pads can't be understated. Reusable products like menstrual cups or cloth pads are often not feasible for those without access to basics like clean water, soap, and privacy; and products made with organic or all-natural ingredients can be prohibitively expensive for many. But it is critical to work toward ensuring safe, eco-friendly, and easily accessible options for all. The health and environmental impact of menstrual products on our bodies—and the entire planet—is decidedly a feminist and social justice issue. That too is explored in the closing series of policy proposals.

At its core, a menstrual movement, and *Periods Gone Public*, is about challenging all of us to face stigma head-on. And about advancing an agenda that recognizes the power, pride, and absolute normalcy of periods. Indeed, President Trump, we *do* have blood coming out of our wherever. Every month. It is not a secret.

These realizations have been nothing short of a life-altering experience for me. Two years after Wonder Woman made an appearance on the cold Brooklyn beach, the moral of my own story may just have to be: don't ever underestimate the determination of a woman with a cape. And a tampon.

JOURNEY TO
"THE YEAR OF THE PERIOD"

chapter one

SURFiNG THE CRiMSON WAVE

We'll never have gender equality if we don't talk about periods, but 2016 signaled the beginning of something better than talk: It's becoming the [era] of menstrual change.
— ***Newsweek**, April 2016*[1]

MENSTRUATION IS CERTAINLY HAVING ITS moment. Periods have been around since the beginning of time—and stigmatized, sidelined or, at best, ignored for just about as long. So why have they suddenly become a topic fit for public consumption, a modern cause célèbre?

When I first dove into the issue on January 1, 2015, public discourse was sparse and cautious to the point of apologetic. According to its records, *The New York Times* used the word *menstruation* just four times a year during the entire twentieth century (415 times in total).[2] Fast-forward to 2015, *menstruation* topped 167 mentions in the five top national news outlets that year, more than triple the four prior years combined.[3] And the coverage was serious and substantive, far beyond glossy magazine ads or fodder for sex and health columns. *Cosmopolitan* magazine trumpeted it "The Year the Period Went Public," and then by the close of 2016 proclaimed a new era of "Period Power."[4] Emblazoned across *Newsweek*'s April 29, 2016, cover was an oversized torpedo-like tampon on a blood-red background with the headline, "There Will Be Blood. (Get Over It.) Period Stigma is Hurting the Economy, Schools and the Environment."[5]

Much of the attention was spurred by activists spanning the globe who had staged protests to demand that government address the economic burden of menstruation by eliminating the "tampon tax" and by helping draw attention to the plight of the impoverished and homeless in accessing menstrual products and hygiene facilities. Petitions calling for policy and action collectively garnered many hundreds of thousands of signatures. Social media ignited an outcry, too—including viral stories and trending hashtags directed at then candidates, now president of the United States, Donald Trump (#PeriodsAreNotAnInsult) and Vice President Mike Pence (#PeriodsForPence) for deriding or otherwise implicating menstruation on the campaign trail. Athletes and artists captured headlines when they talked about periods while running marathons, competing in the Olympics, or walking the red carpet at the Emmys. And a new generation of inventors and entrepreneurs aimed to disrupt the traditional menstrual hygiene market, offering not just more imaginative, healthier options than old-school tampons and pads, but making a modern case for how we talk about periods and consider the ways we manage menstruation.

The question of how we arrived at this loud, proud era requires that we know at least a little bit about from whence we came. Of course, there are myriad mythologies that have surrounded menstruation throughout time—from scripture to superstition, legend to lore, and, in between, countless customs, rituals, and beliefs. These could easily fill volumes, an encyclopedic series. In order to get us to the modern-day story, what follows is something more akin to a "greatest hits" album, a history of the world vis-à-vis periods with a special look at menstrual moments, debate, and developments in the United States and around the globe over the past century.

Keeping the Faith

Nearly all of the world's religions and core spiritual teachings have had something to say about menstruation. The overarching theme is perhaps best summarized by this ominous, apocalyptic quote from the *King James Bible*, Esdras 5:8: "Menstruous women shall bring forth monsters . . . " I've searched high and low for literal and contextual interpretations of this scripture gem (and even the curious word *menstruous*) to see if it might mean something other than the obvious. In any event, in the context of periods, it is hardly an outlier.

Menstruation is commonly assumed to be part of the reproductive package of pain foisted upon Eve in the familiar story of Genesis 3:16. As punishment for succumbing to temptation and eating the forbidden fruit, Eve and her descendants are explicitly burdened with the suffering of childbearing. Scripture would imply that menstruation, too, is a result of original sin, a sign of humanity's grand fall from grace. But beyond the vast array of interpretations of the biblical "Curse of Eve," there is no shortage of explicit examples of distrust, even disgust, for women's monthly blood. Here are some of the ways periods are still regarded today for many of the world's believers far and wide.

According to the Jewish code of law, Halakha, physical contact (including and especially sexual) is prohibited during the days of menstruation and for a full seven days after, also known as the phase of Niddah. The biblical source for this rule, Leviticus 15, focuses on the unclean state of menstruation and bodily secretions. For married women, a state of purity and cleanliness is only restored after immersion in a ritual bath called a Mikvah—still a common practice in many modern Jewish communities.

It is believed in Buddhism that menstruation causes women to lose or leak some of their Qi—life force or spiritual energy.

Islamic women are not supposed to touch the Quran, enter a mosque, or offer the ritual prayer during menstruation. A verse in the Quran specifically forbids sexual contact as well. During the holy month of Ramadan, menstruating women are not permitted to participate in the required fast between sunrise and sunset during the days they have their period.

In the Eastern Orthodox Christian Church, partaking of sacraments during menstruation, especially communion, or touching holy items like the Bible or religious icons is strictly off-limits.

During her cycle, a Hindu woman is forbidden from entering not only temples but also her own kitchen; she must not bathe, take naps, wear flowers, cut her nails, have sex, or touch others. Many are ostracized and banished to remote menstrual huts.

Shintoism keeps menstruating women out of shrines and temples, even off sacred mountains.

And then, just when all hope in any period-loving spirituality is lost, there's Sikhism—which professes positivity around the menstrual cycle and reassures that a woman's blood is a natural and fundamental component of life. Gurus strongly counter and condemn those who deem menstruation unclean and instead assert that impurity comes from the dark recesses of one's heart and mind alone. Accordingly, there are no restrictions placed on menstruating women, who are free to carry out fundamental religious principles—meditation and prayer, visiting houses of worship, and partaking in voluntary, selfless service—as well as go about their daily lives.

Of course, when it comes to religious practice and perspective there is always room for analysis, interpretation, even excuses. Alternative explanations of the passages from Leviticus 15, for example, offer a nod to encouraging the procreative process; for a woman with a twenty-eight-day cycle, the rules make it much more likely that any sex being had is at a time when ovulation, and therefore conception, is most likely. And among the more benign interpretations of the Ramadan fast exclusion, which applies similarly to those who are pregnant and breast-feeding, as well as the sick and elderly, is the acknowledgment that menstruation is a taxing physical state that creates greater need for daily nourishment. Perhaps, but these explanations doth protest a bit too much. Claims of weakness and impurity . . . these are precisely how menstruation has often been leveraged as a means to exclude women from full civic or social participation. It transcends and extends far beyond religious customs and bleeds its way into public life. (I know, I know. Blood humor is an oxymoron.)

Among the Ancients

It is hard to start with anything but the bombastic, oft-quoted proclamation by Pliny The Elder—Roman author, naturalist, and military commander who perished in AD 79 under the lava that flowed from Mount Vesuvius and blanketed Pompeii. Said Pliny: "Contact with the monthly flux of women turns new wine sour, crops touched by it become barren, grafts die, seed in gardens are dried up, the fruit of trees fall off, the edge of steel and the gleam of ivory are dulled, hives of bees die, even bronze and iron are at once seized by rust, and a horrible smell fills the air; to taste it drives dogs mad and infects their bites with an incurable poison."

Does this make menstruation magical . . . or maleficent? Is this a statement of fear of women's extraordinary power? Or disgust with women's bodies and blood?

From the ancient Greeks, the answer appears to be a little of both. Aristotle perceived menstruation as a sign of female inferiority and a deformity; in his treatise, *On the Generation of Animals*, menstrual blood is portrayed as a lesser sort of semen. But he also attributes mystical prowess to menstruating women and wrote in his grand analyses, *On Dreams*, that "if a woman chances during the menstrual period to look into a highly polished mirror, the surface of it will grow cloudy with a blood-coloured haze."[6]

This tension is similarly demonstrated within the etymological roots of the word *menstruation* itself—directly linked to the ancient Latin *mensis (month)*, which in turn relates to the Greek *mene (moon)*, from which the English words for both are derived. Hence, the monthly, lunar cycle. But around the world, there are many more complex and intriguing connectors. For example, the word *ritual* comes from the Sanskrit *r'tu*, which translates to *menstrual* (also rooted in the words *arithmetic* and *rhythm*); and the word *taboo* is from the Polynesian *tapua*, meaning *sacred* and, quite literally, *menstruation*. The American poet, Judy Grahn, author of the 1994 book, *Blood, Bread and Roses: How Menstruation Created the World*, offers a fascinating exploration of some of the most potent derivations and definitions. In particular, she notes the conflicting roots of *taboo* and *sacred*, zeroing in on the alternating fear and awe of menstruation. Writes Grahn, "Besides *sacred*, *taboo* also means *forbidden*, *valuable*, *wonderful*, *magic*, *terrible*, *frightening*, and *immutable law*." She points out that in European culture it is *regulation*, and not *taboo*, that is linked to menstruation: in German, the word *regel*, and the French *regle*, and the Spanish *las reglas* each mean *rule* and *regal* . . . and, again, literally, *menstruation*.[7] How telling that words reflecting a combination of order, regularity, and a dose of something sacred, special, even royal, can convey so much about the ever-present struggle to reconcile the very power *of* women's bodies with the establishment's desire for power *over* women's bodies.

Where in the World?

Around the globe, and since the beginning of recorded time, societies have found ways to segregate, subjugate—and every so often, even celebrate—the menstrual experience. A quick rundown of some of the more notable customs spanning ancient to modern history that I've seen referenced: Native American women of the Tlingit tribe were reported to be prohibited from lying down or chewing their own food during menstruation; they would instead sleep propped up with logs and be supplied with masticated food. The South American Ticunas subjected menstruating girls to flagellation. In Siberia, Samoyed women were segregated and had to "fumigate with reindeer hair" before they could be considered clean. Ancient Persians confined menstruating women to an isolated portion of the house, where no fire was to be kindled, all wood was removed, and the floor was strewn with dust; post-period, they were said to be treated to a washing with bull's urine.[8]

Reindeer hair and bull's urine are hard to come by these days. But there are plenty of assumptions that still abound. Among them, the touch of a menstruating woman will cause milk to curdle, vegetation to spoil, and bread not to rise. In Japan you may have a hard time finding female sushi chefs—not because of fears they'll rot the fish but due to the prevalent myth that menstruation causes an imbalance in taste, thus rendering women incapable of seasoning the unagi.[9] (As if that's not enough, the sushi establishment also claims that women's hands are too small and warm to prepare rice properly.)

Meanwhile, a handful of examples demonstrate menstrual reverence and empowerment, especially when it comes to marking a first period. Ceremonies involving an abundance of food, family, friends, and gifts are customary in parts of South India, Bali, and Bangladesh. Among the Zulus of South Africa, a goat is slaughtered and the girl is secluded with her friends, emerging the next day to be bathed, smeared with red clay, and taught lessons for adulthood by a circle of women. In some parts of Ghana, West Africa, girls may be seated under beautiful, ceremonial umbrellas when they begin menstruating.[10] And try

Googling the phrase *First Moon Party* and you'll discover a surprising array of Pinterest-worthy ideas and parenting blogs that address the ways some modern American families acknowledge and celebrate first periods, including specialty party games like "Pin the Ovaries on the Uterus" and PMS goody bags.

According to Gloria Steinem, there are examples, too, of entire matrilineal cultures—sometimes called "matriarchal," though that implies domination, rather than balanced societies— where reverence for women's bodies was a core tenet. Before Europeans arrived in North America, women often controlled reproduction, and when they menstruated were deemed to be especially powerful: a phoenix who bled yet did not die. Here and in early Africa, for example, men sometimes put menstrual blood on their bodies to denote bravery in battle. Menstrual huts were common, a place where women were separated from the community for various reasons ranging from fear to respect. (Steinem shares a joke told among some Native American women: "What did Columbus call primitive? Equal women!") Suggests Steinem: since patriarchy and control of reproduction may be only about six hundred years old on this continent— and probably no more than five thousand years elsewhere, a fraction of the time humans have been around—it may be more appropriate to say that periods have been stigmatized for as long as *patriarchy* has been around.[11]

An American Story

The modern evolution of menstruation in the United States didn't really begin to unfold in a public way until the turn of the twentieth century. Up through the 1800s, there is scant recorded detail about societal perceptions or, even as a practical matter, how monthly blood flow was managed. A generation of pioneer women donned all-in-one "sanitary aprons" or used homemade cotton pads that they either pinned to their bloomers or held up with belts. (I've always wished one of my beloved childhood heroines, the spunky champion of the northwestern frontier, Laura Ingalls Wilder, had included in the Little House series some telling tales about how she and her sisters dealt with periods on the prairie.) In the south, enslaved black women, whose bodily autonomy was compromised and violated in countless ways, used torn cloth; the onset of menstruation and its signal of fertility meant girls could be bought, sold, and traded away from their families, forced to breed or serve as wet nurses.[12] More generally, all women menstruated for a smaller percentage of their years—periods started later, women bore children earlier and more frequently (and nursed them longer), and lived shorter lives.

By the early 1900s, periods made a public entrance in the context of a new generation of commercial products. During World War I, nurses realized that the cellulose bandages they used to dress the wounds of soldiers absorbed blood better than plain cotton. Those bandages became the inspiration behind Kimberly-Clark's Kotex-brand disposable pads.[13] An advance, interestingly, that coincided with another key historical development: the fight for women's right to vote.

As activists fiercely waged this battle in politics and in protests on the streets, instability caused by menstruation was among the reasons touted to discredit universal suffrage. In 1912, *The New York Times* reported on the purported "militant hysteria" of suffragettes in England: "No doctor can ever lose sight of the fact that the mind of a woman is always threatened with danger from the reverberations of her physiological emergencies. It is with such thoughts that the doctor lets his eyes rest upon the militant suffragist. He cannot shut them to the fact that there is mixed up in the woman's movement such mental disorder, and he cannot conceal from himself the physiological emergencies which lie behind." Following the headline of that article, "Feminism Behind the Suffrage War," was the caption, "And Peace Shall Come When Each Woman in Overcrowded England is Under a Husband's Care."[14]

The year 1920 marked a profound advance on both fronts: Kotex's debut in the commercial market and the ratification of the Nineteenth Amendment to the US Constitution. Not only did women now presumably have an equal voice in American democracy, they were afforded supplies that could better enable them to engage and participate in civic life.

Procter & Gamble's Tampax-brand tampons with cardboard applicators arrived a decade later when the first patent for the product was filed in 1931. The word *tampon* itself comes from the Old French *tapon* and German *tappo*, meaning *plug* or *stopper* (as in that which is stuffed in a gun muzzle).[15] While internal protection wasn't a particularly new idea—over the centuries, women spanning the globe have fashioned tampons from a wide variety of materials including lint, flax, cotton, paper, wool, plants, grass, or essentially anything absorbent—it still sparked concerns among those who feared they were too sexually charged for young girls, virginity-breakers that would rupture their hymens. But as women entered the workforce in greater numbers during World War II, practicality and the need for reliable menstrual care won the day.

With the advent of commercial products, messaging of menstruation was channeled almost exclusively through fierce marketing and advertising campaigns. Starting in the 1920s, discretion was the rule. Packaging was plain and nondescript. Separate payment tins were placed on store counters to ensure no words or sideways glances would be exchanged. A 1928 *Ladies Home Journal* ad touted quiet convenience as a selling point for Modess-brand pads: "In order that Modess may be obtained in a crowded store without embarrassment or discussion, Johnson & Johnson devised the Silent Purchase Coupon presented below. Simply cut it out and hand it to the sales person. You will receive one box of Modess. Could anything be easier?"[16]

Through the mid-twentieth century, imagery began to shift—less about secrecy, though modesty still prevailed, with an overt nod to fashion and self-presentation. Names of products were sweet, diminutive: Lillettes and Pursettes. As for the ads, think crisp, white attire and a parade of confidently demure, always pristine, upscale (and white) women. Later on, a sportier, more diverse and youthful set joined the fray promoting period protection, often perched on a balance beam or ready to take a quick dive in the pool. The message was always the same: No leaks, no stains. No pain. No problem.

Menstruation management, and the efficacy of the products themselves, became embedded in an emerging national ethos of the time. In part, this was a practical result of women assuming a greater role in public life, education, and the workforce. But it also reflected a distinct commitment to middle-class values, including growing reliance on the modern medical establishment, appreciation of (and aspiration for) high-tech convenience products, and a robust advertising economy.[17] Tampons and pads, and the messaging around them, were reflections of the American lifestyle they portrayed. Simplicity, self-sufficiency, and self-control. A win for menstruation? Partly so, perhaps, if it meant more or potentially better options.

Another corporate communication tool of the era: "informational" pamphlets that made the rounds under the guise of sex education curricula, reaching a captive audience of millions nationwide (translation, consumers). The innocuously titled "Very Personally Yours" was a Kimberly-Clark creation, a booklet that cheerily offered up the facts of life and, conveniently, hawked its Kotex products. It also offered tips tempering the use of tampons by teens (not coincidentally, the tampon market was dominated by rival, Procter & Gamble). I vividly remember receiving a copy at my own elementary school assembly years later in the mid-1970s—girls only, of course. We were presented with those palm-sized, pastel-green booklets and a stash of free Kotex product samples, a not-so-subtle nudge to promote early brand loyalty. Upon our return to class, the evidence was quickly tucked away in desks and book bags to avoid the boys' prying eyes and teasing snickers. All the companies produced their own versions of the same during the middle of the century, similarly spun with names like "Accent on You," by Tampax and "Strictly Feminine," by Modess (which offered a parental counterpart entitled, "How Shall I Tell My Daughter?").

Kimberly-Clark had also commissioned a companion to its booklet back in 1946, the Walt Disney ten-minute film, *The Story of Menstruation*—though hardly classic cartoon fare. The Disney company was in a postwar slump and had suffered major financial losses after producing its animated masterpiece

Fantasia, and as a way to boost revenues it brokered contracts with private corporations. As for the film, it was shown to more than one hundred million American students from its release through the mid-1960s.[18] The whole thing is all very Disney-fied, filled with a cast of chirpy characters—no sign of blood and certainly no mention of sex. Girls are urged to keep exercising, keep clean, and keep smiling. All told, it actually offered a surprisingly mainstream gesture to the normalcy of periods—so much so that it was even awarded the *Good Housekeeping* Seal of Approval and a spot in the National Film Registry of the US Library of Congress. And yet, given the context of vast financial interest in and influence over menstrual storytelling, that's still a whole lot of manipulation to absorb.

By the end of the 1960s—on the heels of second-wave feminism and the emergence of the "women's lib" movement, Betty Friedan's *The Feminine Mystique,* and the birth of The Pill—came perhaps one of the only other rebellious, rollicking American period for periods. Menstruation was further integrated into mainstream discourse in the 1970s but, for the first time, this was achieved through women's own voices, questions, and stories—a remarkably powerful expansion. The decade kicked off with a political battle, a smackdown in 1970 of a member of the leadership of the Democratic Party's Committee on National Priorities who was forced to resign after suggesting that women could not hold office because of "raging hormonal imbalances." That same year the ever-controversial Germaine Greer published her feminist treatise, *The Female Eunuch*, a clarion call for female emancipation and the end of gender oppression. In it she posed her now infamous, provocative challenge: "If you think you're emancipated, you might first consider the idea of tasting your own menstrual blood—if it makes you sick, you've got a long way to go, baby."[19]

Judy Blume's triumphant young adult novel, *Are You There God? It's Me, Margaret,* also landed in bookstores in 1970, enabling readers and parents alike to engage in slightly more pragmatic period talk. *Ms.* magazine proudly launched the following year as a *New York* magazine supplement, and then as its own fiercely independent feminist publication in 1972. Next up, the Boston Women's Health Collective released the groundbreaking first edition of *Our Bodies, Ourselves* in 1973, one of the most influential how-to handbooks ever published, created by women, for women—and even today still the penultimate sexual health resource. Four decades and nine editions later, it has been translated in thirty languages and read by millions around the world.[20]

In so many ways, the sum of these publications was and has continued to be both radically life changing and sanity saving. Each succeeded in embracing many of the facets of menstruation as a topic of personal *and* political discourse.

Are You There God? It's Me, Margaret adopts much of the "products as progress" sensibility of the preceding era. The young characters' fascination with and commitment to modern period management is one of my most distinctive memories of the book. Like Blume's suburban sixth grader Margaret Simon, I was among those who anxiously, hopefully awaited my first period, not at all resentful of my own biology or the slightest bit mindful of the perspective of the patriarchy.

I revisited *Margaret* around ten years ago when my older daughter started fourth grade. I bought the latest edition for her and was actually stunned (and saddened) that one key 1970s relic from the book had been scrubbed. Margaret's sweet pink sanitary belt—for fastening to her "Teenage Softies" pads—was replaced with sticky strips. For much of the twentieth century, pads required a bulky utility belt–like contraption to keep them in place (self-stick pads were an invention of the early 1970s). Even when the book was first published, belts had already been innovated into oblivion. As a preteen reading the book for the first time, I'd never even seen one in real life, though I was intimately aware of its every cumbersome mechanism thanks to Margaret and her fearsome foursome of friends: the indelible imagery of Margaret nervously lingering in the hygiene aisle of her local drugstore to choose one and her grateful exuberance when she finally gets to use it for real.

That belt was the source of a visceral, colorful memory, not just for me but for millions of other readers. Removing it from the story wasn't without controversy apparently. Said Blume of the maxi pad upgrade in a 1998 interview: "Some people said, 'Oh no, it's a classic. You can't mess around with a classic.' And I said, 'Look, we're not messing around with the character . . . We're just messing around with the equipment.'"[21] *New York* magazine columnist and author Rebecca Traister wrote a 2006 *Salon* essay lamenting the modernization of the supplies: "It's hard to imagine, but while we've been busy growing up, *Are You There God? It's Me, Margaret* has become a historical novel, one that gives its readers more than just a mirror held up to their own specific conditions. It offers them the thrill of seeing themselves, even in characters who live in different times, in different worlds."[22] I agree. And I think a tiny bit of the magic of *Margaret* is surely lost (though the demise of belts is worth a few cheers).

In another *Margaret* sidebar and twentieth century slice of menstrual perspective, I was intrigued to learn that Blume first dedicated the book to her mother—thanking her, among other things, for introducing two other classics, Anne Frank's *The Diary of a Young Girl* and *To Kill a Mockingbird* by Harper Lee. What Blume couldn't have known then is how profound the menstrual ties that bind would be for this trio of unforgettable protagonists. They share one surprising commonality: Each takes on periods in uncommonly refreshing and honest ways. Anne, even in her horrifying reality as a teenager hiding from the Nazis during the Holocaust, reveled in having her period (she called it her "sweet secret"); precocious Scout, as revealed many decades later in Lee's *Mockingbird* prequel *Go Set a Watchman*, despises her period from the moment it arrives, and her misunderstanding of the "Curse of Eve" is equal parts comical, smart, exhausting, and traumatizing. The stories of Margaret, Anne, and Scout, collectively, have now been read and revered by generations. And all three have the shared honor of being the target of book bans in libraries and schools across the country—the first two explicitly on account of their open discussion about sexuality and menstruation.[23]

Interestingly, *The Diary of a Young Girl* was so deeply beloved by Japanese readers in the sixties and seventies—for reasons having to do with postwar politics, but also high among them Anne's open talk about periods—that the phrase "Anne no hi" ("Anne's Day") became a common slang name for menstruation there.[24]

Back in the United States, 1978 brought what may be the most magnificent of contributions to the menstrual dialogue.

Gloria Steinem's essay, "If Men Could Menstruate," was published in the October issue of *Ms.* magazine that year, a brilliant exploration of an imaginary society where menstrual centrality is the rule, turning the table on patriarchy and oppression.[25] "So what would happen if suddenly, magically, men could menstruate and women could not?" Steinem asks. "Clearly, menstruation would become an enviable, worthy, masculine event." She then goes on to describe all the ways society would normalize and celebrate menstruation:

"Men would brag about how long and how much."

"Sanitary supplies would be federally funded and free."

"Generals, right-wing politicians, and religious fundamentalists would cite menstruation ('*men*-struation') as proof that only men could serve God and country in combat ('You have to give blood to take blood'), occupy high political office ('Can women be properly fierce without a monthly cycle governed by the planet Mars?'), be priests, ministers, God Himself ('He gave this blood for our sins'), or rabbis ('Without a monthly purge of impurities, women are unclean')."

Steinem's satire remains one of the most masterful anthems to the political consideration of menstruation. It has been critiqued, cited, and celebrated by readers around the world in the nearly forty years since it was published, a featured subject of discussion from book groups to middle school lessons to college curricula. It has inspired creative, modern scenarios, including the 2016 "Man-pon" spoof commercial featuring two sweaty dudes in a locker room backslapping over their cycles and clutching a box of turbocharged, NASA-designed menstrual protection. The ad was part of a series that doubled as a fundraiser and public service announcement for WaterAid, a nonprofit that creates sustainable sanitation projects around the world.[26] And it has also prompted more serious, nuanced discussion of gender diversity and inclusion, given the reality that there are transgender men who do menstruate and are uniquely targeted by societal stigma.

I discovered "If Men Could Menstruate" a few years after its release in the mid-1980s when I was finding and exploring feminism on my conservative college campus in the height of the Reagan era. Menstruation in that decade had begun to take on a more pragmatic tone. On the plus side, it swept in new frankness in product advertising. While a ban on discussing menstruation over the airwaves had been lifted in 1972, it wasn't until 1985 when the actual word *period* was uttered out loud on television by a feather-haired teenage Courteney Cox.[27] (Even then, it was still another twenty-five-plus years before actual red blood—not ubiquitous sky-blue liquid—made its first primetime appearance for visual demonstrations of maxi pad absorbency.) And in 1986, *Consumer Reports* named the tampon one of the "50 small wonders and big deals that revolutionized the lives of consumers," an honor shared by air conditioning and running shoes.[28]

This was the same decade that introduced the concept of menstruating in outer space, when Sally Ride became the first woman to join the Challenger mission in 1983. In planning the number of tampons they should pack for her seven-day trip, NASA engineers asked, "Is 100 the right number?" ("No," Ride responded. "That is not the right number.") Before her blast into orbit, the NASA team reportedly aimed to be thoughtful about the options. They deployed a tampon sniffer to ensure scented products wouldn't be a problem in the otherwise tiny space capsule, and some crafty soul connected a supply of tampon by the strings—so that they wouldn't float away one by one.[29]

But the main menstrual headline of the decade was tampon safety after an alarming spate of toxic shock syndrome cases in 1980. That year, 813 tampon-related instances of a severe bacterial staph infection were reported by the Centers for Disease Control leading to the deaths of thirty-eight women. The death toll reached eighty-six over the next five years out of another two thousand–plus reported cases.[30] High-absorbency tampons made of synthetic ingredients were implicated, particularly a newer Procter & Gamble brand, Rely, which it had aggressively marketed as a modern, super-powered solution. ("It even absorbs the worry!") Rely was used at the time by nearly a quarter of tampon users.[31] It was pulled from the market later that year. As more and more cases were reported, over a thousand lawsuits were filed, and public ire (and fear) swelled—as did media coverage. Whereas *The New York Times* published the word *tampon* a total of 255 times between the years 1850 and 2000, more than half of those mentions were coverage of toxic shock cases between 1980 and 1989.[32] In 1982, the Food and Drug Administration began requiring manufacturers to advise consumers about the link between tampon use and toxic shock syndrome. By 1989 the FDA also called for standardized tampon absorbency levels and relevant warnings on tampon boxes. And then by the end of the decade, almost as suddenly as the scare swept in, the number of cases dropped dramatically. The media's urgent watchdog oversight slowed to a halt.

By the early 1990s, product safety once again found its way to public discourse as Congress pressed the FDA on new reports over the link between dioxin, an ingredient found in bleached rayon used in commercial tampons, and cancer. Even then coverage was sparse. Though among the highlights, a 1995 *Village Voice* feature, "Embarrassed to Death: The Hidden Dangers of the Tampon Industry," called out the FDA for sitting on memos revealing this link and for not pushing for testing. To this day, the FDA does not require manufacturers to disclose the ingredients in tampons and pads. Federal legislation was introduced in 1997 by US Congresswoman Carolyn Maloney to require funds for independent research into potential hazards posed by synthetic fibers and chemicals in tampons, as well as to mandate more transparency in testing results.[33] It went all but ignored, back then and still today. The legislation has been reintroduced *ten* more times over the past two decades, most recently in 2017, but has never succeeded in passing, or even come close.

But it wasn't the scathing investigative reporting by the *Village Voice* that sparked a furor. It was the newspaper's cover: the lower half of a naked body with one leg raised and the string of a tampon dangling on the other thigh. There was no blood, nor were there any body parts on display but for a leg. And an inch of clean, white string. The hypocrisy of the outsized outrage over that photo was part of what motivated the article's author, Karen Houppert, to publish the now classic 1999 book, *The Curse: Confronting the Last Unmentionable Taboo: Menstruation*, a "searing indictment of the culture of concealment that surrounds menstruation."[34]

Menstrual memorabilia was quietly amassed in the nation's capital with the 1994 opening of an actual brick-and-mortar shrine, the Museum of Menstruation and Women's Health (also known as MUM, Houppert noted, "as in mum's the word!").[35]

A far cry from the Smithsonian, it was set up in the DC suburb of New Carrollton, Maryland in the basement of a middle-aged bachelor, Harry Finley, an unlikely steward. It featured a collection of more than five thousand individual artifacts, from turn-of-the-century products to vintage ads to classic literature. Finley gave personal tours and developed a loyal (or just plain curious) following but closed the museum's doors in 1998 after a four-year run. For the past two decades he has maintained MUM as a stand-alone website. Exhaustive in content, though cumbersome to navigate, the site is a maze of thousands of pages, and as many links per page, to images and information. While hardly a mainstream medium, it is a rather remarkable resource for those who seek it out. (Many a Google search with the word *menstruation* will still take you to one of MUM's pages.[36])

A decade-plus later, 2009 ushered in one more burst of public rabble-rousing, including several important books released that year. Elissa Stein and Susan Kim's *Flow: The Cultural Story of Menstruation* highlights the modern popular advertising trajectory, featuring an unparalleled array of stunning ad copy and artwork.[37] Lara Freidenfelds's *The Modern Period: Menstruation in Twentieth Century America* explores the overlapping contributions of product manufacturers, educators, advertisers, and the medical community, along with the evolving role of women in the mid-1900s.[38] Rachel Kauder Nalebuff's *My Little Red Book* offers a riveting anthology of more than ninety first period stories, spanning nearly a full century (1916–2007) and as told by women of all ages, religions, and nationalities from around the world. Her aim: "[A] call for a change in attitude, for a new way of seeing periods. In a time when the taboo around menstruation seems to be one of the few left standing, it makes a difficult subject easier to talk about, and helps girls feel proud instead of embarrassed or ashamed."[39] And Chris Bobel, Associate Professor of Women's Studies at the University of Massachusetts, Boston, president of the Society for Menstrual Cycle Research, and one of the nation's leading academic experts in all things period activism (and, in her words, "funky" movements), published *New Blood: Third-Wave Feminism and the Politics of Menstruation*, through which she explores why, despite emerging dialogue and activism, menstruation still had not risen among feminist priorities in the twentieth century.[40]

Simultaneously, a slew of women aimed for shock value throughout 2009 under the banner of "menstrual anarchy" (or . . . "menarchy"). Among these, British artist Ingrid Berthon-Moine snapped a self-portrait and series of photos of women using period blood as lipstick; comedian Chella Quint debuted a zine called *Adventures in Menstruating* to address menstrual stigma with "wit, craftivism and brute force, joyfully inviting audiences to hang ten on a crimson wave," which morphed into a live performance and BBC radio show. By October 2009, *Salon* quipped: "Menstrual activism seems like an overreaction to a taboo that has mostly dissipated. Some advice for the menarchists: Let it bleed."[41]

Perhaps it is true that some of the raw gimmicks employed by activists of the day weren't destined to appeal to the masses or offer a pragmatic enough stab at calling out the perils of marginalizing menstruation. But to suggest that period stigma was a nonissue in 2009—or, really, ever—is just plain folly. Counter to *Salon*'s snarky suggestion, Bobel's *New Blood* is clear and emphatic: open dialogue and activism around menstruation is at the heart of addressing every level of social control over women's bodies. Truly, it always has and always will be.

WHAT A LONG, STRANGE TRIP it has been. "For people like me who have been studying menstruation for decades, we've never enjoyed this kind of attention before," Bobel told NPR in 2015.[42] But somehow this new array of activity has made a case that is at once compelling, reasonable, and meaningful—just the right combination to catapult the issue into the mainstream. And when menstruation landed on the cover of *Newsweek* in April 2016, the feature story perhaps best summed up our forward-looking path: "There's a new movement—propelled by activists, inventors, politicians, startup founders and every-day people—to strip menstruation of its stigma and ensure that public policy keeps up. For the first time, Americans are talking about gender equality, feminism and social change through women's periods, which, as [Gloria] Steinem puts it, is 'evidence of women taking their place as half the human race.'"[43]

chapter two

CODE RED

We're not talking about rocket ships. We're talking about sanitary pads. Yet they both have the same effect. They take you places.
　　　　　　　　—Diana Sierra, Founder, BeGirl[1]

I GREW UP IN SUBURBAN New York City in the 1970s and was hardly immune to the popular lore surrounding periods. I believed that baths were strictly off limits, only showers allowed. Also no swimming, no camping; the blood will attract sharks and bears. These stories didn't do much to damage my sometimes sunny, more often surly preteen worldview, though, nor did they particularly limit my opportunities. Quite the contrary, I was always the first to claim cramps as an excuse to sit out of gym class. And I hated camping anyway.

The same cannot be said for many millions of girls worldwide, back then and still today. Here's the reality: menstruation has created a class of untouchables. Quite literally.

It's not just dear Pliny the Elder—remember his declaration to the ancient Romans how "monthly flux" would sour wine?

That is not a far stretch from some of the beliefs to which millions around the globe still cling. Among these: one should not water the plants, handle or cook food or even step foot in the kitchen, touch animals, milk cows, or sleep in the same bed with another, even a spouse.

And then there's the pickle jar. In India, one of the long-standing superstitions about the dark power of periods is that a menstruating woman will cause a pickle to shrivel and rot by her mere touch. The rumor has the tiniest bit of science rooted within. A pickle is among those fruits and vegetables that are fermented, so the story goes, when its antimicrobial properties are disturbed by unclean human contact, the vegetation will spoil and disintegrate. And, of course, menstruation presupposes a state of unclean.

In 2014, Procter & Gamble's global brand Whisper, marketed in India for the very few who use commercial pads, launched its #TouchThePickle campaign. A print ad and companion commercial encouraged viewers to defy tradition and break taboos (mildly ironic, given the brand name Whisper). The video itself is actually quite adorable. A spunky teenager decked out in white pants playfully pokes at a pickle jar, equal parts bold and coy, and exclaims, "I touched the pickle!" Crowds of older women cheer her on, parade route–style, and offer thunderous applause. She urges: "Girls, let's break the taboos . . . go ahead and *touch* the pickle!" The campaign earned accolades and picked up awards. More than 2.9 million women pledged to #TouchThePickle. [2]

But for all of the girl-power messaging the corporate marketing campaign aimed to harness, the fact is that stigma around menstruation remains rampant throughout India. And it causes real bodily harm—to people, not to pickles. When combined with extreme poverty, little to no practical health education, and a dearth of clean, safe toilet facilities, the problem is dire, if not downright deadly. Access to menstrual products is perhaps the most visible, tangible sign of the problem. A widely-cited study reports that of the 355 million people who menstruate in India, just 12 percent use any sanitary products at all.[3] How do the rest cope? Quite often by using makeshift materials like leaves, paper scraps, or mattress stuffing to absorb menstrual blood. A 2012 *New York Times* op-ed reported a particularly nightmarish story about a young girl who unknowingly used rags infested with lizard eggs, leading to a hysterectomy at age thirteen.[4]

The problem is not unique to India, of course. Around the globe, on any given day, more than eight hundred million people are menstruating. And at least five hundred million of those lack adequate resources—including supplies, education, and facilities—for managing their periods.[5] Factor in societal and cultural stigma and the practical consequences of these realities are startling:

- Worldwide, girls often miss out on education. In Sierra Leone, for example, one study found that more than two in ten girls are reported to skip school during menstruation.[6] Another study showed the figure to be just under 20 percent in Rwanda.[7]
- In the poorest corners of the planet, less than half of all schools and public places have working toilets. In Tanzania, just 11 percent of schools have a sufficient number of facilities, and only half of those have running water. In Nigeria, where one toilet accommodates

every six hundred students, 77 percent of girls reported having no private place to change their menstrual pads.[8]

- Students in Bolivia have been urged by teachers to hold on to used pads all day and dispose of them only at home, not in school, for fear of contaminating the trash, which many believe will lead to illness, like cancer. In fact, most schools there have no garbage bins at all, or only flimsy, cardboard barrels without waterproofing or lids.[9]

- Lack of toilets and sinks in Afghanistan exacerbates a related hygiene problem, the pervasive misconception that bathing while menstruating can lead to infertility (known as *gazag*).[10]

- In rural Kenya, girls are reported to engage in transactional sex or seek out boyfriends to buy them goods, including sanitary products.[11]

- Nearly half of girls in Iran are so lacking in accurate education about menstruation that they believe it to be a disease.[12]

- In parts of Nepal, girls miss out on more than just their education. Many are exiled altogether from society during menstruation. In a ritual known as *chaupadi*, they are shut out of their homes and isolated in makeshift huts with no protection from the elements, even during monsoon season. In December 2016, to the world's horror, two Nepalese teenagers died within weeks of each other, their deaths caused by hypothermia and asphyxiation from fires they made to keep warm in the huts. And in July 2017, yet another young woman died during banishment; she was bitten by a poisonous snake. Although the country's highest court banned this practice in 2005, it remains a grim reality in many remote rural areas.[13]

These practices and beliefs can have potentially devastating public health consequences. Increased likelihood of infection is but one result. But the crisis goes far deeper. Just pause for a moment and think about what this all means. Entrenched stigma marginalizes menstruation and exacerbates the conditions of poverty, not only undermining the health and endangering the safety and lives of women and girls, but also curtailing their opportunities. The result is, effectively, a denial of their equal chance to obtain an education, to acquire the tools to escape poverty and contribute to the economy, and to participate fully and productively in civic life. Make no mistake, this is a core human rights issue. And when half the population is held back, *all* of society suffers as a result.

How is this not a global scandal screaming for a solution? Or, as period slang goes, a "Code Red" crisis?

While menstruation has remained in the margins, there is, however, a generation of progress emerging from the small but robust international field of study and advocacy called Menstrual Hygiene Management (or MHM), an outgrowth of the global water, sanitation, and hygiene sector. These issues are being addressed by scholars and scientists, researchers and engineers, human rights advocates and experts, and entrepreneurs and innovators. It is coupled with a modest investment of philanthropic support in order to more fully understand the complex drivers of this problem and develop viable, scalable solutions. With this infusion of resources, and growing evidence to make the case for public engagement, some governments have become similarly motivated to support a menstrual agenda, link it with broader, systemic outcomes for public health and education, and advance new policies and funding commitments.

And then there are everyday people spearheading truly extraordinary initiatives that aim not only to tackle menstrual taboo and access but also to empower and educate women and girls in that process. This chapter is largely devoted to their stories.

"Popular innovators" is how *The New York Times* referred to this style of social enterprise in a November 2016 article about India's efforts to address menstrual access, reporting that, "The solutions developed by grassroots inventors aim to be just good enough, simple in form and function." Known as "lean innovation" in business school speak, it stands in stark contrast to what the *Times* describes as an "ethic of 'smarter-faster-better' that drives corporations to continually upgrade products" and meet the desires of the masses.[14] In the case of menstruation, simple and local is very often a right-sized and optimal approach. For those who are accustomed to getting by on little—not to mention forced to face down deeply ingrained shame—the ability to creatively pinpoint and address a problem within the confines of community has inherent influence and can yield tangible, lasting results.

India's M.Y.O.P. (Make Your Own Pads) Revolution

In the industrial city of Coimbatore, deep in the heart of southern India, lives a fifty-five-year-old entrepreneur, husband, and father named Arunachalam Muruganantham. He resides in a compact, crowded apartment with his wife Shanthi and their young daughter and owns a modest local factory, commuting there each day through a maze of dusty, twisting streets populated by roaming cows and shabby roadside vendors. He's an unlikely international hero, one who also happens to be known as "The Menstrual Man."

In August 2015, I boarded a plane in New York City and flew fifteen hours to Mumbai and then another four to Coimbatore. I joined an enterprising activist named Annie Lascoe to spend two days in person with Muruganantham. Annie and I had only briefly met once before when we'd both found ourselves at a menstrual cycle research conference in Boston that June, so I was surprised and thrilled when she invited me to accompany her in India. Twenty years my junior and a Los Angeles native, Annie was in the throes of founding a new company, Conscious Period, and seeking a partner for what we soon coined our "menstrual mission." Together we embarked on a whirlwind tour of the country punctuated by interviews with dynamic innovators, starting with Muruganantham.

His life story is as implausible as it is inspiring. A high school dropout and son of a widowed mother, he is the creator of the world's foremost menstrual microenterprise model: a manufacturing device and process for producing low-cost, locally made pads. Even before meeting him, I'd read all about it. In 2014, he was celebrated by *TIME* magazine as one of the world's 100 Most Influential People. He's been the subject of high-profile features by the BBC, PBS, and *The New York Times*, and his story was the basis for both a documentary and a forthcoming Bollywood film, *Pad Man*. Now I'd traveled thousands of miles to see and hear it all firsthand.

Back in 1998, a newly married Muruganantham witnessed Shanthi's struggle to manage (and hide) her bleeding with a stash of old, torn rags. He was aware that disposable pads were sold at the local market, but had no idea they were so expensive. At that time, a package of eight cost twenty rupees—around fifty cents—or the equivalent of half a week of groceries. (Today most commercial products sell for around eight rupees per pad.) He started with a singular mission: to create simple, functional pads for his young bride's use. He molded a wad of cotton wool and wrapped it in a thin layer of cotton. Shanthi tried it but reported that her old rags were preferable to what amounted to a mottled mess.

Muruganantham began to experiment with different materials and combinations, though he knew so little about the menstrual cycle he was disappointed to learn that he'd have to wait another month for Shanthi to test his creations. Impatient, he tried to expedite the process by finding more women willing to participate in the trials—his sisters, nearby college students. Impossible. Not a topic in which any woman would engage, especially with a man. This was also when he discovered that Shanthi's use of rags was more sanitary than what many others resorted to—sand, bark, ash. And many who used rags, like Shanthi, were often too embarrassed to dry them in the sun, which meant that the cloth between their legs was never fully clean, dry, or disinfected. The depth of the problem, and how easily solvable it seemed to him, became a personal crusade.

Desperate to keep testing his creations, he went so far as to construct and wear a rubber bladder filled with animal blood that simulated menstrual flow, so he could assess the pads himself. According to the BBC profile, "A former classmate, a butcher, would ring his bicycle bell outside the house whenever he was going to kill a goat. Muruganantham walked, cycled, and ran with the bladder under his traditional clothes, constantly pumping blood out to test his sanitary pad's absorption rates. He used to wash his bloodied clothes at a public well and the whole village concluded he had a sexual disease."[15]

Neighbors thought he was insane, perverted, and/or possessed by demonic spirits. Shanthi left him. So did his mother. Ostracized by his community, nevertheless he persisted. It took another two years before he finally discovered the right material—pulverized sheets of wood fiber—and still several more before he perfected a manageable production process. By then it was 2004, six years later. The result was a simple machine that produced inexpensive, disposable, good-quality pads.

In 2005, he took his invention on the road, traveling to poor, remote communities in India. But between the stigma—of periods, to be sure, but also of a man bearing the menstrual message—he didn't have many takers. "To speak to rural women, we need(ed) permission from the husband or father," he told the BBC. "We can only talk to them through a blanket." Accustomed to resistance and rejection but determined to succeed, he eventually broke through and got his first taker. Word started to spread. And now, more than a decade later, hundreds of women's groups, rural nonprofits, and job training organizations use his machine, serving some of the most underdeveloped regions of the world, in and beyond India. Most are managed and staffed by women, who make and sell the pads to others in their communities (in India, for approximately 2.5 rupees per pad—a quarter of the price for a single, commercially produced pad).

And therein lies Muruganantham's exceptional vision and exponential genius. He not only created affordable pads, he created jobs. Jobs for women helping other women. The machine doesn't require electricity or any special skills or training. The beauty is its simplicity. Anyone can master it. It is not intended to keep up with the automated processes used by the Procter & Gambles of the world, but one machine can employ ten women and yield up to one hundred thousand pads in a year. These numbers are at once audacious and modest, underscoring the very point of the "popular innovation" model. It need not compete in a mass market. Because the women who produce the pads are able to sell them directly to the customer, this eliminates the middleman (emphasis on "man"). Women buying from women creates community—a sphere that is safe, supportive, and free of shame.

I'd read the articles and watched the film, but I didn't quite believe it all until I was right there on the floor of his factory. Muruganantham led Annie and me through a maze of machines. Dozens were assembled and lined up, ready to be shipped to new sites, each painted bright orange and turquoise. The machine resembles a simple desk, combination drill press and sewing machine. Muruganantham gladly demonstrated the full process. First, the hard, poster board–sized sheets of wood fiber go through a simple grinder, creating a material that looks much like fluffy cotton (though a little sharp to the touch . . . I worried briefly about splinters). Then, the pulverized fluff wads are shaped and cut into rectangular slabs before being wrapped with a cotton sheath.

As if wandering through Wonka's chocolate factory, my Veruca Salt kicked in and I impatiently begged to have a turn at it. I got to make a few pads—clumsily at first but it didn't take too long to get the hang of it. The process requires a bit of muscle and coordination but is not complicated. The pads themselves are thick with squared corners. Utilitarian, not particularly fancy, but they get the job done.

The factory itself was an odd sight, staffed only by men— around a dozen of them, most in jeans, sandals, and hard hats. I asked where the women were. Muruganantham shrugged and said it was not a place for women, given the welding and heavy lifting involved in making and transporting the machines themselves. I pondered that. A men-only haven for the production of menstrual machines in a far corner of India? It was too surreal. But considering that women lead nearly every aspect of the production process outside of the factory, I didn't press the issue further.

Muruganantham's tiny office features a wall covered with newspaper clippings and photos of him in cracked, smudged frames, smiling broadly with recognizable American faces— Bill Gates and Bill Clinton—and numerous world leaders. Still, he's modest, spiritual, and reflective. Major corporations have repeatedly offered to buy and market his machine, but he has resisted the clarion call to scale up. Instead, he's stayed focused on the model he's championed and honed—and the women's stories that led him to all this in the first place.

Later, we headed to his apartment for a meal with Shanthi (a decade later, moved by his perseverance, she took him back!) and their adorably shy daughter Phrithisri, then five years old. His mother lives in the unit next door (she, too, returned to his side) and popped over to say a quick hello. As we sat on the floor and devoured rice on bamboo leaves, it was clear that

Muruganantham's personality is as singularly focused as Shanthi's is sweetly subdued.

Arunachalam Muruganantham, Jennifer Weiss-Wolf, and Shanthi Muruganantham in the Muruganantham's home in Coimbatore. (Photo credit: Annie Lascoe)

In the middle of the meal, he hauled in a gigantic box overflowing with packages of finished pads. Since he provides only the machine and the materials but doesn't treat the production process as a franchise or even his own, women have the autonomy to name their product and design the packaging. The western influence is palpable. Lots of pink and turquoise and modern silhouettes and exclamation points. Names like "Happy Girl" and "Fighty!"

Phrithisri climbed in the box and played with the colorful bundles, first giggling as I encouraged her to toss them around in a game of "hot potato," then hugging them close like a baby doll. It was a moving sight—a father, his child, and heaps of menstrual pads—and perhaps one of the most potent expressions of the deep empowerment that he extends to so many, including and especially the women in his life.

Phrithisri Muruganantham plays with creations from her father's pad press.

Equally remarkable is his willingness to freely share his experience, expertise, and model. Appreciating the vast and desperate need for sanitary products, Muruganantham is open to allowing others to adopt and adapt his creation, without substantial fees or even requesting credit. Over the past decade, more than four thousand related production centers have been launched in India and around the globe, including in Nigeria and Nepal, by innovators who have run with, and even further refined, his invention.

OUR NEXT FLIGHT TOOK US to the lively city of Vadodara, a colorful, vibrant hub in the western state of Gujarat. There, Annie and I were met by a striking woman, Swati Bedekar, a former science and math teacher. Bedekar's nonprofit consultancy, Vatsalya Foundation, brought her to some of the poorest regions of the state in an effort to improve educational outcomes in public schools. After observing that female students were missing classes for several days each month due to menstruation, she jumped right in.

Bedekar had heard about Muruganantham's machines and purchased one in 2010, not looking to reinvent the wheel. But the women who used it, many of whom were quite petite, complained that the some of the mechanisms—in particular, a heavy, cumbersome foot pedal—were difficult and caused back pain. So Bedekar began tweaking aspects of the machine, making it easier to use. She also went on to refine the boxy pads it produced, too, developing a slimmer, more modern style with rounded contours and adhesive "wings," beloved by Indian women who adore the American touch.

Seeking a locally viable production and distribution plan, she sought out and formed women-run cooperatives whereby members would manufacture sanitary pads in their own homes and villages. Bedekar has since launched forty production sites that produce a collective fifty thousand pads per month. Each is run by women who are paid per pad, which are then packaged and sold under the name *Sakhi*, Hindi for *female friend*. The workers also receive training in menstruation education—which they then impart to women and girls, men and boys alike—as well as basic financial management.

Swati Bedekar demonstrates the pad making process in Vadodara.

Bedekar took us to visit two Sakhi production sites. The first was in the tiny home of a young widow named Amitaben, whose husband had died in a local uprising just two years prior. She now raises her young sons in a one-room, open-air house. Menstrual products stacked and strewn about the house are as normal a sight as the dusty cows and goats that wander up to the windows off the streets.

A closet-sized alcove is the heart of her production site, which has just a single machine. After welcoming us to crowd in close and observe the process—shoes off, masks on—she pulls out a canister full of already ground wood pulp, swiftly presses it into the frame, and molds a pad. Another woman wraps it in a cotton cloth, sealing it all together. Even the children gather to watch; they too are involved with simple steps in the production and delivery process. These two women make fifteen hundred pads a day, which they sell locally in smaller quantities, four pads for ten rupees.

The ability to earn an income is a source of great pride to Amitaben. So too does she relish being an "expert" on menstrual health, making sure locals know the benefits of using pads and not hiding or fearing their cycles. And because she includes her sons and their young friends in her work, menstruation is nearly devoid of taboo in her home. She is far more of a renegade than she even realizes and smiles shyly when I tell her as much.

We are joined that day by two special education teachers from Mumbai who plan to bring a machine to their school as a way to offer job skills and an income-producing activity to their students, another often ignored segment of Indian society. Similarly, one of the sites we'd visited with Muruganantham was a vocational program for young adult men with cerebral palsy, who were otherwise capable of managing the machines.

The second Sakhi site was in the outskirts of Vadodara, Baska Village, a Muslim community. There we meet the young woman, Akthar, who runs the production site—a space so cramped, just a few feet deep and wide, that only three people can fit in it at one time. Village rules require that she keep the site within a few yards of her home and husband. She explained how gratifying it is to be able to contribute financially to her household and proudly added that she has become so deft at producing pads, she has orders from all over the state as well as two local stores that sell her products. She is a natural entrepreneur and success story.

One of Bedekar's Sakhi pad production sites.

We're later joined by Bedekar's husband, Shyam, a textile engineer and farmer who has completed the circle of invention with his own special creation, a low-cost incinerator he calls the "Ashudhdhinashak" to dispose of used pads in an environmentally sound way. This is especially important for rural areas where there is no system in place to manage garbage collection. Made from terra-cotta or cement and resembling a large decorative flower pot, the incinerator's brilliance is its utilitarianism. Because it doesn't require electricity, it can be operated discreetly, burning up to twenty used pads at a time and turning them into ash without spreading smoke. It also eliminates odor—and, therefore, embarrassment and shame. Among the other advantages of the incinerators, production has become a source of livelihood for local potters, and the ash that is produced, when mixed with soil, is beneficial to locally grown plants. The Bedekars have taken care to consider the many ways menstruation may impact a community—the needs for pads, the need for disposal, the need for discretion, even the need for mulch!—and taken the "lean innovation" model to its most useful and powerful extension. Their holistic consideration of every aspect of the problem shows no detail is too minor.

The Bedekars, and especially Swati, have been recognized and celebrated across India and the world for these contributions. And since 2015, the Vatsalya Foundation has provided six thousand girls each a year's supply of free pads and underwear.

Among recent global partners, the Bedekars have teamed up with British activist Amy Peake to ship a dozen machines, raw material, and incinerators to the Za'atari refugee camp in Jordan.[16] For the estimated sixty million people around the world displaced by war, conflict, or natural disaster, the challenges for those managing menstrual hygiene are particularly severe.[17] Menstrual stigma and discomfort can inhibit women from moving freely and accessing needed services, according to the United Nations Population Fund.[18] Through Peake's initiative, Loving Humanity, the Bedekar's machines are being used not only to address the shortage of menstrual products for refugees in the Jordan camp, but also to make incontinence pads, which are terribly needed and in short supply, particularly for the elderly, disabled, and war wounded, as well as traumatized children. It is no small thrill to see just how far this model can extend. Menstruation is an essential global connector.

NEXT ON OUR TRIP WE spent time with yet another entrepreneur committed to enhancing Muruganantham's model: Jaydeep Mandal, founder of Aakar Innovations, a Mumbai- and Delhi-based operation. Meeting with Mandal was our third stop and first big-city exploration. At his request, we joined him in what seemed a peculiar meeting place, a bustling street outside the Dharavi Slum in front of the local police station. It is one of the most densely populated and impoverished communities in India, rocketed to fame by the blockbuster movie *Slumdog Millionaire*. As we awaited Mandal's arrival, Annie and I drew curious stares from the crowds of local passersby. We tried to act cool and nervously cracked jokes about how we would explain ourselves should anyone inquire as to why two Western women were lingering on the crowded corner. ("A menstrual mission? Oh, but of course!" Indeed.)

Mandal, a savvy young businessman, soon pulled up in a sleek black Uber, hopped out of the car, and led us to our next destination. After turning a few sharp, quick corners, we found ourselves in the heart of the slum. Sun-scorched and dusty, it was teeming with people. Old men sprawled out on the dirt, teenagers played games with sticks, lines of small school children in tidy uniforms joyfully swarmed us as class let out.

We headed to the small office of one of several on-site agencies, the Society for Human and Environmental Development. Known to locals as SHED, it offers a range of social services to residents, from grammar schools and day care, to adult literacy and family counseling, to elder care and medical clinics. Among SHED's most notable programs are its peer advisors for domestic violence and sexual assault victims, and specialized health programs for sex workers. Given the dearth of healthy opportunities for slum-dwelling women, the array of vocational programs SHED offers are a lifeline for many, especially its sanitary pad partnership with Mandal's Aakar Innovations.

Of all the production sites we visited, the Dharavi site was the largest and most efficient, with as many as a dozen women able to work a single shift. Aakar Innovations has brokered a total of forty women-run and women-staffed sites throughout urban areas in India, as well as in Kenya, Uganda, Bangladesh, Nepal, and Bhutan. As with the SHED arrangement, most are established in connection with local nonprofits. One of the benefits of this model is that the work experience is bolstered by a full array of social and educational services. Another is that it enables women to be paid a regular, reliable stipend, rather than on a per-pad basis. Each site employs fifteen to thirty women who produce 1,600 to 2,000 pads per day, enough to meet the needs of five thousand women and girls in the local schools each month.

Like Bedekar's Sakhi pads, Aakar Innovations has further refined the actual products—in Mandal's case, by developing a formula for pads that purport to be 100 percent compostable and biodegradable. As a result, Aakar Innovations' sanitary pads may actually meet a higher environmental standard than much of what is on the global commercial market.

Variations on the Theme

Around the world, similarly imaginative people have crafted initiatives reflecting the same spirit, creativity, and economy of scale as Muruganantham's model. Shortly after I returned from India, I arranged to meet with several more of these pioneers to get a better handle on the many ways menstrual innovation was being applied.

In early September 2015, I sat down for coffee in New York City with a young powerhouse innovator whom I'd seen profiled everywhere from *PBS NewsHour* to Nicholas Kristof's *New York Times* column, Harvard Business School and Kennedy School of Government graduate Elizabeth Scharpf. She shared how her menstrual moment of shock became inspiration back in 2005 while she was interning for World Bank in Mozambique. At the time, she had toured a small sewing factory and asked the owner about her ideas for improving efficiency. She hadn't predicted the owner's response: address the productivity of employees who would miss as many as twenty-four days a year while they were menstruating because they couldn't afford pads. Stunned, Scharpf couldn't shake her immediate instinct to seek a solution. She turned her focus to Rwanda, where there was evidence of the same problem. There she deduced that the workdays missed due to menstruation amounted to $215 of lost income per person, per year, which added up to a potential $115 million loss to the national GDP annually. Other draws included working in a country that has majority-women representation—Rwanda has more women in Parliament than any other country in the world—and a host of business-friendly policies.[19]

Scharpf committed to developing a locally, economically, *and* environmentally sound business model. In this case, that meant tapping existing natural resources to create affordable, quality, eco-friendly pads, and coupling the development of a product with the provision of health education and policy advocacy. She spent several years with her team in Rwanda, blenders in hand, experimenting with various kinds of naturally absorbent materials. The winner? Banana trunk fibers. Double bonus, banana trees are everywhere in Rwanda. It's like spinning gold from straw, almost a fairy tale solution.

She secured seed money and launched Sustainable Health Enterprises (SHE) in 2008 to bring her plan to scale. Like Muruganantham, Scharpf's goal from the start was not only to help broadly expand access to affordable menstrual pads, but also to create employment opportunities and to sustain communities. SHE currently provides twenty-eight production jobs in the local district of Ngoma in the Eastern Province of Rwanda, where the main facility is located. It also generates business for six hundred banana farmers, the majority of whom are women. Another local team earns income by managing distribution, both of menstrual education curricula and the pads themselves. To date, SHE has made and provided two hundred thousand pads to ten thousand women and girls throughout the country. Across the sprawling local economy, SHE's approach brings layers of intrinsic value—with menstruation as the focal point.

AMONG THE MOST COLORFUL PERSONALITIES I was fortunate to encounter is Colombian designer Diana Sierra, founder of BeGirl. Sierra herself is as bright and dazzling as the three-pack of underwear—neon turquoise, electric purple, and lacy fuchsia—she tossed my way just minutes after we met for the first time in late September 2015. After examining pulverized wood fibers in India, to me, her sleek panty products were a near-blinding sight. They look like something straight out of a Victoria's Secret catalog except for one key difference: a waterproof bottom and a secret mesh pocket that can be filled with whatever absorbent material is readily available.

"You just go MacGyver-style with these," Sierra jokes, her classic one-liner. "Just stuff them with anything that will work, whether a pad or cloth rags or even a handful of leaves."

Sierra's menstrual epiphany came during a United Nations internship in rural Uganda, when she learned why girls were missing out on a crafting class she was offering. Determined to help offer a solution, Sierra set about fashioning makeshift pads from mosquito netting right then and there. But when she learned that underwear could be as hard to come by for the girls as pads, she concocted the panties as a one-stop solution. She also created a line of reusable snap-in pad holders using the waterproof nylon bottom of an umbrella.

*Diana Sierra removes umbrella fabric for use in developing BeGirl creations
(top) and shows off a prototype of BeGirl's reusable pads (bottom).
(Used with permission)*

What stands out most about the BeGirl products are their eye-popping colors and modern design. Sierra's prior career in industrial design for slick companies like Nike is part of the reason she is so focused on aesthetics. But she puts herself in the position of the people she serves. The product can't just be utilitarian, basic, or "good enough" to suffice. "I would never assume just because someone is poor they deserve any less than the rest of us," she tells me. When she tested her prototypes, the girls responded that they wanted items that were stylish and fun. Sierra wants them to believe that they are worthy of the very best.

When one user wrote to her that the panties made her feel proud to "be girl," the name was set. BeGirl was launched in 2014. Today, Sierra sells her products commercially and also employs a donation model that enables her to distribute them for free in Uganda, Rwanda, Tanzania, Malawi, and ten other countries, as well as poverty-stricken corners of the United States. Her message to girls everywhere, embodied by her design and products: "Love your body. Design your life. Achieve your potential."

AROUND THE SAME TIME, I had begun reading about another novel rendition of the menstrual social enterprise model. Spearheaded a decade ago, a group called ZanaAfrica focuses primarily on the needs of teen girls and women in Kenya. Very happily for me, some of its staff is based in New York City and we immediately arranged to meet locally.

ZanaAfrica manufactures, markets, and sells its own disposable pads under the brand name *Nia*, which translates to *purpose* in Swahili. The packaging is polished and inviting; the products high quality and affordable. But improving access to commercially produced pads is just one part of its three-pronged integrated approach: the other components include provision of reproductive health education through a distinct pairing of culturally and age-appropriate, body-positive curricula, which is further bolstered by regional and national policy advocacy to advance menstrual access and girls' education. ZanaAfrica is now undertaking extensive, essential research to examine and report on the impact of the combined effects of free pads plus health education over the course of girls' years in school.

I've since joined the advisory board of ZanaAfrica and have worked closely with their team on-site in Nairobi, as well as in New York, to link their research and the successes they've achieved in influencing menstrual policy reform to the emerging US agenda. It is a meaningful global partnership, one we are all proud to forge.

One of the key points driven home by ZanaAfrica, based on its extensive research, is that the girls it serves are most comfortable using disposable pads and prefer these to other menstrual products. While not surprising, this spurred my interest in exploring groups that focus on providing other alternatives, like cloth pads and cups. I next met with Madeleine Shaw and Suzanne Siemens, the cofounders of a Canadian company called Lunapads. Shaw and Siemens are both long-standing global leaders and social entrepreneurs involved in manufacturing, distributing, and retailing reusable menstrual products. I'd sought them out, eager for information about the current usage of cloth pads, in particular, and to better understand their pros and cons, especially for impoverished communities. Though less expensive and less wasteful, they do require time and certain resources—like access to privacy, running water, and soap—to be properly washed and dried. The care and keeping sounded mildly daunting to me, but Shaw and Siemens assured me that it is all, in fact, very easy.

While Shaw had originally conceived of Lunapads in the early 1990s as a solution to persistent allergic reactions to tampons, the company began receiving inquiries from organizations around the globe, particularly those working to support girls' health and education. Far from the company's traditionally Western eco-minded customers, this new demographic of Lunapads users included adolescent school girls with scarce access to products or private bathrooms, let alone landfill capacity for disposable menstrual products.

Among their partners is a social enterprise in Uganda— AFRIpads, founded in 2010 by an American and a Canadian, Sophia Grinvalds and her husband Paul, after their own bout of frustration in obtaining menstrual products there. When the Grinvalds realized the depth of the plight for those who are young and poorest, much like other innovators described here, they decided to act. They'd received a set of Lunapads and sought to develop a model in Uganda that similarly focused on reusable cloth pads. Today, AFRIpads are manufactured locally and provide jobs and economic opportunity for more than 150 workers—nearly all of whom are women in dire need of an income and are otherwise without formal skills, education, or job training.

To ensure the broadest reach, AFRIpads collaborates with hundreds of nonprofit organizations, international relief agencies, and private companies that purchase its menstrual kits (which include a set of four reusable cloth pads and a storage bag) and distribute them widely in Uganda, East Africa, and beyond. Among these are high-profile entities like Save The Children and UNICEF. The model is thriving. AFRIpads kits are now in the hands of more than 1.5 million women and girls worldwide.

AND THERE ARE STILL MANY, many other organizations forging equally ingenious operations around the globe. Here are just a few with which I've had the pleasure to cross paths:

- Huru International, which holds workshops for girls in Tanzania and Kenya to deliver locally produced menstrual kits (containing cloth pads, underwear, soap, and a waterproof storage bag), along with training in essential life skills and HIV education.
- The Cup Foundation, based in Nairobi's Kibera slum, which works to empower young adults by providing menstrual cups, sexual health curriculum, training and mentorships for girls and boys, and a 24/7 helpline.
- Days for Girls International, which deploys teams from every continent to make and distribute cloth pad kits and education throughout South America, Asia, Africa, Europe, Canada, and the United States.
- Binti—which means *young lady* in Swahili, *daughter of* in Arabic, and *request* in Punjabi—assists in the creation of pad-making micro factories in India and Kenya and is a strong leader in global awareness-raising campaigns.
- Femme International, which operates in East Africa and partners with schools to provide menstrual cups, reusable pads, and all-purpose packs—filled with soap, a towel, and

steel bowl for boiling and sterilizing—along with essential health education workshops for both girls and boys.

BUT MENSTRUAL INNOVATION STRETCHES FURTHER than the provision of sanitary products. Some, like Indian-born author Aditi Gupta, are reaching women and girls through materials that meld practical health information with humor and pop culture. Gupta is the creator of *Menstrupedia*—a fun, taboo-busting series of graphic novels intended to help girls in India understand menstruation and "stay healthy and active during their periods and throughout their lives."[20] According to Gupta, what makes *Menstrupedia* stand apart is that she knows—and *is*—her audience. The series is able to strike the balance between acknowledging cultural beliefs, shattering misconceptions and shame, and offering no-nonsense advice.

Since launching in 2014 as a result of a successful crowd-funding campaign, *Menstrupedia* has made the rounds throughout India's villages and cities and has been translated into Hindi and fifteen other Indian languages, as well as Spanish and Russian. It is now accompanied by an assortment of spirited blogs, chats, and online tools with impressive Facebook and Twitter followings—hundreds of thousands likes and check-ins. Says Bangalore-based journalist Priti Salian, "the blog and the question-answer section feature some of the most freewheeling discussions of puberty and menstruation of a kind that would have been unthinkable in India even a few years ago."[21]

Similarly, comics are wildly popular in Kenya. Nearly ten million teenagers read *Shujaaz*, which translates to *hero* in Swahili, soaking up its trendy characters and messages about everything from HIV prevention to peacekeeping to conflict resolution.[22] But Kenyan girls rarely see their own stories and experiences reflected in this medium. ZanaAfrica aims to change that and has adapted the model to make menstrual and reproductive health information and guidance readily accessible. *Nia Teen*, a companion to their same-named sanitary pads, is a special magazine that celebrates the lives and experiences of girls and offers answers to the most frequently posed questions (collected from participants in ZanaAfrica's school programs). Each issue offers the fun-loving relevance of a snappy fashion magazine with the absorbing read of a comic book, and adds up to a dose of education that is at once enjoyable and relatable, filled with period-positive messages.

In 2016, a UNICEF team in Indonesia launched a two-in-one comic—a ten-page booklet that can be flipped inside out, one side geared to girls, with practical information about personal care during periods, and the other side for boys so they can learn what happens to (and how to be supportive of) their mothers, sisters, and friends. A punchy animated video short accompanies the booklet. The content and ideas were provided not only by global hygiene experts, but from the target audience itself, one hundred teens from six provinces who shared firsthand experiences with menstrual stigma and shame. As reported by NPR, early testing of the book and survey findings are promising. The percentage of girls who felt that periods should be kept a secret dropped from 38 percent to 20 percent; and the percentage of boys who considered it wrong to bully or tease a girl for menstruation increased from 61 percent to a whopping 95 percent.[23]

And in rural Madagascar, a similar message is being spread through a video, "Girls Just Wanna Have Pads," a spoof of the Cyndi Lauper eighties hit. Girls twirl and dance across the screen with pads in hand, crooning, "I want to be the one to take on the world . . ." The video was released by Projet Jeune Leader, a group that operates under the broad mission statement: "Every girl has a right to clean, affordable, and reliable menstrual products. Every girl has a right to enter puberty confident and informed. Let's give girls their rights." A year-long middle school curriculum combines access to menstrual products with educational materials and peer leadership on reproductive and sexual health, and sessions in which girls create their own menstrual kits containing eight washable cloth sanitary pads, a small carrying bag, a care sheet, and a cycle-tracking calendar.[24]

But . . . what works?

From my vantage point, the global menstrual hygiene community's collective approach is nothing short of revolutionary—defying commercialism, creating locally sound products and processes, and forging meaningful connections by, with, and among women and girls. More than anything I've ever experienced in my own US-based activism and advocacy, this network is energetic, dynamic, open, and engaging beyond belief. Perhaps it is the near-universal experience of having a period that makes the quest for a solution so profound.

But can it really be all that simple? Not exactly. A 2016 report issued by nonprofit strategy and evaluation consultant FSG, commissioned by the Bill & Melinda Gates Foundation, cautioned that despite rising momentum among many of the leading institutional players—governments, researchers, and funders, as well as the array of innovators and social enterprises—these efforts are too often "disparate and siloed." It recommends that better collaboration could help avoid unnecessary duplication of efforts, bridge gaps in everything from research to production, and keep the price of menstrual products low (while ensuring that access remains high).[25] Fair enough. Cohesion and coordination are a perennial challenge across all movements—but, when prioritized, offer undeniable benefits. All too often, though, that's far easier said than done.

More complicated, perhaps, is consideration of the impact of the various models and interventions. "There is always this hope for a magic-bullet answer—the perfect product—that will solve what is a deep, pervasive, and complex condition," says Dr. Marni Sommer, associate professor at Columbia University's Mailman School of Public Health. I was fortunate to first connect with her in late 2015. Sommer is one of the world's preeminent researchers on menstrual hygiene management.[26] She has traveled the planet on behalf of this work, published prolifically, and, more than most, understands the enormous array of interconnected obstacles: How bringing disposable products into communities without adequate garbage disposal facilities, for example, can create sanitation problems. Or how reusable cloth pads and menstrual cups aren't feasible for those who don't have access to private spaces with clean, running water to wash and disinfect the cup, or a safe place to dry cloth pads in the sun. Or that menstrual cups and other products that are used internally are laden with a whole additional layer of taboo in many cultures. Or why any pads are useless to girls who don't have underwear. And how all the products in the world don't address a lack of toilets and adequate sanitation, or a community environment that doesn't support or empower girls as they navigate puberty and periods.

To date, hard evidence about the efficacy of menstrual hygiene management programs and school-based interventions is scant, largely due to lack of sufficient funding to support long-term research, and therefore still too limited to be consistent or conclusive. Among the findings, for example, a 2012 study in Kenya reinforced the belief that girls who were provided with disposable pads saw health benefits but found they did not increase school attendance.[27] Research in Nepal examining the distribution of menstrual cups also found no impact on school attendance, although it did show an increase in girls' free time due to less need for washing cloth pads.[28] A report out of Ghana compared the impact on school attendance for two interventions: the provision of health education with and without the pad distribution. The study found that while both interventions increased school attendance, the group that received education actually had slightly higher school attendance than those that also received pads, pointing to the critical importance of information.[29] And, most recently in Uganda, a study that offered girls four options—a seventy-five-minute lecture on how to handle periods, a free AFRIpads kit (along with some soap to wash them and three pairs of underwear), neither, and both—showed vastly better attendance rates for girls who chose the lecture, the kit, or both. No interventions at all produced the worst outcome.[30]

What does this say about the provision of products? Do they matter when it comes to school attendance? Of course. When offered with safe, sanitary places to use them, pads and cups are a simple intervention that can drastically improve daily life, no doubt. But the need for accurate, sensitive health information, in particular, and efforts to address stigma are clearly also critical parts of the equation. These, too, are not without complications. Facts and figures compete with cultures that have been rife with menstrual secrecy and shame for generations.

Sommer herself has created a nonprofit called Grow and Know that provides basic guidance on menstruation, body changes, and peer pressure. More than a million copies of her puberty books, part of the Girls and Boys Puberty Book Project, have been tailored and distributed for young readers (ages ten to fourteen) in Tanzania, Ghana, Cambodia, Ethiopia, and Madagascar, with new versions to be introduced in Pakistan and the United States. Each edition is developed in partnership with local government officials, and includes participatory research with the target audience; even the illustrators, translators, and publishers are all hired locally to ensure a culturally appropriate end product.

Yet undoing thousands of years of taboo is a sensitive, long-term process. Stories and practices carried down from grandmother to mother to daughter—aunties and sisters, too—have real, often impenetrable power and create a layer of resistance, even suspicion, in the face of what may otherwise appear to be a perfectly objective, factual curriculum. Considering this, part of Procter & Gamble's #TouchThePickle campaign's subtle poignancy was the overt nod it gave to intergenerational influence and approval. Even for younger women, who may strive to be more modern in their approach, the consternation and acceptance of their elders matter.

Any hope of a lasting solution will require engaging whole communities and committing to a full array of interventions—access to hygiene and disposal facilities, accurate information, a supportive environment among peers and adults, *and* sanitary products—needed for girls to manage menstruation and lead healthy lives. In order to ensure equity when it comes to access to education, in particular, it really is the complete package that matters. Without any one of the components, risk remains high.

And, for that matter, the goal needs to go beyond aiming that girls simply attend school but also ensuring that they are comfortable and confident while there. Later, when they venture out into the world, they'll carry with them the belief they are worthy of the same dignity and respect. It is about educational opportunity, yes, but encompasses so much more: economic empowerment, bodily integrity, and an understanding that menstruation is deeply rooted in the broader case for human rights.

Which, inevitably, takes us back to the production models like Muruganantham's pad-making machine, and the many others he's inspired. What makes them so meaningful is that they, too, demonstrate how menstrual solutions can at once be a local, communal, and intergenerational undertaking. This process of change is sometimes slow, painstakingly so. But very well worth the effort. The gains being made along the way are vital.

BY THE TIME I ARRIVED back home from our menstrual mission across India, I felt certain of at least this much: if menstruation is a global issue, the solutions are at once local *and* global. So what, if anything, might be replicable or even resonate in the United States? Here are some of the takeaways that I wrote in September 2015 in a *New York Times* essay about that trip:

- *Collaboration:* We must aspire to be forward-thinking and generous in sharing winning ideas and letting others improve upon them, just as Muruganantham has done with his machine.

- *Education:* We must be holistic, linking education, dialogue, and information to products, whether handmade, purchased, or donated.
- *Ownership:* We must think about enterprise, activism, and advocacy not just as a way to provide for immediate needs, but also to enable all players to participate and define the interventions that work best for and fully empower them.

That was how the path ahead looked to me in 2015 as "The Year of the Period" continued to pick up steam. It was onward and forward—and due time to explore and expose the scope of the problem for Americans, and start charting potential solutions, right in our own backyard.

chapter three

AUNT FLO AND UNCLE SAM

Nothing else so absolutely ordinary reminds you that you have a vagina—something other people are quite willing to viciously harm you for—like having a period while homeless.
—Kylyssa Shay, formerly homeless blogger[1]

EVER SINCE MY FATEFUL NEW Year's Day discovery of "Girls Helping Girls. Period." and its flyer calling for tampon and pad donations for a local food pantry, I wondered frequently how the United States fared. And how our nation's poorest and most vulnerable managed the costs of menstruation—those living paycheck to paycheck, without a paycheck at all, on the streets, or in government custody. I'd begun to see firsthand the reality across the globe, both the depth of the problem *and* the promise of innovation. But as far as I could tell, there was no real attention being paid to the idea of menstrual access as a domestic matter.

With some rudimentary research, I pretty quickly catalogued the ways in which we *weren't* helping make tampons and pads more accessible and affordable as a matter of public policy: they're ineligible for purchases made with public benefits like food stamps; they're not routinely or consistently offered (free of cost or otherwise) in public shelters or crisis centers; they're not mandated or provided in any uniform way in jails and prisons; in the vast majority of states they're not exempt from sales tax; they're not covered by health insurance or Medicaid, or included in Flexible Spending Account allowances; and they are not readily available in school or workplace (or any) restrooms.

The takeaway for Americans: you're on your own.

More power to you if you can clip coupons or order in bulk. And grassroots donation drives, like the one in my hometown, have started cropping up and gaining traction. But given that one in three American women—that's 42 *million* adults and another 28 *million* children—either live in poverty or are right on the brink of it,[2] suddenly this was looking potentially like a nationwide problem. And one that called for more action than even a full-service charity operation in every city could possibly fix.

I kept writing about the issue, posing questions, and proposing ideas for interventions. But I also wanted answers. Where were the studies? The data? The reporting? Were American students missing school for lack of pads? Were low-wage workers sacrificing income? How were those who were homeless or incarcerated coping each month?

This lack of information is a critical part of the story, of course. Identifying a solution is exponentially harder to do when the problem itself is so hidden, so invisible—because it is entrenched in shame, dismissed as a "female matter," or otherwise disregarded—that any discussion of it has been off-limits. The fact that menstruation itself—and the intersection of menstruation and poverty, in particular—has been wholly absent from any national public discourse (or even most private discussion) also has meant that people who need help are unlikely to feel comfortable enough to ever say so. And, conversely, those who might be willing to offer to help often weren't even remotely aware that the need existed. Prior to 2015, I was living proof of that.

The global issues of menstrual stigma and access, and the resulting conversation and innovation, have provided us with some comparative context for how to start and frame the dialogue here at home. It may have seemed distasteful to pose the inquiry—why it is that developed nations like the United States are lagging behind, as if we are somehow bigger, better, more compassionate, more capable—but the media did indeed start asking that very question. How do Americans feel about potentially allowing what amounts to a "third-world crisis" to unfold in their country? Could this really be happening, right here, in our own communities?

And with that, the coverage—and the real-life stories—began to . . . well, flow. This chapter compiles and shares many of them. Both compelling and, at times, disturbing, these narratives are the fuel we have so clearly needed to make the case that menstrual equity is indeed a first-world, American problem worthy of our consideration.

Blood in the Streets:
Periods and Homelessness

*"Pads and liners, please. They go the longest way in keeping a single pair of
underwear—and that's all I've got—as clean as possible during my period."*
—Dawn, homeless in San Francisco[3]
(Photo credit: Laura Epstein-Norris)

As one might imagine, experiencing homelessness while menstruating can be an especially horrid combination—uncomfortable, unsanitary, and unsafe. Hygiene facilities and privacy are scarce. So too is clean or spare clothing. Shelters and food banks aren't typically afforded public funds for tampons and pads and menstrual cups; most struggle just to keep enough food on the shelves to meet demand. Desperate for products, some homeless women report using anything from rags, bags, newspaper, socks, paper towels, or toilet paper, to just bleeding right into their clothing. Of course none of these options are a quick fix but actually are used for several consecutive days, the full duration of a period. Now picture the least palatable and most grotesque version of any of these items: newspapers and bags salvaged from dumpsters, toilet paper stockpiled in dank public restrooms, discarded socks pulled from donation piles. Menstruation becomes not just a source of humiliation, but utterly and undeniably a health and safety risk.

Lack of access to toilets, sinks, and showers takes a considerable toll, too. Periods are a 24/7 condition when they strike, but public restrooms—whether in gas stations, bus depots, fast-food joints, or public buildings—are not always open or available around the clock. Homeless shelters may have restrictions or offer toilet facilities that are neither safe nor secure. Privacy is needed simply to change a tampon, let alone to wash oneself or rinse a blood-soaked rag or stained pair of pants. For those who are transgender, a growing population in the overall homeless head count, the need for discretion, especially while menstruating, can be a matter of personal safety, or even life or death.

Even the inability to secure one's own belongings poses risks for menstrual hygiene. Kylyssa Shay, the blogger quoted in the chapter opening, shared with me that during the time when she was homeless, her tampons and pads were as likely to be stolen as any other valuables: "It was a miracle I even kept one item through my whole ordeal, my ratty old teddy bear, and that was actually returned to me after my pack was stolen. A man who'd seen me with it found the remains of my possessions while dumpster diving and it was the only salvageable thing. I honestly have no idea how many times I had to start from scratch again after getting knocked around and robbed."

While a 2016 report by the US Department of Housing and Urban Development shows that homelessness is down nationwide, the overarching numbers are still pretty sobering. Nearly 550,000 people in America are currently without a roof overhead, 40 percent of whom are women and just under 1 percent are transgender.[4] Not surprisingly, however, formal research about the experience and impact of menstruating while homeless in the United States is practically nonexistent. A 2014 study conducted by the National Law Center on Homelessness and Poverty, presented to the United Nations Committee Against Torture, only briefly acknowledges lack of access to menstrual products as a problem for women.[5] And recently in New York City, a team of graduate students from The New School for Social Research spent a year assessing the city's shelters and interviewing residents about managing their periods; more than half said they had been forced at some point to forego menstrual supplies.[6] That's about it.

With so little data, but a lot of assumptions and anecdotes, amassing personal stories is about as potent an arsenal as we can aim for. And so it happened that "The Year of the Period" kicked off with a media breakthrough achieving just that. On January 13, 2015, *Al Jazeera America*'s Lisa De Bode reported on the lack of adequate hygiene facilities and menstrual products for women who are homeless in New York City.[7] It was a riveting and widely read piece—"Hygiene and heartache: Homeless women's daily struggle to keep clean"—with firsthand accounts of the challenges posed by periods. Among these, one woman described how heavy bleeding kept her from even walking or moving about freely each month. Response articles and blogs followed over the next few days in *Huffington Post* and *Vice*. Something about the synchronicity and synergy of this coverage resulted in a surprising platform. Unlike the misogynistic fury a few months prior that came on the heels of Jessica Valenti's 2014 *Guardian* piece, "The Case for Free Tampons," the response this time was the exact opposite: a massive outpouring of compassion and firestorm of activity—a real call to action. Looking back, it was a major turning point.

What made for such a drastically different reaction? My theory is that the early 2015 wave of coverage came from such an unusually rich and varied array of sources and messengers, high-profile and pragmatic enough to be taken seriously, and bolstered by compelling firsthand stories. Rather suddenly, and without much fuss, a swift and certain wave of activism took hold.

Among the most immediate and direct, the hashtag #TheHomelessPeriod, a United Kingdom–based initiative started by three enterprising advertising executives, went viral—including jaw-dropping visuals, a fundraising campaign, and a correlating petition, now signed by more than eighty thousand people calling on Britain's National Health Services to allocate funds for free menstrual products in shelters.[8] More recently, #TheHomelessPeriod worked in a coalition with lawmakers, activists, and shelters to successfully persuade private partners, including Procter & Gamble and Britain's largest, swankiest pharmacy chain, Boots UK, to contribute to national donation projects.[9] And the simple, clever hashtag itself has spurred several similar donation drives and fundraising campaigns in the United States and around the world. Among some of the newly formed and highest impact organizations are the following:

- Support the Girls, based in Washington, DC, and now with forty-eight global affiliates, which has collectively donated over 800,000 menstrual products (and 135,000 bras) to 215 shelters and organizations over two years' time.
- #HappyPeriod from Los Angeles, and now with eight chapters in major cities across the country, which hands out care packages of period products directly to people living on skid row and city streets.
- RACKET., a Broadway-based donation drive that has tapped stars of the Great White Way, from *Hamilton* to *Book of Mormon*, to raise awareness and benefit New York City's biggest shelters.

With many of the new projects specifically citing De Bode's reporting as a driving motivation, the correlating uptick between donations and her January 2015 article was clear and measurable. In fact, the initial article had included an interview with Care for the Homeless, a New York City shelter and provider of health and social services, which reported at the time that it had completely run out of tampons and pads (along with its sister branch in Orlando, Florida, even after a local fundraising campaign specifically for menstrual products). Thanks to the wave of media and increased awareness that followed, De Bode reported just four months later that at Care for the Homeless donations were already five times greater than those for all of 2014. "We're blown out of the water," they said.[10]

My first essay ran in *The New York Times* just two weeks after De Bode's piece, in late January 2015. When I first read it, I recall feeling honest-to-goodness shock to discover that there was another person having the same exact revelation, and desiring to share the very same story at the very same moment in time. Truly, proof that the universe acknowledges the power of a good idea! In the weeks that followed, the collective consequence of our work only fueled my resolve to dig in deeper. These were clearly stories that needed to be told.

LATER THAT YEAR, I HEADED out to San Francisco to further explore the issue of homelessness and menstruation. More than most, it is a city that has grappled with the challenges of rapid economic growth and sweeping gentrification. It is hardly unusual for street dwellers to camp out a stone's throw from the headquarters of superstar companies like Uber and Twitter. Though national levels of homelessness are declining, California's rate remains on the rise and San Francisco claims the second highest per capita rate per square mile in the country, trailing only New York City.[11]

Annie Lascoe, my traveling companion in India, had beckoned me to the Bay Area after she'd been introduced to a local nonprofit organization called Lava Mae, which provides free mobile hygiene facilities. It is the "mobile" part that makes this idea so novel. Lava Mae transforms out-of-service municipal buses into roaming showers and toilets, powered by fire hydrants. Its small fleet traverses the city, parks in neighborhoods most convenient for those who are homeless, and offers people twenty minutes in a private bathroom—hot and cold running water, sparkling-clean facilities, and a dose of what Lava Mae's founders call "radical hospitality." This philosophy of service underlies its mission to offer a meaningful, dignified experience to every person it helps.

Annie had just launched Conscious Period and was initiating a partnership with Lava Mae as a donation site. Joined by her partner, Margo Lang, and professional photographer Laura Epstein-Norris (who also has traveled with me to explore menstrual hygiene and policy in Kenya and Nepal, and provided the photos in this chapter), we set out to distribute tampons and pads to Lava Mae clients, talk with them about what it is like to manage periods while living on the streets, and then, with their permission, publish and share their stories and photos.

Our menstrual crew met up at a gritty stretch of Polk Street in the city's Tenderloin district on a blustery December morning. Dozens of men and women had already formed a line, waiting their turn to take a hot shower on the Lava Mae bus that was stationed there for the day.

Leah Filler, director of global communications for Lava Mae,
stands with a Lava Mae mobile hygiene facility.
(Photo credit: Laura Epstein-Norris)

Smack in the heart of the city, the Tenderloin is a rough neighborhood with an outsized homeless population. It is just blocks from swanky Union Square, where the holiday windows twinkled that day and rising tech bros were headed to work. On this teeming corner, though, what the scene lacked in festivity it made up for in purposeful activity. Lava Mae staff chatted with regulars, making sure they were keeping their appointments, signing up for meals, getting needed medications. Among the numerous resources that are made available throughout the week: haircuts, clothing, veterans' information, voter registration, and information and referrals to allied neighborhood health and service providers.

We went unnoticed in the commotion until Annie pulled out a giant sack of brightly wrapped care packages like some sort of tampon Santa. We drew surprised stares as we announced we had come to talk periods and take photos. Gratefully, we had a willing and chatty crowd. Our resulting photo essay, "Blood in the Streets: Coping with Menstruation While Homeless," featured several of the women we met there:

A forty-something woman named Anne tells us that what is hardest about having her period is the lack of private, safe bathrooms in the residence where she sleeps. Constant intrusions and a broken lock on the door make it hard to use the toilet, change a tampon, and wash her hands and body. Predators linger around bathrooms, knowing women will be there alone. Get in and out as fast as possible is Anne's advice. When offered tampons, she'll take as many as she can carry.

Ruth lets out a hearty laugh and a raspy "no thanks" when offered a package of pads. Happily, the hassle of periods is a thing of the past for her. But now, rather than struggling to access tampons, Ruth needs insulin for her diabetes. The Lava Mae team intervenes and informs her that the bus is strategically parked right next to a building that houses several service providers to which she can go for help with her medical needs and for meals.

And then there is Dawn. She has lived on and off the streets since she was a teenager. She's fiery and energetic, and, she tells us, a would-be writer and staunch feminist. With her husband and her dog, Lucky, she's now homeless again. Like Anne, she remarked on the prohibitive expense of tampons—impossible to afford. A whole box wouldn't fit in her duffle bag, anyway, which she carries at all times. She relies on the spare, sometimes unwrapped tampons that she finds at the circuit of shelters and meal programs she attends. She prefers pads, though, simply because they help her to keep her underwear clean.

Among the coverage that followed our segment was a jolting video produced by *Bustle* later in 2016 highlighting several homeless women in New York City as they walked viewers through a "day in the life" and discussed the challenges and indignities of managing their periods.[12] It quickly amassed more than three million views on YouTube alone.

All of this attention kept the issue high on the public radar. There is no formal count (or any group doing the counting), but since 2015, the public's interest in meeting the menstrual needs of the homeless continues to grow and has practically become a mainstay of volunteerism and the heart of a burgeoning policy agenda. Headlines and article captions like "People Across the Country are Handing Out Tampons to Homeless" and "Mountains of Pads, Tampons Collected for Homeless" are an increasingly common—and welcome—sight.

Among the activists elevating the issue is a motivated Harvard undergrad who herself experienced a bout of homelessness and a weekend stay at a battered women's shelter as a high school student in Portland, Oregon. Nadya Okamoto learned firsthand about the challenges of managing menstruation and heard them as well from other women living in shelters—how they rarely had access to pads and tampons and improvised with pillowcases and mattress stuffing, causing infections and skin irritations. After Okamoto's family moved back into a permanent home, she launched a youth-led nonprofit, PERIOD., which is dedicated to raising awareness by delivering care packages of tampons and pads to women in need in the United States and around the world. Now in college, she oversees more than fifty campus chapters at universities and high schools across the United States and abroad. As a teen herself, she fills a unique role in the movement, engaging youth leaders and educating and rallying students to advocate and take up this cause.

Periods are the New Black: Menstruation Behind Bars

Much like surviving life on the streets, for those caught in America's prison industrial complex, menstrual hygiene is an oxymoron. There's nothing healthy or even resembling hygienic for those who are behind bars. Not once a month. Not ever.

Our jails and prisons were initially built with men's bodies and biology in mind—largely because it was men who were primarily those being arrested and filling the cells. For most of our nation's history, women have been a rarity in the criminal justice system. But times have changed. Today there are more than two hundred thousand female inmates in America. And there are countless ways their reproductive health is compromised. For example, while women represent just 13 percent of the local jail population, they make up more than two-thirds of the victims of staff-on-inmate sexual abuse.[13] And for women who find themselves pregnant in a state prison, in twenty-nine states it is legal to be shackled during medical appointments and even labor.[14]

As for periods, it is unlikely this bodily function was given much meaningful consideration at all. In correction facilities across the country, the number and varied ways in which menstruation is disregarded or disrespected is staggering.

A damning report about the New York State prison system, *Reproductive Injustice*, issued in 2015 by the Correctional Association of New York, calls out the routine failure to provide an adequate supply of maxi pads to inmates. According to the study, the state-mandated allocation is twenty-four pads per cycle. Women who need more—and over half (54 percent) said they did at least once—must apply for a special medical permit, a process that is both time-consuming and intrusive. One of the reasons women stated that they used more than the allotted number was that the products provided are low-quality and barely absorbent, making doubling and even tripling up a necessity.

From the same report, one prison required women to save and present a collection of used, blood-soaked pads when requesting new ones. The medical director was quoted saying,

"We need to have evidence . . . a bag of used sanitary napkins to show that she actually has used them and needs more."[15]

In New York City, women incarcerated at Rikers Island tell of horrifying, brutal conditions. Reported incidents of sexual abuse by staff there are more than double the national rate according to the Department of Justice.[16] As for menstrual matters, until last year the official policy had been to provide a weekly 144-count box of thin, nonadhesive pads to be shared among every *fifty* inmates. If equally distributed (assuming the person who has that job does so fairly), that would amount to a paltry eleven pads per period, only enough for a change every twelve hours during the duration of one menstrual cycle. As reported by *The New York Times* in April 2017, inmates suggested that distribution was indeed distorted, limited to particular housing units, and even then, "only dispensed to certain individuals—you had to be sort of chummy-chummy in order to receive them."[17]

In Michigan, eight female inmates filed a federal class action lawsuit in 2014 against Muskegon County's jail for "inhumane and degrading policies." Among many problems cited was the refusal to provide an adequate supply of menstrual products, forcing inmates to routinely bleed through their clothes and then to fail to provide a change of clothes until laundry day. When one inmate requested pads, an officer told her she was "shit out of luck" and threatened that she "better not bleed on the floor." A new jail opened a year after the case was filed, which addressed some of the concerns raised about the condition of the facilities themselves. As for the question about access to menstrual products, the court found that only deprivation, but not a delay, in receiving menstrual products amounted to a legal violation of rights under the standard for "cruel and unusual punishment."[18] (For those wondering, the judge in the case was a woman. Disappointing.)

According to *Reproductive Health Behind Bars in California*, a 2016 report issued by the American Civil Liberties Union of California, women in county jail who "hoard" menstrual products are subject to punishment. Said one inmate, "Pads are not dispensed as they are supposed to be. We are forced to reuse them, we are forced to beg for what we need, and if an officer is in a bad mood they are allowed to take what we have and say we are hoarding."[19] It's a lose-lose proposition—damned if you try to plan ahead, damned if you have to beg a guard.

And in 2016, a Kentucky judge was stunned to find a female defendant appear in court for arraignment wearing no pants and menstruating. She explained that correctional officers refused to give her pads or a change of clothes when she told them she had her period, despite repeated requests. Footage from the courtroom went viral—an intense scene in which the outraged judge called the jail staff from the bench, demanding an explanation and shouting to the courtroom, "Am I in the *Twilight Zone?* What is happening here?"[20]

Often when it comes to accessing products, inmates are recommended to turn to the commissary to take matters into their own hands and purchase a personal supply of tampons, pads, and other hygiene items. But given that more than 70 percent of female inmates come from poverty, that turns out to be a near impossible luxury. The poor only get poorer while they're locked away. And it's not as if there are jailhouse bargains, either. Jacked up commissary prices in facilities run by private vendors stand to profit off prisoners' backs (or, in these cases, vaginas). The Federal Bureau of Prisons Commissary Price List posts that a box of eighteen generic tampons costs $7.65.[21] The commissary of the Muskegon County Jail in Michigan, which was at the center of the lawsuit, sells a package of eight for $6.57 and individual tampons for fifty cents apiece.[22] Among New York State prisons, where women earn an average of seventeen cents per hour for the jobs they work, commissaries sell individual tampons and pads for about a quarter.[23] Meanwhile, on the outside, on average a forty-count box of generic tampons can be purchased for around six dollars—still a stretch expense for the poor, but at more than double the price behind bars, it is simply an impossibility.

For prisoners, the physical effects of menstruation are as daunting as trying to secure menstrual products. A 2009 Australian study published by the *Internet Journal of Criminology* suggests that incarcerated women experience exacerbated PMS and menstrual discomfort, from cramps to moodiness to headaches.[24] And when women in prison menstruate simultaneously—not unusual given the crowded quarters—the overall conditions and collective health issues become exponentially worse.

And then, of course, there is the psychological burden of rationing and requesting menstrual products, a dynamic that creates an unhealthy and humiliating power imbalance. A 2012 letter from an inmate in Washington, published by the Committee Against Political Repression, describes scenarios where pads are used as bargaining chips or leveraged to manipulate prisoners. She describes menstruating in prison as "an experience that either intentionally works to degrade inmates, or degrades us as a result of cost-saving measures: either way, the results are the same. Prison makes us hate part of ourselves; it turns us against our own bodies."[25]

As with so many aspects of women's lives, existing within the penal system is all about control. "The reasons for keeping supplies for women in prison limited are not purely financial," wrote Chandra Bozelko in June 2015 for the *Guardian*. Ivy League–educated and by every measure a thoughtful, tenacious communicator, Bozelko spent six years at the York Correctional Institution, a high-security women's prison in Connecticut and has blogged extensively about her experience. Her essay, "Prisons That Withhold Menstrual Pads Humiliate Women and Violate Basic Rights," was among the first mainstream public accounts of menstrual inequity in prisons and one of the few told from a firsthand perspective. Bozelko's words are haunting: "Even though keeping inmates clean would seem to be in the prison's self-interest, prisons control their wards by keeping sanitation just out of reach. Stains on clothes seep into self-esteem and serve as an indelible reminder of one's powerlessness in prison. Asking for something you need crystallizes the power differential between inmates and guards."[26]

Bozelko has been out of prison for several years now and has since become an ardent advocate for fair criminal justice policies, especially as they impact women. When we first met in person, I was taken by her calm, kind demeanor, intense focus, and utter clarity about the harm of depriving inmates of their agency via hygiene, in particular. Part of what makes her stories sting are the tiniest details, the minutiae that amount to some of the cruelest affronts. Like the challenge of having to evenly share the *five* pads per week that were provided for her and her cell mate—an odd number making the negotiation more fraught than need be if there simply was an even split. Or because pads were only distributed on weekdays, Friday would mean the looming dread of having to ration over the weekend. Even worse, when Bozelko developed a cervical polyp that went undiagnosed, she wound up with vaginal bleeding that lasted for two years *straight*. Pad negotiations with guards and other inmates became a daily, rather than monthly, humiliation.

When sent to solitary confinement where all personal belongings were forbidden, her sole option was to beg a prison guard for a pad and even then, just one was offered at a time; an arbitrary denial meant bleeding right on the floor. During regular cell searches for contraband, she told me how dirty clothing was often ridiculed then confiscated, with period-stained underwear a frequent target for both fates. And the sheer horror of prisoner transport—a process she described as so dehumanizing that many do all they can to bypass it, even if it is to their detriment (such as missing an appointment with a doctor, lawyer, or social worker). Bozelko explained that transport necessitates shackling, often for as long as eighteen hours and a ban on carrying anything at all. Those who are menstruating have to rely on guards to sneak a pad or tampon and then are left to change it in full view while handcuffed. Handwashing is out of the question, even if tampon-changing fingers are bloodied.

And it is not just access to products. Bozelko also reports that it is fairly common for women to be denied access to showers for up to five days, even during menstruation. Broken toilets are common in prison, which Bozelko attributes to the same power dynamic. She wrote in the *Guardian*: "[They] seem to like to keep people living in a situation where there's either blood, urine, or feces on a toilet and there's no way to clean that up because paper towels are contraband and toilet paper is in short supply." Toilets and showers are not monitored and are off-limits from cameras (an otherwise beneficial practice and the result of the Prison Rape Elimination Act's prohibition on cross-gender genital viewing). But this means that unhygienic toilet conditions—from backups caused by flushing of pads to the regular leaks and streaks left by menstrual blood—go largely unseen by the powers that be.

Deprivation of hygiene in the broadest sense—broken toilets, refusal of showers, inadequate products—is unhealthy to start and further exacerbated by menstruation. It also makes women especially easy targets for abuse, which is why Bozelko insists that the most damaging aspect of periods for inmates is their lack of agency. She quotes the Russian author Dostoevsky: "The degree of civilization in a society can be judged by entering its prisons." As we talked, she analogized that the ways society writ large uses menstruation to marginalize women plays out most vividly in the correctional setting. The words she said out loud were stark: "Given that there is no other way for prisoners to get the supplies they need except from an authority—either a guard who passes out free pads or commissary staffer—this shows just how subjugated menstruating women are. In prison, access to supplies is not about finances but an outgrowth of policies where men control everything and need us to be dependent. There is fluidity in a homeless or low-income woman's life that allows her the freedom to manage her affairs, even if imperfectly.

She can walk to a shelter, a food pantry. Borrow from a friend or stranger. In some ways, those women's plights don't crystallize the problem with periods quite the way that prisons do."

The media began to communicate this story in fits and starts in 2015, capturing an overlapping interest on the part of the public in national calls for criminal justice reform. Several noteworthy articles joined the chorus of "The Year of the Period," particularly Bozelko's account of menstruation and hygiene and also moderate coverage of the published report on the New York State Prison system. The Netflix favorite *Orange Is the New Black* aired an entire episode in the fifth season focused on a prison-wide maxi pad shortage, spurring a slew of related commentary in 2016. But overall, the issue remains a widely underreported phenomenon and frustratingly unsympathetic cause.

Unlike the explosion of interest in aiding the homeless, there has been a dearth of calls to action to offer help for inmates. Lack of empathy is perhaps one of the biggest barriers. Women behind bars tend to be among the most invisible and least understood in our society. Or the most despised. To hear President Trump rail about "American carnage," it is not surprising that many are prone to equate arrest with depravity. It harkens the old adage, "Don't do the crime if you can't do the time." But the majority of women who are swept into the system are punished for committing nonviolent offenses—crimes like drug possession, shoplifting, and prostitution—and are often victims of abuse themselves.[27] Breaking the law should not be viewed as an invitation to bodily degradation.

But even if people were so inclined to initiate local donation drives, for example, it would be nearly impossible to ensure that menstrual products reach prisoners. Tampons and pads aren't accepted in most facilities, which typically only facilitate book donations. And those that do allow items from the outside often have daunting requirements; these may need to be purchased from a sanctioned wholesaler (meaning its employees and delivery people undergo background checks) or inspected for smuggled contraband.

As a result, there are sparingly few charitable interventions. As of this writing, only two national nonprofit organizations specifically address inmates' menstrual needs: Pads2Prisons; and A Woman's Worth, which provides services for domestic violence survivors and the homeless, and recently launched a menstrual product collection project called Dignity Behind Bars.

All of these challenges speak to the real and urgent need to press for systemic change. Unlike the many new projects focused on the homeless, where public interest now runs high and the ability to get products *en masse* to those in need has proven feasible, the obstacles for doing the same for the incarcerated are too steep. Here, full-blown policy reform is needed, with an explicit focus on the importance of access to hygiene, generally, including and especially menstrual products.

It Doesn't Add Up: Periods in School

Whereas the stories and statistics describing how girls in developing countries struggle to manage school and menstruation are prevalent (and shocking), there's been no comparable attempt to document if and to what extent the same issues might exist for poor students in the American educational system. Here's what we do know: a majority of public school students—51 percent—come from low-income families.[28] Nearly one in five teenagers age twelve to seventeen live in poverty,[29] which, for a family of four, means getting by on $24,600 each year.[30] After rent, food, and other bills, even with the help of public benefits, that doesn't leave much room for anything else. Not all the things a student needs. Like books. Like shoes. Like maxi pads.

As highlighted from reports around the world, helping girls to properly nourish and care for their bodies bolsters their ability to learn. In the spirit of this knowledge, during the school day the US federal government offers free and reduced-price breakfast and lunch programs for students who qualify. It is a matter of good nutrition and health, part of what students need to be productive in class.

But in order to be fully engaged in the classroom, menstrual products and support are as much of a necessity as a square meal, or as the pencils and paper on their desk—and yet, tampons and pads are not provided, either at all or with any sort of systematic approach. The need is perhaps doubly great for younger teens who are more prone to be caught off guard by the arrival of their period (which is less likely to be regular), more embarrassed by it, and more likely to be without budgets of their own to buy what they need, when it is needed.

In October 2015, a group of high school students was convened by New York City Council Member Julissa Ferreras-Copeland to participate in a discussion and focus group about this very issue. They were given the space to be frank and honest about periods and how they affect their daily lives at school. Many shared how hard it can be to be productive in class, or to attend school at all, when they don't have any or enough menstrual products. In a subsequent series of related media reports out of the United Kingdom in March 2017—spurred after a police officer in the small town of Leeds, England, discovered that lack of access to menstrual supplies was leading to notably high truancy rates—British students echoed identical concerns.

A desperate statement offered over BBC radio by a girl who started her period at age eleven, one of five children in her family and unable to afford pads: "I wrapped a sock around my underwear just to stop the bleeding, because I didn't want to get shouted at. And I wrapped a whole tissue roll around my underwear, just to keep my underwear dry until I got home. I didn't know what else to do."[31]

Across the board, these were the most common of the teens' reflections as reported from both sides of the pond: how panic sets in when their parents can't afford to buy tampons or pads on the very day they are needed. And how they're sometimes reluctant to ask for them at all, knowing how stretched the family's income is, or when it is still many days before a paycheck is due. If necessary, they'll try to get by using just one tampon or pad per day. Alarmingly, and understandably, concerns about smelling badly or staining their clothes—and subsequently being made fun of or bullied for it—pose greater worries than the potential health risks caused by infrequent changing of products.

And among the New York City students, some shared that while the nurse's office in their school may offer an emergency stash, having to ask in front of a room full of people can be embarrassing, intimidating, even detrimental to their attendance. One young woman told of a time she had to endure a long wait at the nurse's office, and an improperly signed hall pass, resulting not only in missed class time but after-school detention. Nearly all said it was hard to concentrate in class and do their best when they were worried about leaks, stains, and where the next tampon or pad was coming from. Some even said they'd be interested in using a menstrual cup as a more affordable option if there was a way to wash it privately in school.

When asked what they *did* need, the answer was utterly obvious to them, as it should be to all of us: for tampons and pads to be readily available in bathrooms. Without having to ask someone or see the nurse. Or wait in line. Kind of like . . . the toilet paper and soap and paper towels that are already provided. It is a logical equation and one that contributes to a better learning experience. It just adds up.

The media reported widely on the issue throughout "The Year of the Period" and public reaction was overwhelmingly supportive, especially in outlets that reach young readers like *Teen Vogue* and *Seventeen*. Unlike the outcry in response to the plight of the homeless, though, the school issue did not result in a spike in comparable local donation projects. It did, however, generate interest and enthusiasm from policy makers who have introduced and passed new laws and called for more research into the problem, as well as from numerous school boards and administrators around the country, and even students themselves who pressed their principals to take action. In fact, some of the very best commentary I've ever received has come from feisty middle schoolers seeking advice about how to raise the roof on this issue.

COLLEGE CAMPUSES ACROSS THE COUNTRY—from NYU to UCLA, and from the University of Nebraska to the

University of Arizona—have taken up the cause of menstrual access, too.

Most have done it under the banner of gender equity and fairness, though it certainly is part of the fallout of rising income inequality and a growing cohort of college students who live in poverty. According to NPR, "as the cost of college grows, research shows that so does the number of hungry and homeless students."[32]

Among the success stories: the vice president for finance and administration at Connecticut College proudly backed students who proposed a plan for making menstrual products free on campus, calling it, "an equity issue, social justice, kind of a women's rights issue."[33]

The student body president at Brown University decided that rather than petition the powers that be, the student government itself would raise funds to buy menstrual products and distribute them in all nonresidential bathrooms—women's, men's, and gender-neutral—highlighting the need for trans inclusivity.[34]

And as reported by the *Columbia Spectator*, students wrote public letters like this one: "That these requests needed to be made indicates the university's utter lack of support for people who menstruate, a group that includes a significant portion of the student body. Sure, I can easily find a free condom on Barnard and Columbia's campuses, but why can't I find a free tampon in the bathrooms? Why does the administration care about my sexual protective rights, but not how I handle my monthly menstrual cycle?"[35] Columbia University itself later experienced a bit of a roller-coaster implementation after administrators were eventually persuaded to provide free menstrual products in the Health Medical Services Center in March 2016, but then

announced the program would be discontinued due to perceived lack of interest. The student council pushed back, and
the tampons and pads reappeared by the next semester.

At Grinnell College in Iowa, one student initiated a campus-
wide caper that transformed into a productive protest. She used
bobby pins to break open campus dispensers, making available
all the tampons and pads for others to use. "I freed your tampons kept behind lock, key and quarter," she wrote in a public
letter to the college. "Bleeding bodies deserve to think about
Foucault and micro-organisms and the history of the bleeding
bodies that came before them. When we menstruate, however
unexpectedly, we should not feel fear in the pits of our stomachs
because of your lack of foresight. We are a part of this college.
Provide free menstrual products to students who need them so
I can stop picking the locks on your bogus machines."[36] The
president of Grinnell, a former deputy director of the National
Institutes of Health, agreed with her argument. "It's not unrea-
sonable to provide free menstrual products everywhere, including on campuses, especially in an affluent society and at an institution like Grinnell," he announced. "We have free toilet paper,
so wanting the same for menstrual products is not extreme.
This is a normal human function."[37] When students returned to
campus in September 2016, all of its bathrooms featured new
machines stocked with free products.

It is worth noting, too, that in 2013 Grinnell granted
$100,000—a prize it makes annually to young innovators in
social justice—to Sustainable Health Enterprises, the group
described in chapter two that makes low-cost pads out of
banana fibers in Rwanda. In light of that award, "to continue
to not offer tampons and pads for free on [our] campus," the

college president said, "would be hypocritical." Better late than never.

COMBINED, THESE STORIES AND SITUATIONS start to paint a vivid picture. We may not banish or deliberately shun women and girls during menstruation, but among our poorest and most vulnerable, many are indeed suffering for lack of access to adequate menstrual hygiene. For those who are marginalized—by lack of resources, by lack of power, by lack of agency—they are rendered exponentially more at risk by their periods. Requesting help or a "handout," even a "hand up," in any circumstance is hard enough. Asking for the same to manage menstruation is still clearly a whole other league of humiliation in our society.

So for anyone still wondering if we have something of a menstrual calamity on our hands here in the United States, I would wager the answer is a solid yes.

And while a groundswell of period positivity and stigma smashing may slowly start to reverse that, and even as new laws are introduced to mandate the provision of menstrual products, we still have a long way to go. But it is only in shining a light on the problem and sharing the stories that we can hope to begin raising solutions. We surely succeeded in sparking the conversation. And now, the world actually appears to be to listening.

PERIODS GONE PUBLIC

chapter four

CARRIE AT THE PROM

While I had the freedom to reject my own shame that day, millions of people who menstruate around the world do not because of the stigma still associated with periods. I ran to say this stigma—it does exist—and we overcome it every day.

—Marathoner Kiran Gandhi[1]

WHEN IT COMES TO BOLD activism, a good period moment is hard to stage. That's part of the dual charm and challenge of menstruation, of course. Its timing is rarely in our control. In many ways, it's that very unexpectedness that captures what was so groundbreaking about "The Year of the Period." There was no prefab plan, no gimmick, nor even any coordination— at least at first. Just as I'd had my moment of menstrual revelation on New Year's Day 2015, so too were others coming to realize the same. And then, remarkably—simultaneously—taking that knowledge and translating it into uniquely individual expressions of rebellion. Artists, athletes, journalists, gamers, illustrators, students, and others all lent voice to a growing chorus.

This chapter's period slang title reflects perhaps one of the most watched and expertly executed, albeit fictional, period events ever. In the real world, though, unlike Stephen King's 1974 dark, menstrual-harnessed fantasy, opportunities for action and activism (minus the tragic humiliation, thankfully) present themselves at unexpected times, just as periods are prone to do. That is how Kiran Gandhi's story started. It was April 26, 2015, when Gandhi's long-awaited day of personal triumph—her first marathon run—also became a catalyzing emblem for the emerging "Year of the Period."

I had been training for the 2015 London Marathon for a year. I knew that I was going to get my period at some point, but I didn't know I would get it right then. Like many women who have been caught on their cycles unprepared, I started evaluating my options. I could have used a pad, but chafing is a problem for all marathoners, and I didn't want to hurt myself. Tampons were another option, but I didn't want to have to run twenty-six miles while holding a backup tampon, ready to change it at any moment. These options seemed so unnecessary, so uncomfortable. To me, it made far more sense to do the race without any foreign objects in my body. To just . . . run.[2]

A striking twenty-eight-year-old Indian American woman raised in New York City, educated at Georgetown University and Harvard Business School, and a rock star to boot (she's also a professional musician and drummer who got her start touring with hip-hop performer M.I.A.), Gandhi ran all 26.2 miles of the London Marathon while "free bleeding." Photos of her crossing the finish line decked out in a pink monogrammed tank and bright-orange, blood-stained tights, beaming proudly as she posed with her father, brother, and friends, went viral following an online essay she published, "Going with the Flow: Blood & Sisterhood at the London Marathon."

Kiran Gandhi (center) at the London Marathon.
(Used with permission)

Gandhi's story soon drew major media attention, offering her a platform to reveal a more audacious motive and mind-set. "A marathon itself is a centuries-old symbolic act," she proclaimed. "Why not use it as a means to draw light to my sisters who don't have menstrual products, or who hide their periods from the world, in shame, pretending it doesn't exist?"

She's since shared her story many hundreds of times—with me, with countless reporters, on college campuses, and even with leaders at the White House and the United Nations, through interviews, her own writing, and as an accomplished performer and presenter—offering a mile-by-mile account of her emotions on the day of the race and in its aftermath. She has incorporated the topic of menstruation brilliantly into her music, an eclectic, electronic, and decidedly feminist brand, which she writes and performs under the moniker Madame Gandhi. And she has joined forces with other artists, innovators, and activists from all over the world. In doing so, Gandhi has become a refreshing voice and leading force in helping to spark public discussion about menstrual health, comfort, and access. She is adamant: "Women must own the narrative of our own bodies. Speaking about an issue is the only way to combat its silence, and dialogue is the only way for innovative solutions to occur."

This is a key tenet of a movement built around a verboten topic, of course: women's bodies and realities will be routinely ignored or dismissed or denigrated unless and until we force the conversation.

Simple and straightforward as her act was, she was also aware of the shock value it entailed. At the time of her marathon run, "The Year of the Period" was brewing but not quite yet embedded in the mainstream. On a good day, the Internet has not historically been a terribly kind or welcoming place for women's voices, especially those of feminist ilk. That is doubly true for those who bleed from their vaginas for the world to see. And so, along with the positive media coverage also came a barrage of ridicule and criticism, especially among right-wing pundits. "And people wonder why we mock progressive feminism. THIS. This is why," huffed the writers from *Chicks on the Right*, a conservative blog and radio show.[3] "So far, so third-wave feminism," jabbed the bloggers at *Breitbart*, which went on to claim that the act of free bleeding—which "has existed in the outer corners of the feministisphere for years"—was actually a hoax to troll feminists by getting them to join "made-up crusades to humiliate themselves."[4]

Ultimately though, efforts to undermine Gandhi were met with her defiant retort that menstruation's long history of being subject to stigma and shame are the very essence of what she's combating. Her actions did not set off a wave of free bleeders by choice; nor has she made an ongoing practice of eschewing menstrual products. But if they had . . . and she did? Well, so what?

In early 2016, *New York* magazine's Noreen Malone took a stab at defining period feminism: "[If] menstruation is a wholly natural part of life for anyone born a woman . . . feeling obligated to hide the smells and the stains and the cramps is as symptomatic of the patriarchy as unequal pay and sexual harassment. And there's a little fun to be had in the shock value of it, too: the modern day equivalent of bra burning."[5] As this concept has unfolded in the public eye, Gandhi has emerged as a most compelling, even irresistible, spokesperson—young, bold, articulate, intelligent—who has used her art and music, and her newfound menstrual celebrity, to raise the profile of the issue and promote smart policy reform and global charitable efforts.

I have a particular affinity for Gandhi, whom I've come to know and deeply admire as we collaborated closely on policy issues and discussed her marathon story. Truth be told, at around the same time in the spring of 2015, I free bled my way through a (much shorter) race as well. I ran under similar circumstances as Gandhi, a coincidental bout of silent protest. As part of my New Year's Day creed and polar bear determination, I joined my friends in a race called "MuckFest"—a giant obstacle course designed to send runners through enormous puddles of mud, chest- and chin-deep at some points. My period started unexpectedly just as I arrived at the starting line and, not surprisingly, there was not a spare tampon to be found. Mildly mortified and panicked, I decided to complete the event out of necessity, not so much to make a statement but because it beat the alternative (stand alone with toilet paper wadded in my shorts and wait for my group at the finish). But as I traversed the course and slogged through the mud, I became acutely aware of the women for whom lack of access to menstrual supplies is a regular reality, not a temporary inconvenience or flash of embarrassment. By the time I finished the race, caked in mud and minimal bloodstains, I felt something close to fierce. I briefly considered blogging about my story; I hadn't yet heard of Gandhi or her marathon run. Ultimately I concluded the world would not be enchanted by a forty-seven-year-old menstruating on a muddy suburban course.

Lesson for movement builders: the messenger matters.

This role was made for Gandhi. She wears it well. (As proof of her cool factor, she even taught me how and when to properly use the word "dope," which has both impressed and mortified my kids. She is so dope.)

And so, in mid-2015, a free-bleeding, rock star marathoner became the face of a wave of conversation-provoking acts in the name of menstruation. In Gandhi's own words, "it was radical and absurd and bloody in ways I couldn't have imagined." So, too, has been the trajectory of this movement.

The next high-profile protest that would ultimately help catalyze and define "The Year of the Period": a public smack-down of Instagram. A few weeks prior to Gandhi's run, another bright star and ambitious millennial, poet, and artist Rupi Kaur, posted a photo to her account. The picture was part of a series called *Period.*—a project she'd created for a course at the University of Waterloo. A self-portrait, the image is of Kaur lying in a rumpled bed, her body curled—a haunting, yet all too familiar portrayal capturing just what it looks and feels like to manage dull, persistent menstrual pain. A dark-red stain is visible on the backside of her gray sweatpants along with a telltale leak on the bed sheets.

Instagram not once but *twice* removed the photo, claiming it violated its "community guidelines," which otherwise bans images of sexual acts, violence, and nudity. In response, Kaur posted on her Facebook and Tumblr accounts, "Thank you Instagram for providing me with the exact response my work was created to critique." And then continued with the blistering words of a poet: "Their patriarchy is leaking. Their misogyny is leaking. We will not be censored."

"I wondered why I scurry to hide my tampons and pads from the world and why I'm too ashamed to tell people I'm in pain because of my period," Kaur told the *Huffington Post*, describing her initial inspiration for the project. "As if it's a bad thing to have. This was just a small part of it. The issue is so much deeper. Some women can't visit their places of worship, or leave their homes or cook for their families while menstruating because they're considered dirty. We're laughed at in public if we have leaks. It goes on and on really."[6]

Public reaction to Instagram's censorship was intense and rapid and generated far more attention (and views) than the photo likely would have otherwise. Instagram eventually reinstated the image and issued an apology but not before Kaur's story accumulated hundreds of thousands of social media hits, and significant mainstream coverage, too, including in outlets like the *Washington Post*. In the court of public opinion, menstruation scored another meaningful win.

As the year went on, in part spurred by these stories but also by the growing body of quality, substantive reporting on menstruation and related activism, the issue continued to register on the public radar. Twitter, in particular, became the go-to medium and method for engaging the masses. Campaigns to normalize, publicize, and "out" menstruation rapidly accrued within a few months. #JustATampon featured selfies of prominent Brits holding, yes, a tampon. RACKET.'s New York City–based collection drive organized Broadway stars to pose with maxi pads using #PeriodsWithoutShame. #HappyToBleed was formed in India to counter the famous Sabarimala Hindu temple and shrine's centuries-old ban on women, and its latest call for full-body scanners to ensure the exclusion of menstruating women. #FreeTheTampons made the case for all private businesses and public restrooms to provide tampons and pads as they do toilet paper and soap. And after *The New York Times* ran a 2015 article called "Our Bodies, Our Feeds," arguing for a "microprotest against a modern paradox" to reject stigma and shame, #LiveTweetYourPeriod called upon women to share their menstrual woes online.

oaksmash ● · 10 months ago   + Follow

❤ 6,873 likes   💬 113 comments   *Instagram*

Hamilton star Okieriete "Oak" Onaodowan's
#PeriodsWithoutShame post
(Used with permission)

But it took the brashest of them all, then presidential candidate Donald Trump, to unleash a menstrual maelstrom that inspired not just hashtags but front-page news. In August 2015, right after FOX News hosted the very first Republican debate, Trump essentially charged Megyn Kelly with menstruating while moderating. At the time, it was still early in the campaign and there were a whopping seventeen presidential hopefuls seeking the Republican party nomination. Ten of them crowded the stage in Cleveland, Ohio, perched behind a line of podiums on a steamy Friday night. Trump's crass demeanor throughout the debate was par for the course and certainly didn't surprise anyone as he jostled with his rivals and the moderators. Nor did Kelly's blunt questioning about Trump's long string of prior insults about women strike the audience as out of line: "You've called women you don't like 'fat pigs,' 'dogs,' 'slobs,' and 'disgusting animals,'" she asserted, and then followed with, "Does that sound to you like the temperament of a man we should elect as president?"

The next morning on the weekend talk show circuit, CNN anchor Don Lemon grilled Trump about his performance at the opening debate, to which he responded that it was Kelly who should be called out for asking "ridiculous" questions. He went on to complain, "You could see there was blood coming out of her eyes, blood coming out of her 'wherever,'" a phrase immediately assumed to mean menstruation. Trump vehemently denied it. (So did conservative firebrand Ann Coulter on his behalf.) The charge spread like wildfire nonetheless and landed the word *menstruation* smack in the middle of the election coverage—on the front page of nearly every major national and small-town newspaper in between.

While that in itself was noteworthy, so too was the swift reaction of American women who fired back on Twitter, Trump's own forum of choice. People began live tweeting the details of their periods to @TheRealDonaldTrump using #PeriodsAreNotAnInsult to make the point that mockery of menstruation is juvenile, harmful, and, quite frankly, part of the very pattern of misogyny for which Trump came under fire. Quite ironically, it now seems, we have the POTUS to at least partially thank for elevating the issue.

Months later, another Internet sensation emerged. #Periods ForPence was the brainchild of an anonymous citizen who later "outed" herself—Laura Shanley, an Indiana mom, social worker, and activist extraordinaire—to protest then Governor Mike Pence for his extreme antiabortion stance. A state law that Pence signed in 2016 was one of the most intrusive and punitive in the nation, not only forcing women to disclose their reasons for terminating a pregnancy but requiring that miscarried fetal tissue be interred or cremated regardless of the duration of the pregnancy. In other words, mistaking an early miscarriage for a heavy period could subject women to criminal penalties. The #PeriodsForPence response: flood the governor's office with detailed talk about periods. "Let's make our bodies Mike's business for real, if this is how he wants it," was its initial Facebook call to action. And many thousands did. Hoosier women jammed the phone lines and took to social media to report the nitty gritty of their menstrual flow, from cramps to clots, and birth control to bloating.

When Pence became Trump's vice presidential pick, the public shaming campaign went national, calling out the sheer irony that the top two men on the presidential ticket had both stirred controversy over periods. #PeriodsForPence's Facebook page (renamed #PeriodsForPoliticians) was joined by another, #TamponsForTrump, and ballooned to a collective one hundred thousand followers. The week prior to the 2016 election, I joined the group for its first public rally at the Indiana Statehouse, where it spurred perhaps the first-ever Get Out The (Menstrual) Vote task force.

Periods again trended on Twitter during Women's History Month in 2017. *Hidden Figures* actress and singer Janelle Monáe kicked off a call for period pride, offering the simplest three words: "Menstrual Period Blood. #WomensHistoryMonth." Her tweet set off a barrage of responses, many of them supporters who thanked her. But she was not without a cohort of agitated critics, which prompted her to clap back with some political edge: "It's sad that there are prob folks more grossed out by and/or ashamed of menstrual period blood than they are the current administration." Shortly after, on International Women's Day, March 8, 2017, *TIME* published a beautifully written essay by actress, activist, and humanitarian Meghan Markle (who also happens to be Prince Harry's significant other), "How Periods Affect Potential." Markle decried the plight of period stigma and lack of access to hygiene—and its impact on education and opportunity—for girls in India, after returning from a menstrual tour similar to my own.[7] Her piece spurred even more supportive Twitter commentary, including that from all-stars like Serena Williams and Priyanka Chopra.

When it comes to breaking taboos, I'm a firm believer that online engagement really does matter and isn't simply a lazy case of armchair activism, a.k.a. "slactivism." Social media is a living laboratory where ideas can be test driven, where conversations can start, where awareness is raised. It's true that dialogue can quickly turn nasty, even threatening, and is often unproductive—and that 140-character messages don't always lend themselves to substantive or meaningful interaction. (Just follow @TheRealDonaldTrump for proof of that.) But for an otherwise off-limits topic like menstruation, the mere ability to place periods front and center, in a way that might not be possible in real-life exchanges, is a remarkably effective way to chip away at stigma. Relatedly, over the past year, Twitter offered an essential forum for personal storytelling related to political activism—for example, regarding sexual harassment following the release of the Trump's "pussy-grabbing tapes" (#NotOkay). And in anticipation of the US Supreme Court 2016 ruling on abortion rights, #ShoutYourAbortion encouraged women to go public with their personal experiences as a way to dismantle stereotypes and reclaim the narrative. With hashtag activism comes visibility, as well as community. It catalyzes conversation that can lead to action, especially for issues or groups that have been deliberately stifled. In the case of menstruation, even simple tweets like "Hey @RealDonaldTrump, I had my period last week and was still 1000x more awesome than you the whole time" (an actual tweet by an actual awesome user) not only allow the messenger to revel in her own moment of anonymous empowerment but also to convey confidence to countless others who just may be inspired to abandon their shame and silence, too.

POPULAR FIGURES—ACTORS, SINGERS, ATHLETES—speaking causally and openly about menstruation helped to generate media and bring period talk into the mainstream in ways that paralleled, even fueled, activism. While not necessarily rebellious or even deliberate, a celebrity's unconventional commentary still makes for great power of persuasion. One of my favorites came from the acid-tongued comedienne Sarah Silverman in a December 2015 tweet:

Sarah Silverman ✔
@SarahKSilverman

Menstrual Cycle Haiku:

Crime scene in ur pants.
Ain't no man could handle that.
Maybe a marine.

But among the all-star period moments, one of the most celebrated followed the 2016 Golden Globe Awards. Best Actress winner Jennifer Lawrence brought the discussion to the red carpet through her matter-of-fact banter with *Harper's Bazaar*. The reason she wore a (gorgeous) sleeveless red Dior dress? Her period. "That was my Plan B dress," she shared in the May 2016 issue. "Plan A was a dress that I couldn't wear because awards season is synced with my menstrual cycle." "[The red one] was loose at the front," she further explained, "and I didn't have to worry about sucking anything in. The other dress was really tight, and I'm not going to suck in my uterus. I don't have to do that." The comments were notable enough that out of the feature-length article, that particular segment was shared and re-shared. "JLaw" is the everywoman-turned-movie star who trips awkwardly at awards ceremonies, takes goofy (and naked) selfies, and can have a laugh at her own expense. While her period quip feels like an inside joke between old friends, really it is creating a safe space for the millions of fans who admire and want to emulate her.

Later in 2016 at the Emmy Awards, while walking the red carpet, comedienne Amy Schumer went for crass, her signature style, when fielding the ritualistic question, "who are you wearing?"

"Vivienne Westwood, Tom Ford and an o.b. tampon!" Her response prompted cheers and virtual fist bumps across the Internet.

And teen superstars Demi Lovato and Miley Cyrus opened up with the nitty gritty details of their respective first periods. Poor Miley's was on the set of *Hannah Montana*. Both have partnered with Betty.co.uk, a British health, wellness, and gossip website for teens, in a campaign to erase the embarrassment and "encourage young girls to embrace the natural menstruation process." Even Katy Perry offered details of her period with her ninety-six million Twitter followers to dispel pregnancy rumors. Hardly revolutionary, but certainly role model–esque—and, again, helping create a comfortable, open environment for periods, especially for the younger set.

What is notable about these examples is just how mundane they are. And they acknowledge that in many ways, periods are nothing but normal—just another part of life for half the population. And yet, we've been unable to talk about that reality in polite, open discourse. It has been a relief, even a revelation, to see those boundaries stretched. It's a reminder, too, of how far we still have to go to make periods apart of the regular ebb and flow of conversation.

Like pop stars, athletes are an influential messenger. In some ways even more so, given the fierce physical nature of their jobs and lives. The 2016 sports world was rocked by menstrual mentions, too. British tennis star Heather Watson first broke the code of silence when she suggested her poor performance at the Australian Open was due to "girl stuff." True, she didn't actually say the word *period*, but it was still a rarity in the industry to even acknowledge menstruation. Martina Navratilova weighed in on that challenge in a BBC radio interview suggesting, "It's a bit of a taboo. You don't want to use it as an excuse, but it can affect some players in a big way."[8] Shortly after, Watson's Wimbledon competitor Petra Kvitová joined her in admitting that periods are "difficult" for female players.[9] This seems more than believable considering that Wimbledon may just be the ultimate menstrual purgatory: mandatory white outfits and one bathroom break per set? Clearly, rules that were not set by people who are thinking about periods.

Stigmas were further smashed, maybe even a full stroke closer to obliterated, at the 2016 Summer Olympics in Rio. Swimmer Fu Yuanhui of China remarked unapologetically about her disappointing performance in the 4x100 meter medley relay, acknowledging that she had her period that day. She said it in such a natural, breezy tone (she was constantly called "adorable" by the media), but it was the public response that turned heads. The story blew up social media, and in the best possible way. Messages of support flooded the airwaves and an overwhelming consensus that acknowledging menstruation by athletes shouldn't be shocking (or cause for keeping them out of pools either). Not only did period pragmatism "win the Internet," so claimed CNN, but even conservative outlets like *Breitbart*, the original roughshod critic of Gandhi's run and Valenti's *Guardian* column, posted an uncharacteristically even-keeled and supportive essay commending Yuanhui's openness. It was *The New York Times* that linked the positive response to our growing movement here in the United States. It reported, "In many parts of the world, menstruation is still regarded with shame and distaste, though that is changing. In the United States, creative hashtag campaigns on social media and online petitions have challenged the discomfort about period-related topics."[10]

Nighttime television and comedy news programs reinforced the story too. These are perhaps my favorite sources of sharp, satirical discourse and I was especially impressed by how vigorously the shows took on the topic of periods. *The Daily Show* scripted regular segments on menstrual policy advances. *The Nightly Show* instituted a weekly feature called "Tampon Tuesday" to keep up with all the breaking news in mid-2016. On one earlier episode, Nicolle Wallace, communications director for former president George W. Bush, joined the banter, telling former *Nightly Show* host Larry Wilmore, "Yes, I worked in the White House, and yes, every twenty-eight days I bled. But the country went on."[11]

Comedy Central's *Broad City* season three finale featured a full-blown period parable as told by Ilana Glazer and Abbi Jacobson. The episode leads with two main characters on an overnight flight when Abbi unexpectedly starts her period. They spend the episode crowded in coach class and in pursuit of the ever-elusive tampon, only to learn they're available in abundance in first class. They dish out some serious dialogue about the plight of the poor: "This must be how homeless women feel," Ilana says. "If you get a couple of bucks, do you buy food, or do you buy tampons?" Abbi follows with: "Tampons should be free. Every woman should have access to tampons." Definitely a case of real-world activism meets comically on-point social commentary.

This infusion of menstrual perspective into such a wide array of social and cultural outlets closely mirrored, even mimicked, the movement's progress. Every time yet another public period moment transpired, I would cheer it on and enjoy the thrill—and for a little while, even, I'd feel genuine, earnest surprise. But I soon came to appreciate that, really, this was simply a natural evolution of an increasingly successful campaign. All that was brewing in real-life activity—from collection drives to marathon runs—was being ricocheted right back at us, and then reflected out to the greater public. It helped keep momentum high and offered mainstream credence and cover to conversations around menstrual health, policy, and activism.

Fun and Games

Periods as gaming fodder? Another unexpected medium where creativity transpired was through artistic and technology projects that both captivated and charmed the public—and turned out to be a prime platform for taking a menstrual stand.

Imagine a high-tech video game in which players chase down and shoot up the bad guys. However, in this case, in lieu of guns, zombies, and other weapons of mass destruction, players are armed with tampons. Welcome to *Tampon Run*.

Conceptualized and created by two high school students who met at Girls Who Code camp—an organization that aims to narrow the gender gap in the technology industry—Sophie Houser and Andrea Gonzales joined forces to combine their love for gaming with a desire to celebrate girls, destigmatize menstruation, and push back on the reality that our society treats menstruation—rather than guns and violence—as the unspeakable taboo. As Houser told *TIME* magazine, "It seemed so silly to us that it's so normal that you can have a video game where you can hold a gun and shoot it but none of us can talk about something so normal like menstruation."[12]

The girls' mettle is even more admirable given the culture of violence against women so prevalent in the gaming industry. They created *Tampon Run* on the heels of "Gamergate"—a brutish social media harassment campaign that personally targeted prominent female game developers. The cohort of men who railed against them were described by the *Washington Post* as a "motley alliance of vitriolic naysayers: misogynists, anti-feminists, [and] trolls." Watching Gamergate unfold "was horrible," Houser shared with *Salon* in 2015. "But it strangely made me want to be here more. I want to stand here like a woman. I want to hold my ground."[13]

Tampon Run, which launched in 2014 just before "The Year of the Period," went on to garner a loyal following and spurred high-tech upgrades. The coding duo was invited to give a TEDx Talk on gender and technology. They've even launched their second game called *Catcall Run* in which the player flings "tools of empowerment"—pencils, computers, and notebooks—at oncoming buffoons.

The year 2016 saw the introduction of old-school gaming, too. The Period Game, a board game for tweens, was created by two students at the Rhode Island School of Design. A throwback to classics like Life, Sorry, and Trouble, the board circles around a model reproductive masterpiece: a uterus, ovaries, fallopian tubes in all their 3-D glory. Twist an ovary and one marble "egg" drops down and guides the next move. Game pieces are as cute as the Monopoly terrier and thimble; players move a tiny tampon, pad, and menstrual cup around the board. Cards drawn teach about the mechanics of the menstrual cycle, PMS symptoms, product choices, and proper hygiene and care—all in kid-friendly lingo ("You're ovary-acting"). As *Slate* reported: "The past few years have seen a significant shift in the public culture of adult menstruation: There's more room for humor, irony, grievance-airing, and frank discussion than ever before. Girls should get to enjoy that same variety of period talk from the start."[14]

And the fun-loving spirit has continued with America's coloring craze. Though youngsters have cornered the Crayola market, the latest trend is coloring books for adults, with researchers and art therapists alike touting the calming benefits. It's a booming business: according to Nielsen consumer market testing, more than twelve million adult coloring books were sold in the United States in 2015, up from just one million in 2014.[15] And now, periods have joined the craze with the 2016 release of the *Period Coloring Book*—a thirty-page visual journey through all the ways we bleed, including to-be-shaded drawings that depict cramps, bloating, tampon insertion, period sex . . . you name it. The creator, Andrea Yip, called the rise of menstrual activism her "guiding force." An artist and designer, she underscores the vast benefits: "It's an easy entry point for people to start thinking and talking about periods, and that we can learn something different by visualizing the experience. I think coloring is a meditative and playful way to explore topics that may be considered serious or taboo—topics like menstruation."[16] Yip provides the blank canvas. We just get to color it.

No doubt, each of these endeavors is more than a little bit quirky. But to me, each is living proof that periods are such a vital, integral part of our lives, that their appeal can resonate even in the most unlikely outlets. One sign of a vibrant social movement is its ability to employ a wide variety of mediums and messengers to make its case. The menstrual field is meeting that benchmark in spades.

Acts of Compassion

Another direct, and heartening, response is the outpouring of charitable support from the next generation. But the most surprising twist is how strongly the inspiration has resonated with boys. Among the stories that have gone public is that of a group in New Haven, Connecticut, who founded the Kiyama Movement to promote self-improvement among African American men and mutual respect across genders via five guiding principles: respect for life, sexual responsibility, commitment to fatherhood, respect for womanhood, and economic accountability.[17] When one of its members read an article on menstrual access—in particular, a poll that showed that 86 percent of girls and women have reported starting their period unexpectedly in public and without the supplies they needed[18]—the group folded into its mission a fundraiser to provide free tampons and pads for classmates. An informative, inspiring video featuring their period project racked up an amazing eight million views and generated kudos across the Internet.

Another trending moment was an Instagram post by a fifteen-year-old boy from Miami, Jose Angel Garcia, alerting classmates that he carries an emergency stash of tampons to share with friends in need. He posted: "To every girl that follows me. You are completely welcome to ask me for a pad at any time without receiving a negative response or dirty look. We should all help each other out like this so you don't have to thank me at all." He concluded with the hashtag #realmen-supportwomen. His message had more than thirty thousand likes and received an outpouring of public support after it was blasted out by *Buzzfeed*. Actions like these not only motivate peer-on-peer compassion and action, but are endearing to adults as well.

Local, teen-based collection drives, too, have multiplied in communities across the country, similar to projects like my hometown's "Girls Helping Girls. Period." One of these is "Flowing Forward," which flowed from a ninth-grade English class in suburban Chicago, where fourteen-year-old Lily Alter was assigned to write a mock grant application. She chose menstrual access as the topic and pitched "Flowing Forward," which has morphed into a successful fundraiser and ongoing partnership with Chicago-area homeless shelters that receive "FlowKits" filled with tampons, pads, and wipes. Even the big brands are claiming a piece of the action. U by Kotex spearheaded a nationwide contest called "Power to the Period," collecting suggestions from students across the country and implementing the ideas of the winners. One was an awareness-raising Period Pop-Up shop that ran for a week in New York City; another was a national collection drive through which participants collected more than 165,000 pads, tampons, and other products that were donated to homeless shelters.

Creativity on college campuses is also a growing part of the movement, going well beyond the petitions for free products for students described earlier. In Athens, Georgia, a team of University of Georgia students took top prize in 2015 in the prestigious Public Policy Challenge hosted annually by the University of Pennsylvania's Fels Institute of Government for their proposal to provide "(fem)me kits" to area shelters. The kits are stocked with tampons, pads, and other essential products (sanitary wipes, Midol) and accompanied by a series of affirmative health messages for recipients. In Cambridge, Massachusetts, a team of Harvard Business School students was inspired to use seed money for an entrepreneurship course to launch a "buy one, give one" mail-order company that enabled subscribers to donate a box of tampons or pads for every order purchased to a local women's shelter. Over the year, as I connected and collaborated with projects like these, the message I heard, over and again was: "I never even thought of access to menstrual products as a problem until I read about it. The solution seems so simple. We couldn't not act on it."

Youth-led activism—so much of it happening in traditionally male-dominated contests and venues, no less—has been a real catalyst. There's much for which to be hopeful in the next generation of menstrual activism.

Global Momentum

Acts of rebellion have been part of an exploding international movement. In London, white trouser free-bleeding sit-ins have been staged outside of Parliament since 2015 as part of the campaign in Britain to eliminate the national taxation of menstrual products. Women in Zurich, Switzerland, protested the same by dumping red food dye into more than a dozen city fountains, making them appear to bubble over with blood.

"Pads Against Sexism" was the handiwork of a German activist who stuck sanitary pads, scrawled with piercing takedowns of sexism—"Imagine if men were as disgusted with rape as they are with periods"—all around the city of Karlsruhe, plastering its public walls and poles with the message. Photos of the pad messages were viewed over one hundred thousand times on Instagram and Tumblr and inspired a group of students in New Delhi, India, to take to the capital's streets and similarly cover walls with pads and messages about everything from abortion to street violence. A group of students at Calicut Medical College in Southern India formed "The Red Cycle," a period poetry contest to mark International Women's Day in 2016. They solicited haikus and short poems about periods, which were then published in a student literary magazine and shared widely on social media. A daring display, it wasn't without detractors. But even some who voiced discomfort ended up acknowledging that the depth of emotion and experience reflected in the poetry was eye-opening:

Just remember,
A man bleeds for death,
for agony and for misery.

Do you know why a woman bleeds?

She bleeds for glee,
for happiness,
and to create a new life.
                    —Greshma

Locked in a room,
Food served in turns,
Get out, they warned.
For it seemed,
We ruined the godly places!
Funny, I said.
For we bleed to give a life.
                                    —*Anuna*

All of this momentum comes together under a grand umbrella—the advent of a worldwide annual Menstrual Hygiene Day. The brainchild of WASH United, a global sanitation and hygiene organization and driven by Berlin, Germany-based advocates Danielle Keiser, Ina Jurga, and Denise Rack, Menstrual Hygiene Day has fully linked all of this emerging activism with the broader movement for menstrual access. Since 2014, it has taken place each year on May 28, chosen because May is the fifth month of the year (and most periods average five days) and a menstrual cycle is approximately twenty-eight days long—a sort of belated Mother's Day celebration. By 2017, it attracted more than four hundred partners in thirty-three countries that staged hundreds of public events—exhibitions, concerts, educational workshops, and gatherings—to engage in "action, advocacy, and knowledge-sharing" and, in so doing, to "recognize the right of women to hygienically manage their menstruation wherever they are."[19]

HELPING ELEVATE ALL OF THESE actions, from the raucous to the beautifully charitable and creative, has been a deeply engaged and responsive media that has proved willing and able to amplify the story that periods are, above all else, normal. Considering the old journalism adage, "If it bleeds, it leads," it's kind of ironic, isn't it? In this case, that which is normal is newsworthy. NPR called the coverage an "epic" phenomenon. Periods made headlines in a wildly diverse array of sources—from traditional women's magazines, including *Cosmo*, *Glamour*, *Teen Vogue*, and *Marie Claire*, to millennial-focused websites like *Upworthy*, *NowThis*, *Vox*, *Fusion*, *Mic*, and *Refinery29*, to classics like *The New York Times*, *Washington Post*, and *Wall Street Journal*—all of which reported on the issue regularly and enthusiastically.

Where exactly did all this activism and media coverage get us? To a place of greater mainstream recognition, yes. That alone is remarkable and gratifying. But also, to a political and social landscape ripe for policy advocacy—the realm in which I have been fortunate to participate—and ready to seriously consider and pass new laws that aim to solve many of the problems we've discussed both domestically and internationally.

chapter five

LADY'S DAYS

Tampons and sanitary towels . . . have always been considered a luxury. That isn't by accident, that's by design of an unequal society, in which the concerns of women are not treated as equally as the concerns of men.
—Stella Creasy, Member of British Parliament[1]

WITH MENSTRUAL ACTIVISM ON THE rise, it had become increasingly clear by mid-2015 that if there was ever a time to go full-on political with periods, this had to be it. This was the charge I'd begun to envision back on New Year's Day of that year: how to chart a viable policy agenda and demand a top-down message that menstruation, well, *matters.*

I pondered the options—whether fiddling with tax codes or leveraging public agency regulations could be the ticket to achieving better menstrual access. I also quickly saw that my wonky enthusiasm wasn't universally embraced and appreciated, at least initially. Friends and colleagues warned that arguing for more government intervention and free (or tax-free) stuff—free tampons, no less—was a losing proposition, a one-way ticket to being labeled a feminist socialist of the bloodiest kind. They countered that donation drives were already making a difference. Why not organize more charity? They pressed me on the "popular innovation" model that was driving global solutions and social enterprise like those I'd seen in India and elsewhere. Couldn't we just borrow or adapt some of that here? While I'm a fan of these interventions, they're simply no substitute for—and not nearly as impactful as—meaningful systemic change. I see two primary reasons for this. First, introducing and implementing laws is the most efficient way to benefit the widest swath of the population. But, as importantly, the laws we pass make a societal statement about the very values for which we stand—a critical ingredient in stigma smashing.

Menstruation had never been the heart of US policy debate or even at the fringes of it. Suffice it to say, taking tampons to the hallowed halls of government was neither an inevitable nor enviable next step. There were myriad potential challenges. Even with growing public interest in and discourse around periods, the majority of politicians do not menstruate and, thus, were more likely to misunderstand, or worse, mock and trivialize the issue. And there was the risk of just being roundly ignored. As we discussed earlier, proposed federal legislation to address tampon safety and research has languished for nearly two decades in Congress.

More generally, policies pertaining to women's bodies are too often marginalized, cloaked in societal bias. It's a funny topic, periods. They toe the line between being a reproductive function, just plain biology, and public health. I get asked all the time, "Tampons in schools? What about condoms?" As if these items are interchangeable or serve even remotely the same purpose. On the one hand, if menstruation wound up too readily or inextricably tied to more divisive reproductive issues like abortion and contraception, it might invite toxic partisan rancor. But if introduced and cordoned off carefully and strategically, periods could offer an incredibly rare opportunity to talk about many of the touchy subjects—starting with our bodies and the basics of how they function every month—in as near a neutral and noncontroversial legislative setting as possible. Stigma aside, when pressed, who can argue that periods happen? Or blame people for having them? Unlike other women's health matters, menstruation just might be the way to bridge the political divide between right and left, anti- and pro-, Republican and Democrat.

The time was ripe to test this theory and start making policy moves part of "The Year of the Period." The game was on.

The Tampon Tax: An Opening Salvo

It was the "tampon tax"—shorthand for the fight to exempt menstrual product purchases from sales tax—that burst onto the US scene in 2015 on the heels of similar campaigns around the globe. The gist of the argument: after shelling out five to ten dollars for tampons and pads each month, any additional charge for sales tax, the norm in most places, smacked of unfair, even illegal discrimination. Over the course of the next year, the phrase was bandied about at the highest levels of government, including by then President Obama and other world leaders.

It was the subject of many major national and international news programs, articles, and editorials. And the real accomplishment? Related legislation to change tax laws was introduced or debated by twenty-four US state legislatures. In sum, a tremendously successful record for any new advocacy initiative, let alone a first crack at mixing periods and politics.

Before describing the campaign itself, though, let's start with a quick primer about the mechanics of the law and what the US tampon tax is—and what it isn't.

Sales tax is primarily a state issue.

Sales tax is legislated and levied state by state. Each state makes its own decision about what items to include and exempt, at what rate items will be taxed, and if/how sub-bodies like counties or municipalities can do the same. Prior to 2015, there were five states ahead of the curve that had already begun exempting menstrual products—Maryland, Massachusetts, Minnesota, New Jersey, and Pennsylvania. Another five—Alaska, Delaware, Montana, New Hampshire, and Oregon—collect no sales tax at all, and therefore don't tax these items. By 2017, Connecticut, Florida, Illinois, and New York joined the list of states that have successfully scrapped the tax.

A "luxury" tax?

"Tampon tax" is a catchy phrase, with alliteration and a cadence that makes for a decisive battle cry ("Axe the tampon tax!"), but the tax itself is not a special or additive levy. Rather, it is regular sales tax applied to menstrual products—tampons, pads, liners, cups—ranging from roughly 4 to 10 percent depending on the state tax code. Generally, and as a matter of historical practice since sales taxes were first implemented in the United States in the 1930s, states exempt food and other items deemed necessities of life, such as medicine and prescription drugs, from sales tax.

Nor is it a "luxury" tax, a common misnomer. The term is a by-product of the vernacular of the European Union's value-added tax (VAT), a consumption tax that specifically applies to "non-essential luxury items." Other than on a Monopoly game board, though, the United States does not currently collect a special luxury tax. But since it does exempt necessities, and the opposite of necessity implies something unnecessary—in other words, a luxury—the phrase has caught on.

What is a necessity?

Lack of consistent classification of "medical necessities" from state to state has resulted in a complicated maze of laws and outcomes. Prescription drugs—ranging from the life-saving (insulin) to the life-enhancing (Rogaine and Viagra)—largely are tax exempt. So too are incontinence pads, dandruff shampoo, and lip balm under this classification. Meanwhile, other items that seem comparable to menstrual supplies and that may also be deemed basic (if not medical) necessities, are often taxed—toilet paper, soap, and bandages among them.

Therein lies the 120-million-dollar question (roughly, the amount in sales tax collected each year by all the states). Are menstrual products a necessity?

Let's get real. For the most part, without them, anyone who has a period is prone to humiliation, not to mention potential infection, and an overall state of compromised hygiene. Whereas one can make do without a bar of soap, improvise a bandage, and find free toilet paper in any public restroom stall, we have little choice but to purchase products that absorb menstrual blood. (For what it is worth, I would argue that toilet paper *is* a necessity that should be tax exempt, too, and I believe menstrual products should be provided for free in public restrooms.)

The costs.

A year's supply of tampons and pads for one person costs in the ballpark of $70 to $120, depending on where one lives, how heavy the flow, and the ability to take advantage of cost-cutting measures. (Reusable alternatives like menstrual cups and cloth pads have upfront costs but are obviously more cost-effective over time.) All told, the expense can add up to more than $4,000 over a lifetime, and sales tax adds another several hundred dollars to the grand total. The amount of annual tax revenue states collect on the sale of these products is based on the number of menstruating people in the state—ranging from $1 million in Utah to $20 million in California, for example.

It is worth noting some painful subjectivity to those figures that make periods an especially costly experience for those who are poor. Whereas middle-class families can take advantage of things like bulk discounts or shopping at wholesale retailers—to buy a year's supply of tampons (or cans of tomatoes, or dog food, or whatever)—those who live in poverty often cannot. The poor end up paying considerably more for the exact same items, whether it is because they're subject to the inflated prices charged at convenience stores, or they can't afford a price club annual membership, or they are only able to expend precious dollars one necessity at a time. Add to that the exorbitant check-cashing fees for those without bank accounts or credit cards—and factor in the inherently regressive nature of sales taxes—and the burden only deepens.

Is the "tampon tax" the same as the "pink tax"?
The phrase "pink tax" is a popular euphemism for the phenomenon where goods or services marketed for women often cost more than the men's version for no apparent reason other than price gouging. A 2015 New York City Department of Consumer Affairs study, *From Cradle to Cane: The Cost of Being a Female Consumer*, found that this happens a whopping 42 percent of the time. Among the examples cited: shampoo and conditioner in the women's aisle cost an average of 48 percent more than that in the men's; women's jeans are 10 percent more expensive; dry cleaning bills for women's shirts run an average of $4.95 as compared to $2.86 for men's. Pink razors consistently outprice navy blue ones; same for pink bicycles and scooters.[2] Yes, an educated consumer can buck the system and reject the pink, but it is insidious all the same. And while the technicalities of the tampon tax are entirely different, the crux of the economic equation is the same. Add in low-paying, pink-collar jobs, not to mention wage disparities and glass ceilings, and it becomes clear that the American economy bleeds women dry at every turn.

SIMPLY STATED, HERE'S MY CASE for what's wrong with the tampon tax. Menstrual products are used by half the population—month after month and year after year—to be productive members of society. Taking on and taking down the tampon tax has the potential to accomplish four key objectives: it lifts a small financial burden; it challenges laws that are archaic, unfair, and discriminatory; it helps inch toward a model of economic parity and gender equity; and it is a gateway for getting people to talk and think about the wider implications of menstruation—social, economic, and otherwise—in our policy making.

Fighting the Tampon Tax Around the World

Outcry against taxation of menstruation was making international news throughout the summer of 2015, well before the issue made its debut in the United States. That July, Canada eliminated its national Goods and Services Tax on menstrual products. The effort was fueled by a Toronto activist, Jill Piebiak, who secured nearly seventy-five thousand signatures on an online petition and led a series of protests. This had been a multi-decade fight led by two members of Parliament, Irene Mathyssen and Judy Wasylycia-Leis, which culminated in a unanimous vote by the major political parties, Conservative, Liberal, and New Democratic (the sponsor of the bill). Though Conservatives had long stood in the way of this reform, in the face of a growing and favorable new media environment, they suddenly saw fit to switch course, claiming to be the party that cares about women *and* lowering taxes. A winning combination, indeed.

At the time, then British Prime Minister David Cameron and then prime minister of France Manuel Valls would have been wise to take note. Both soon found themselves engulfed in high-profile battles over the issue, complete with lively floor debates, vigorous protests, and massive media campaigns.

The tampon tax became the pawn in a fascinating multi-year struggle among Britain's political parties and the European Union. Though a national tax on menstrual products had been reduced from 17.5 percent back in 2000, a remaining 5 percent surcharge lingered, required by the European Union and its mandatory value-added tax. Reducing the VAT to zero was long considered a nonstarter.

Enter a plucky University of London student, Laura Coryton, who fueled the debate when she launched an online petition in May 2014. One of the most successful tampon tax petitions in the world, it has now garnered more than 350,000 signatures. Coryton highlighted the absurdity of the policy in terms only a true Brit can say with a straight face. That is, while menstrual products are among those taxed, notably excluded from the VAT are alcoholic jellies, flapjacks, crocodile meat, and Jaffa cakes. Coryton has penned brassy op-eds and is a force on camera and behind the megaphone. She rallied several prominent Labour Party leaders, including member of Parliament Paula Sherriff, Shadow Minister for Women and Equalities, to champion the cause. She has staged several protests, including one where she delivered her petition directly to 10 Downing Street. Chancellor of the exchequer George Osborne was even forced to debate the issue, beet red in the face, on the floor of Parliament.

The issue took an even more curious turn in late 2015 when the chancellor announced that the millions in annual tax revenue it collected from the sale of menstrual products would be funneled as charitable contributions to groups that work to improve the lives of disadvantaged women and girls, including those who have been affected by domestic violence. Worthy causes, no doubt, but a tax paid solely by women, footing the bill for the aftermath of actions perpetrated almost entirely by men? Talk about blood money. Even more controversy broke out in 2017 when it was announced that one of the tax fund recipients would be an antiabortion organization.

Together, Coryton and I concocted the first ever US-British alliance against unfair taxation—sort of a reverse Boston Tea Party. I flew to London to join her in coleading a rally in Parliament Square outside Big Ben, where our feisty group of activists young and old, including my teenage daughter, wielded catchy, colorful signs and chants—"Not a Bloody Luxury!"—and garnered international media, while delighted tourists snapped photos from atop double-decker buses.

The US-British alliance against unfair taxation protest in London in May 2016.

Ultimately, though, changing the rules for the VAT meant a showdown with the European Union. The fight took some truly bizarre twists and turns—a *House of Cards*–like series of political machinations and not-so-hidden agendas. A faction of far right-wing Tory members of Parliament, the UK Independence Party (UKIP), were, at the time, campaigning hard for Britain to exit the European Union—better known as Brexit—and jumped in to announce its full support for eliminating the tampon tax. Why? To highlight what it saw as the European Union's overreach and Britain's lack of agency. It was also a convenient chance to court women, given UKIP's reputation as a haven for misogyny—especially from its own Nigel Farage, one of the more opportunistic converts to the tampon tax cause. Farage, who has been described by NPR as "Donald Trump's political kindred spirit," had stirred outrage over the years for incendiary remarks like calling maternity leave "lunacy" and suggesting that breast-feeding mothers should "sit in the corner." Unreal as it sounds, the tampon tax became a pawn in one of the most sweeping political revolts of the century.

In an attempt to keep the Brexit insurgency at bay the chancellor and prime minister, together with MP Sherriff and the coalition earnestly fighting the tampon tax, did what it took to change the EU rule. In this case, it meant scrambling to get all twenty-eight of the EU member states to agree to reduce the VAT on menstrual products to zero. It was a deft, quick maneuver, despite the devastating Brexit vote a few months later.

As for the fate of the tampon tax, not surprisingly, Brexit has complicated the process immensely. Even after the successful EU ruling, a national law to affirmatively eliminate the VAT on menstrual products languished in Parliament for months with no commitment to act. By September 2016, Labour members pressed firmly for a deadline, which is set for April 2018—and only then, if doing so remains a legal option "at that point under EU law."

Even with such an improbable backstory, the British battle has gone a long way to highlight how public attitudes toward menstruation pose daunting obstacles. Said MP Sherriff in a December 2016 interview with the *Guardian*: "When I started campaigning in this House on the tampon tax, some honorable members recoiled, while others did not even want to talk about periods or tampons, as if the words themselves were obscene. I do not regret providing such a culture shock to this place—quite the opposite—but that reaction exemplifies why the issue . . . is so terribly underestimated."[3]

Meanwhile on the other side of the Chunnel, the French parliament voted in December 2015 to reduce the national tax from 20 to 5.5 percent. Earlier that year, a vote rejecting that reduction outraged activists and spurred angry protests. While then Prime Minister Valls said the move was "a step in the right direction," there's been no further public demand that the tax be eliminated altogether.

Beyond France's borders, additional petitions and citizen activism emerged throughout Europe, from Switzerland to Austria, and Germany to Australia. In 2017, activists in India pressed for the same using the viral hashtag #lahukalagaan, which translates to *tax on blood*, garnering more than 300,000 signatures on a petition launched by member of Parliament, Sushmita Dev.

An inspiring success story of reform came to light in the midst of all of this activity. These fights had been won more than a decade ago in Kenya, which was the first nation in the world to eliminate the sales tax on menstrual products in 2004. Kenya also ended an import duty on sanitary pads in 2011, helping to reduce costs significantly. And there's still more: by law, Kenya budgets the equivalent of $5 million per year to distribute free pads in schools. As reported by NPR, much of the credit belongs to the country's female leaders.[4] There is even a "County First Ladies Association" to help ensure that the menstrual products funded by the government are coupled with education, disposal facilities, and a supportive social environment at the county level.[5] While there have been challenges with implementation of these laws—tracking is cumbersome, schools don't always get the products they need, or have the capacity to store them— these are model policies and far ahead of most other Western countries. Meanwhile, the Kenya Ministry of Health continues to take the fight even further, forging new ways to promote menstrual health as a human rights issue and to prioritize menstrual hygiene, access, disposal, and education solutions.

Fighting the Tampon Tax in the United States

Early on, I became convinced that the tampon tax was an ideal starting place for policy advocacy here at home. People were already starting to talk about the economics of menstruation in the broadest sense, thanks to publicity around Gandhi's marathon run and the media's robust reporting. The narrow scope of the tampon tax held promise for cross-party appeal: for every person who saw the tax as unfair to women, discriminatory, or an outgrowth of menstrual stigma (read, Democrat), there were potentially as many others who would be eager to get on board to support a potential tax break (Republican). And, if successful, it offered a platform for priming further-reaching arguments and reforms.

Still, there were considerations to weigh, unique to several distinctly American legal and political limitations. Unlike in other countries where a singular national tax was the target, here we faced state-specific tax codes and as many state legislative bodies and leaders, each with their own quirks, challenges, politics, and personalities. And needed to determine how to ratchet up the pressure among a broad array of constituencies—from red states to blue, small states to sprawling—in a collective, powerful way. A centralized petition would address that concern by calling out all culprit states at once. In order to spur legislation, the discussion would have to go national and garner widespread popular support and a whiff of inevitability. Politicians would need to feel the pressure—for some, to be inspired to lead by example, and for the rest, to resist the burn of being publicly shamed.

One morning in September 2015, I received an innocuous message from an editor at *Cosmopolitan*. She was preparing a story on periods for the magazine's November issue and wanted to chat for a quick fact check. When I called her back, I was thrilled to learn that the story was part of a full feature section that would be dedicated to menstruation—not just classic health and sex tips but articles that would offer a serious dive into the plight of low-income and homeless women. We ended up talking for well over an hour. To be honest, I hadn't picked up *Cosmo* in more than twenty-five years and had no idea that it had become such a powerhouse. I checked out the politics page on its website and was blown away by the smart content: essays by dynamic politicians and thought leaders, as well as savvy reporting about everything from abortion to voting rights. There was no doubt that having the support of a major magazine with a readership of more than three million would be an invaluable benefit. I took a chance and asked if they'd partner with me on a tampon tax petition. Not only did they respond with a resounding yes, they were also motivated to create a full online complement to the newsstand issue, a standalone web page dedicated to period activism. They arranged a donation drive with a New Jersey–based national collection group, Distributing Dignity, and planned for a series of op-eds and articles, including one of the first—and best—overviews of the tampon tax, and profiles of homeless women and how they manage menstruation.

What is now the flagship US petition, "Stop Taxing Our Periods. Period.," went live on Change.org a few weeks later, in early October. To date it has garnered more than sixty-six thousand signatures and spurred a few similar petitions, each picking up as many or more signatures. But the goal was never to simply amass numbers and names to hand off to a particular leader or legislative body. No, the ideal outcome was national media attention to elevate the dialogue—and ratchet up the pressure. *Cosmo's* readership and brand helped us land a plug by the do-good sharing site *Upworthy*, known for its "clickalicious" headlines and reported reach of ninety million. It was a strong start.

The next step was to line up a cadre of legislators willing to take the lead. Having a winning public message mattered little if there were no lawmakers introducing bills. California rose to the task. On January 4, 2016, Assembly members Cristina Garcia (D) and Ling Ling Chang (R) introduced the first tampon tax exemption proposal of the 2016 legislative session.

The following week, the issue scored its first viral moment when President Obama was schooled on the tax during a live interview with Internet it-girl Ingrid Nilsen. Beloved by four million viewers for her lifestyle and fashion YouTube channel—she's been a CoverGirl rep and *Project Runway* judge—Nilsen was one of three young interviewers chosen to broadcast a live chat with the president, the theme of which was issues that matter most to millennials. And she chose to use that platform to raise the issue of the tampon tax. (She didn't get it quite right, asking him why in the United States "menstrual products are taxed as luxury goods," which he repeated back in his response, "I have no idea why states would tax these as luxury items.") Obama's impromptu if not slightly awkward retort as to why this is the state of affairs, though, was right on: "I suspect it's because men were making the laws when those taxes were passed." And there it was. The leader of the free world talking about periods in a thoughtful, positive way. The media loved it and a surge of coverage followed—"Obama Pretty Sure Clueless Men are the Reason Tampons are Taxed!"—overwhelmingly supportive of eliminating the tax, taking the matter to a whole new level of public awareness.

Interestingly, it was just a few weeks prior that I had gone to San Francisco to research the photo essay on homelessness and menstruation described in chapter three. The haul of donations that we brought to the clients of Lava Mae had been collected by Nilsen via Conscious Period, which was when and how she learned about the tampon tax and what led her to ask the question. The menstrual world is indeed a small one.

Shortly after Nilsen's Q&A with Obama, *The New York Times* published a prominent editorial that urged states not only to stop taxing menstrual products but also to ensure their affordability for all. Serious policy and fiscal analyses were soon offered up by heavy hitters like *The Economist, Washington Post*'s *Wonk-blog,* and *Wall Street Journal.* The American Medical Association, the largest association of physicians in the United States, issued a statement urging states to exempt menstrual products from sales tax as sound health and medical practice.[6] Preeminent constitutional scholar and dean of the law school at University of California at Irvine, Erwin Chemerinsky, penned a hard-hitting op-ed critiquing the discriminatory impact of the tampon tax, calling it a question of "fairness and constitutionality."[7] This series of endorsements came from heady, well-respected mediums and messengers and added substantial credibility to the arguments we were making—important endorsements that have helped bring lawmakers and other key influencers along.

And the progress we've made is solid. Since the petition was published, proposals to exempt menstrual products from sales tax have been introduced or debated in legislatures in Arizona, California, Colorado, Connecticut, Florida, Illinois, Indiana, Louisiana, Maine, Michigan, Mississippi, Missouri, Nevada, New York, Ohio, Oklahoma, Rhode Island, Tennessee, Texas, Utah, Vermont, Virginia, Washington, Wisconsin—as well as the District of Columbia, New York City, and Chicago.

The city of Chicago was actually the very first US jurisdiction to scrap the tampon tax in 2016; it passed its own ordinance, eliminating the portion of sales tax city residents otherwise would be charged (1.25 percent) on their menstrual purchases. When I was asked to testify in favor of the exemption before the Chicago City Council, I had the privilege and joy of listening as Gloria Steinem's "If Men Could Menstruate" was recited out loud on the floor by a member who proudly led the public hearing before the full chamber. No doubt, a first!

Several states successfully followed suit that year, including New York and Illinois, where the bills passed unanimously and were signed into law by the states' respective governors—one a Democrat (Andrew Cuomo in New York), the other a Republican (Bruce Rauner in Illinois)—that summer. New York's exemption went into effect on September 1, 2016, but got off to a rocky start when many stores, from major chains to corner bodegas, missed the memo to remove the tax from their cash register programs. A rapid-response #TweetTheReceipt campaign urged consumers to snap a photo of their receipt and tweet it to Governor Cuomo, resulting in the creation that same day of a statewide reimbursement hotline. Gratefully, the Illinois exemption had a seamless introduction on January 1, 2017.

The third state to scrap the tax in 2016 was Connecticut, where the exemption was built into the state budget, rather than by passing a law. It was a shrewd move by a young, freshman legislator, State Representative Kelly Luxenberg, who had introduced legislation that was rejected earlier in the year. By the end of the 2016 session, she found herself in the position of casting the deciding vote on the budget. She conditioned her support on the inclusion of a line that covered the costs of the exemption of menstrual products from sales tax and refused to sign without it—otherwise holding the budget hostage. Talk about a menstrual badass. (In a reverse situation, the District of Columbia seamlessly passed legislation in November 2016 eliminating sales tax on tampons (and diapers), but fell short on assigning funding in the budget to cover the exemption—meaning the tax persists.)

And then in the 2017 legislative session, Florida successfully passed a tax exemption for menstrual products, which was quickly signed by Governor Rick Scott (another Republican).

Unfortunately, the journey has not been smooth in California. After debuting the first bill of the session and passing it unanimously in the senate and assembly, Governor Jerry Brown issued a disappointing veto in September 2016. Because the tampon tax exemption came to his desk packaged with seven other tax breaks totaling $300 million, he took the stance of fiscal savior and allowed none of them, arguing they all amounted to new spending since the revenue would have to be recouped. The veto spurred backlash—angry protests at the statehouse, crushing editorials, and a stream of angry tweets. But the fight goes on. The tampon tax landed right back on the legislative floor in 2017 with the introduction of the Common Cents Tax Reform Act, this time coupling the exemption for menstrual products with a clever provision to increase the tax on hard liquor (excluding beer and wine)—making the case that any lost revenue should rightfully be collected on booze since "liquor is a choice and a luxury, but biology is not." Perhaps the most clever caption came from the *Washington Post*, which reported in March 2017, "There's No Happy Hour for Menstruation." (Since the liquor tax is an increase, rather than an exemption, it has to win by a higher vote, a two-thirds supermajority of the legislature. Not likely to ever happen, but a smart messaging strategy to drive home the absurdity of the reality.)

Backlash . . .

Despite the California setback, elimination of the tampon tax quickly became the policy darling that nearly everyone loves—*loves!*—to support. Feminists. Humanists. Antitax libertarians. Democrats. Republicans. It is one of those issues that proved to have a little something for almost everyone on the political spectrum. Even the conservative political blog, *The Resurgent*, decried the tax as "ridiculous" and "grossly offensive and yes, sexist."[8] *The New York Times* ran a post-Inauguration Day op-ed in January 2017, "What Republicans Have to Learn from the Women's March," in which a Republican strategist urged that state legislators would be wise to introduce and support sales tax exemptions for menstrual products.[9]

Among the handful of denouncers, *Washington Post* opinion writer Catherine Rampell published a January 2016 column, "The Tampon Tax Fraud," which led off with a glib poke: "Maybe this makes me a traitor to my sex, but I support the tampon tax."[10] *The Daily Beast*'s Samantha Allen belittled "the mainstream feminist issue *du jour*" in her October 2015 essay, "The 'Tampon Tax' Outrage is Overblown."[11] Both framed their opposition on the argument that menstrual products are not subject to any specific, additive tax (which is a common retort). Wrote Rampell: "Politicians didn't decide one day that periods were gross and therefore ought to be made more expensive." And from Allen: "It is not a state-sanctioned war on periods." Yes, that's quite clear—and also misses the point. Whether or not it was a question of nefarious intent (doubtful) or clueless oversight (likely), the reality is that legislators hadn't ever even been called upon to consider menstruation at all in the evolution of tax code exemptions. And now they were.

It wasn't all snark and discord. Allen did acknowledge gender bias was at play. And Rampell zeroed in on the unique burden of menstruation on the poor, suggesting that direct cash assistance is the solution, given the tiny cost savings per person from sales tax exemptions and the fact that both rich and poor benefit from them. Rampell's critique was echoed in a *Los Angeles Times* editorial a few weeks later. After relegating tampons to the category of things that are nice to have, but not required, such as deodorant—while meekly defending the tax-exempt status of Viagra as a reasonable way to "improve quality of life"—the newspaper's editors offered that meaningful reform should instead focus on more targeted tax subsidies for the poor.[12]

I don't disagree, though I do find these arguments somewhat specious, if only for their defense of absurd preexisting exemptions. (Rampell offers a cute quip: "Maybe it seems unfair that in so many states Twizzlers don't get taxed while tampons do." Yup.) And I argue similarly that a menstrual equity agenda requires going further than simple sales tax reform. The difference is that I view these proposals as "both/and"—sales tax exemptions *and* other subsidies—and not "either/or." The more holistic policy agenda to advance menstrual access that has been charted, and is discussed later in this chapter, makes this case. Further, the very fact that the sales tax question has shined a light on the issue of the economics of menstruation—and has gotten elite media outlets to report and editorialize on it at all—is alone a tremendous advance and fuels our ability to keep making other more nuanced policy arguments.

Nor has support among legislators been universal. Early on in 2016, proposed sales tax exemptions were swiftly dismissed in several states. In Indiana, one state senator actually argued that since eliminating the tampon tax would alleviate a financial burden for *only* women, it is therefore a sexist proposal. Apparently the fact that it is only women who *pay* it sits just fine with him.

Utah's Hygiene Tax Act was killed in committee by an all-male panel in February 2016 (and again in 2017). They might have guessed the optics alone would be trouble. The fact that there was no representation on the original committee by anyone who has actually had a period was mentioned in nearly every headline when the story first broke. Among the reasons for rejecting the bill were fears of a too-subjective tax code and concerns about recouping $1 million in lost revenue. Tellingly, the legislators didn't consider making up the difference by taxing alternative items consumed equally by both men and women, nor did they flinch when confronted with the list of items already chosen for sales tax exemption—"necessities" like arcade game tokens, vending machine potato chips, and snowblowers.

The Utah committee's twisted logic reeked of political nonsense. How widespread might the slew of exemptions really be? On assignment from Ms. magazine, I undertook the most unglamorous of research projects: an examination of the sales tax code of each of the states that didn't exempt menstrual products. My initial goal in doing so was to highlight some of the more curious (read, unnecessary or ridiculous) items for which sales tax exemptions have been allowed and to demonstrate that there is no shortage of the very kind of subjective exemptions that Utah claimed it sought to avoid. On a cold mid-February weekend, I hunkered down to scour some of the most dense, dry language ever crafted by humans. It was Valentine's Day 2016, and if ever there was a romantic gesture I've been granted in my life this was it. My husband's gift to me was to split up the states and help parse through the codes for examples that would further boggle the mind. Who needs flowers or (tax-exempt) chocolate?

Our research turned up this almost implausible list of items specifically called out for exemptions by the same states that were taxing tampons at that time:

Alabama: casings used in molding or forming wieners and Vienna sausages
Arkansas: purchase of kegs by wholesale manufacturers of beer
Arizona: asses, sheep, and swine
California: Pop-Tarts
Colorado: bagged salads
Connecticut: subscription magazines
Florida: marshmallows
Georgia: tattoos and piercings
Idaho: chainsaws (over $100)
Illinois: beef jerky
Indiana: barbecue sunflower seeds
Iowa: kettle corn
Kentucky: Pixy Stix
Kansas: fees for National Hot Rod Association
Louisiana: specialty items for Mardi Gras events
Maine: Bibles
Michigan: doughnuts
Mississippi: coffins
Missouri: bingo supplies
Nebraska: zoo and aquarium admissions
Nevada: newspaper ink
New Mexico: souvenirs at minor league baseball stadiums
New York: Fruit Roll-Ups
North Carolina: meals served at fraternities and sororities

North Dakota: pastries
Ohio: gift certificates
Oklahoma: tickets to professional baseball, basketball,
    football, and hockey games
Rhode Island: golf club memberships
South Carolina: sweetgrass baskets
South Dakota: entry fees for rodeo participants
Tennessee: fishing tournament registration fees
Texas: cowboy boots
Utah: arcade game tokens
Vermont: garter belts
Virginia: leasing of films for public exhibition at motion
    picture theaters
Washington: Christmas tree production
West Virginia: manicures and massages
Wisconsin: gun club memberships
Wyoming: swimming pool and athletic facility admission

Pixy Stix? Barbecue sunflower seeds? Wiener casing is some-thing that one buys as a stand-alone item? Cowboy boots are a necessity in Texas? (I guess so.) *Cosmopolitan* uncovered an especially peculiar scenario:

In 2006, Iowa attempted to impose its 5 percent sales tax on pumpkins sold as jack-o'-lanterns, arguing that the gourd's "predominant use was for decorations" thanks to Halloween. After the press got wind of it, the public was outraged. With an impressive sense of urgency, a week after the story broke, then-Iowa Gov-ernor Chet Culver called on the Department of Revenue to "do the common-sense thing and suspend collection of this tax and offer refunds to consumers or retailers who have been affected," the *Des Moines Register* reported. Inedible gourds are still subject to sales tax in Iowa, but pumpkins have been exempt from the sales tax ever since (and alas, tampons are not).[13]

The exercise was truly an *Alice in Wonderland*–esque trip down the rabbit hole of oddball questions and archaic considerations. State tax codes are riddled with seemingly bizarre inconsistencies and loopholes. Among them, what is "prepared" food? Is a marshmallow an ingredient or is it candy? Is a garter belt clothing? How might one differentiate between a rodeo and a circus? Is dandruff shampoo a cosmetic, personal grooming product, or medical supply? The answers are not forthright, logical, or even consistent from state to state. But it is safe to say the above examples demonstrate more than considerable subjectivity among allowable sales tax exemptions. And it highlights that numerous items far less necessary than tampons (pumpkins!) often make the cut.

Tell It to the Judge

Another avenue for advancing change: courts of law. Nearly two decades ago, a group of women in Chicago won a lawsuit, successfully arguing that the city should follow the statewide sales tax exemption for tampons and pads as "medical appliances." But in 2009, the Illinois legislature reclassified tampons as "grooming and hygiene products," effectively reversing the outcome. Now, of course, the Chicago City Council has passed its own ordinance exempting menstrual products from the city's sales tax, as has the state of Illinois. But the lawsuit demonstrated that the courts can potentially be part of the arsenal for taking down the tax.

In March 2016, a new lawsuit was filed, this time in New York State. Five women signed on as plaintiffs to a sweeping statewide class-action lawsuit, *Seibert v. New York State Department of Taxation and Finance*, charging that the tampon tax is both unlawful and discriminatory, in violation of New York State Tax Law, the US Constitution's Fourteenth Amendment, and the New York Constitution's equal protection clause. The core legal argument is best summarized by the opening language in the brief: "The tampon tax is irrational. It is discrimination. It is wrong."

The case was conceptualized and spearheaded by New York City attorney, Laura Strausfeld, based on research she had done twenty-five years earlier as a student at Columbia Law School. For two decades she intermittently tried to spur the interest of the legal community. After watching "The Year of the Period" unfold, Strausfeld knew it was time to have at it again. She dug up her strategy memo in which she had prolifically mapped out the core legal and constitutional arguments. Amazingly, it was ripe and ready to be deployed. She got on the phone with a well-known civil rights law firm and readily convinced them to file the case. The lawsuit certainly was timely; even though proposed legislation was winding its way through the state legislature, and the media was acting as a good watchdog, there needed to be more incentive to deepen public pressure and ensure its eventual passage.

Among the plaintiffs was a Broadway star, Margo Seibert, and a prize-winning author, Cathy O'Neil. The attorneys held a press conference complete with a show-and-tell of maxi pads, candy, and ChapStick, quizzing reporters, "Guess which items are taxed?" The governor quickly weighed in, assuring that he would do right once the legislature passed a law for him to sign—which it did, just a week later. Once he signed the bill into law later in the summer of 2016, the suit went on to be settled. While those of us fighting for the end of the tampon tax cheered when the new law went into effect, it was a minor shame that it mooted the lawsuit. The practice was and is discriminatory and deserves a formal judgment declaring as much. And seeing as New York had long illegally collected this tax—millions of dollars' worth for nearly eighty years—the potential for a statewide cash refund would have been a welcome and appropriate remedy.

As these legislative battles raged on in other states, more lawsuits were filed making the same claims, including in California, Florida, and Ohio. It is important that one of these cases wins the muscle of a court ruling on our side. None have thus far. But however we have to get there—whether it is a matter of new laws passed, budgets approved, or lawsuits won—until all fifty states have done away with the tampon tax, the larger fight will continue.

Beyond the Tampon Tax . . .
Menstrual Access and Availability

As indicated earlier, the road ahead requires far more than pushing for sales tax reform, which really only scratches the surface. In terms of practical relief for those who are struggling and truly unable to access or afford the expense of menstrual products, a tax savings of pennies on the dollar likely isn't going to make enough of a dent. It is a start, for sure. But there is far more we can do.

Making the case that menstrual products be freely available to those in need—yes, free—defined the simultaneous policy agenda forged in "The Year of the Period." It was the Big Apple that stepped out as the national and global leader. And the woman at the center of it all: the indomitable New York City Council Member Julissa Ferreras-Copeland.

A rising star in city politics, the forty-year-old representative from Queens is known as a dynamic, diplomatic legislator and champion for the rights of women and girls. Early in 2015, we were introduced by a mutual friend. She needed no convincing that menstrual access was an issue she wanted to tackle. Ours was an immediate synergy. I'd brought a wide-ranging list of proposals to her office for her consideration. She honed in on those that were the most realistic and achievable—namely, the provision of products in public agencies. A master of the interplay between budget and policy, Ferreras-Copeland chairs the city's finance committee and oversees its $83 billion budget. She's got that rare ability to think big while also maintaining a razor-like, pragmatic focus on what it takes to achieve a winning outcome.

We both believed strongly it was important to hear from those directly affected by poverty and periods, and convened community leaders and organizers from around the city—from its shelters, food pantries, after-school programs, correctional services, health and legal service providers, among others—to offer testimonials. That group, later designated the "menstrual equity roundtable," first met in June 2015 and continued to strategize throughout the next year.

Participants reiterated the challenges for youth, in particular, given that most (79 percent) of the city's public school students are from low-income families. We heard how menstrual products would fly off the shelves in food pantries whenever a donation came in, and that volunteers would often resort to opening boxes of tampons and rationing them out to stretch the supply. The situation was the same in after-school programs, whose staff shared that there were rarely enough supplies to meet the demand.

Next on the information-gathering mission came teenage focus groups. After listening to students talk about lost classroom time and the sheer embarrassment of it all, Ferreras-Copeland wasted no time launching a pilot project in her own district to provide free tampons and pads (all donated) in the girls' restrooms. In September 2015, the High School for Arts and Business in Corona, Queens, unveiled the model the rest of the city would soon follow. The immediate results were heartening: a modest increase in attendance rates (though not enough data to affirmatively demonstrate causation) and daily expressions of gratitude and appreciation from the student body.

From the start, media coverage was plentiful and extraordinarily favorable, which honestly, had been a major concern. The campaign unfolded in tandem with the national tampon tax debate but required a wholly different set of talking points—more focused on equity and access, and less so on discrimination—and called for a not insubstantial leap in awareness and empathy. It was entirely possible that the public could simultaneously support lifting an unfair tax, while rejecting what *Breitbart*'s chief-provoker Milo Yiannopoulos considered the poor's proclivities for being "helpless and hopeless" and guilty of a simple case of "financial mismanagement."[14] Advocating for free or publicly subsidized anything isn't usually a winner in conservative circles. But somehow this campaign largely avoided knee-jerk criticism. And, as so many compelling personal stories continued to be aired and publicized, support for proposed legislation only grew. Exponentially.

By March 2016, Ferreras-Copeland staged the introduction of a groundbreaking trio of bills—the most comprehensive legislation of its kind in the world. The farthest sweeping of the three proposals required the city to make tampons and pads freely accessible (via dispensers in bathrooms) at its eight hundred public schools reaching three hundred thousand students. The second provided a budget for all shelters overseen by the Department of Homeless Services and the Department of Health and Mental Hygiene to provide free menstrual products—an estimated two million tampons and 3.5 million pads yearly—to approximately twenty-three thousand residents. And finally, a bill that eliminated the cap on the number of pads given to women in custody of the Department of Correction, which as we discussed in chapter three had previously amounted to a mere eleven thin, unabsorbent pads per period.

Students should be able to concentrate on their studies, New Yorkers in shelters should be able to focus on rebuilding their lives, and women in our Correction Department should be able to work toward rehabilitation and release without the indignity of inadequate access to tampons and pads.

—New York City Mayor Bill de Blasio[15]

A few months later, in June, came a public hearing with hours of testimony—from students to health providers to correction officers—followed by the council's unanimous 49–0 vote to approve the measure. Before Ferreras-Copeland introduced the legislation for the vote, she whipped out a tampon from her purse and waved it in the air exclaiming, "They're as necessary as toilet paper!" She added that in all her time overseeing the city's budget, "No one has ever interrogated me over the toilet paper budget . . . or referred to it as government-funded toilet paper." (She had indeed been interrogated about the costs of menstrual products, which add up to a tiny percentage of the city's overall budget.) Mayor Bill de Blasio proudly signed the bill in July 2016 in a sweltering high school gym in the Bronx packed with students and reporters. And with that, New York City made menstrual history.

Among the immediate highlights of the victory was the city's first lady Chirlane McCray's delightful ode to the new laws, a poem called "Tampons for ALL," which she shared with the world in a five-part series of tweets:

Consider the tampon
So essential, so taboo.
For decades we've been silent
Because they make some men go "Ew!"

But finally we are talking
We say is "Enough is enough."
Menstruation is part of life,
If you can't handle it, then tough.

Our latest big win
-And this really is cool-
Is bringing free tampons
To twenty-five schools.

It started with Council Member
Julissa Ferreras-Copeland.
She saw we needed more supply
To match all the demand.

This is one small step for NYC
And one giant leap for womankind.
When it comes to menstruation
We all deserve peace of mind.

Ferreras-Copeland's office in Queens remains the penultimate menstrual headquarters with free products available in the bathrooms, of course, and a piñata that hangs in the lobby filled with . . . what else? Tampons.

In the spirit of the "popular innovation" model championed in the developing world, so too is this legislation's brilliance in both the simplicity of its construction and the ease with which it can be replicated. Inspired by New York City, for example, Columbus, Ohio, started a pilot program in 2016 to provide free menstrual products in the city's recreation centers; Wisconsin's Dane County (which includes the city of Madison) passed a resolution that would make menstrual products readily available in eight county buildings, including its correctional facility and the sheriff's office. And, in 2017, Colorado added an amendment to its budget that will subsidize tampons in all state prisons.

The issue has gained traction in England and Scotland, too, where there's now a growing push for a comprehensive assessment of the problem of menstrual access and affordability and consideration of legislation similar to New York City's provision for homeless shelters and schools, in particular. Another policy on the table may result in the possibility of a special card that could be presented at a pharmacy or doctor's office in exchange for a monthly supply of hygiene products. The Scots have aptly dubbed the issue "period poverty."

Even my own community has made tampons and pads part of the annual public library budget. It's a completely local and scalable solution that can make an impact at every rung of government. There's no venue too small. Importantly, it can go bigger and also be implemented statewide. Really, any government agency can require the same for the facilities it oversees.

At the federal level, too, there are ways to leverage the law to make menstrual products more affordable and accessible. We are fortunate to have a champion in US Congresswoman Grace Meng who is leading the charge in the nation's capital. She convinced the Emergency Food and Shelter National Board Program, administered by the Federal Emergency Management Agency (FEMA), to allow homeless shelters to purchase menstrual products with grant funds. It was a matter of simply adding them to a list of acceptable purchases of "personal necessities," that already included cots, blankets, pillows, toilet paper, soap, toothpaste, toothbrushes, cleaning materials, limited first-aid supplies, underwear, and diapers. This adjustment was a no-muss-no-fuss change and received quick approval from the Department of Homeland Security. Benign neglect before she spoke up? Perhaps. All it took was asking.

This is just one of the creative legislative steps Congresswoman Meng has taken. She's also responsible for introducing the Menstrual Equity for All Act of 2017 (H.R. 792), the first ever omnibus bill of its kind which, if passed, would:

1. allow individuals to buy menstrual products with money they contribute to their flexible spending accounts;
2. provide a refundable tax credit to low-income individuals who regularly use menstrual products;
3. require each state to provide menstrual products to female inmates and detainees, at no cost and on demand, as a condition of receiving funds from the Edward Byrne Memorial Justice Assistance Grant Program; and
4. direct the Secretary of Labor to require employers with one hundred or more employees to provide menstrual products to their employees free of charge.[16]

Collectively, these provisions would help make menstruation more affordable for millions. Whether Congress has the will or ability to move on these is quite another story. Advancing federal reform requires an entirely different approach than what it might take to change state or municipal policy, especially given how polarized the political landscape is right now and the palpable hostility toward women's bodies and well-being. But with vast defensive fights on deck for reproductive health, it may also well be that menstrual policy—with its rare glimmer of bipartisan interest—remains a uniquely viable opportunity to advance affirmative reform.

"THE YEAR OF THE PERIOD" has proven that periods can indeed be political—and that a policy agenda is not only feasible, but here by popular demand. Looking back on these successes, it's important to remember how it was possible that menstruation was excluded from this part of the public arena for so long. In part, I suppose, it is as President Obama remarked: a result of the lack of women at the decision-making table. That said, though, stigma is squarely part of the equation, too. President Trump made incendiary comments about menstruation early in the campaign; California Assembly Member Garcia was rudely nicknamed by male colleagues for her efforts on the tampon tax ("Miss Menstrual Flow"). When women are mocked for biology—in an overt attempt to bully or quiet us down—the ability to promote policies that improve our lives is compromised.

But, perhaps, we too suffered from limited imagination and support and sheer will. That is, up until now.

chapter six

SHARK WEEK

Menstrual products are long overdue for innovation . . . while politicians are fighting to control our bodies, today's investors are now more excited than ever to back one of the most taboo product categories of all.

—Lauren Schulte,
Cofounder of FLEX[1]

THE ACTIVISM AND PUBLIC POLICY advances that marked "The Year of the Period" were met by yet another phenomenon—a simultaneous wave of private sector enterprise and innovation. A new crop of start-ups stormed the market in 2015, seeking to revolutionize not only our choices in products for managing menstruation but also how we talk and think about periods. "Shark Week" may be period slang, but much of the Silicon Valley–style development that has recently rocked the menstrual hygiene industry is straight out of an episode of *Shark Tank*.

Slow March of Progress

The evolution of menstrual product advances in the United States has been a sluggish, mostly uninspired slog: a burst of activity at the turn of the twentieth century, followed by simple advances every decade or so. Today the industry claims a more than $19 billion global market, a quarter of which is US based.[2] The big guns and their domestic brands are all well-known household names—Procter & Gamble (Tampax, Always); Kimberly-Clark (Kotex); and Energizer Holdings (Playtex)—and together control 85 percent of the market. Johnson & Johnson, the other longtime player, sold off its brands—Stayfree, Carefree, and o.b.—in 2013. Not surprisingly, tampons and pads comprise the vast majority of the domestic market and, between the two, pads are the preferred option; a study by the Centers for Disease Control indicates that pads (62 percent) are more popular in the United States than tampons (42 percent).[3]

To get you up to speed, here's a quick, condensed timeline of product progress over the past hundred-plus years. The very first commercial pad was produced and marketed in 1896, made out of cotton muslin and manufactured under the name "Lister's Towels" by Johnson & Johnson, in honor of scientist Joseph Lister, the same namesake of Listerine mouthwash. Kimberly-Clark's Kotex-brand disposable pads, made with absorbent cellulose, the name intended to reflect the intersection of "cotton" and "texture," were launched in 1920. Just over a decade later, tampons made of compressed cotton, featuring cardboard applicators and removal strings, were patented in 1931 under Procter & Gamble's behemoth Tampax brand (the name, here, a medicinal sounding combination of "tampon" and "vaginal packs").

Over the next seventy years, each of these products saw a series of incremental improvements. Belts to secure pads went by the wayside in the early 1970s; the inaugural version of these self-stick pads, Stayfree minis, was introduced the same year Neil Armstrong landed on the moon (as the saying goes, "If we can put a man on the moon . . ."). Slimmer pads, individually encased pads, dri-weave pads, and the ultimate stain-blocker—pads with wings!—came on the scene every five to ten years throughout the latter part of the century.

Meanwhile, the 1970s marked the replacement of cardboard tampon applicators with pearly domed plastic, followed by no-applicator tampons, the o.b. brand (which translates from the German *ohne binde* or *no pad*). Deodorant tampons with chemically induced "fresh scents" to mask supposed odors also were marketed. In the 1980s, absorbency classifications from "junior" to "super" became part of the legally mandated tampon vernacular in response to the spate of toxic shock syndrome cases caused by super-absorbent synthetic tampons. From the late 1990s up through the present came more patented perks like "leakguard braid" removal strings and compact applicators—even specially marketed, softer, quieter wrappers. That's about it.

Organic and toxin-free tampons and pads have occupied a small, but growing corner of the mass market since being first introduced by the British company Natracare in 1989. And a handful of alternative products have enjoyed a limited, though fiercely loyal, following. With little public hoopla, menstrual cups have entered and exited the marketplace every decade or so since the 1930s, with varying degrees of success, though they have seen a tremendous surge in popularity in recent years. On a lesser scale, so have other reusable options like washable cloth pads. (Another niche product is actual sea sponges. Naturally absorbent, they're harvested from the sea and can be inserted like a tampon, washed and reworn for up to six months. It is worth noting that their usage has been critiqued by the Food and Drug Administration.) Among the early leaders in refining and commercializing reusable menstrual products are companies like Lunapads, GladRags, and DivaCup. Once limited to the aisles of specialty and health-food shops, over time "all naturals" and reusables have become increasingly mainstream and now line the shelves of even the big-box mega-retailers like Target and Walmart.

But by 2015, a group of savvy, upscale menstruation entrepreneurs began capturing headlines with a diverse array of offerings. Some inch toward the radical: specially designed super-absorbent, leak-proof, moisture-wicking "period underwear" into which one can bleed directly, eliminating tampons and pads altogether, or worn as a backup. Others cater to healthy, eco-conscious lifestyles: tampons and pads that feature better quality ingredients (nontoxic, 100 percent organic, hypoallergenic, chlorine-free, biodegradable cotton), minimal packaging (therefore minimal waste), and even the very first reusable tampon applicator made of hospital-grade silicone. And then there is the straight-up sexy: a newfangled version of a disposable menstrual disc packaged slickly in a black, condom-like wrapper to promote its usage for mess-free period sex.

Menstrual innovation has also gone high-tech. There are now more than two hundred apps for cycle tracking that assess everything from the date of a last period, amount of flow, pain levels, shifts in mood, cervical fluid, and fertility. And even a "smart" menstrual cup that uses Bluetooth technology to monitor, measure, analyze, and track flow and issue alerts (including a warning before the cup runneth over). Subscription services are popular with the Amazon Prime generation—from period starter kits for tweens to customized monthly tampon and PMS packages delivered right to one's doorstep.

Kickstarter Generation

It isn't terribly clear what drove the synchronized timing and proliferation of the more than a dozen high-octane period focused start-ups in 2015—other than good ideas whose time had come—given that most had already been in development for several years prior.

But what most have in common is vision. They aim to offer not just quality, healthy options, but products that consumers actually enjoy and feel good, even empowered, about using. In an industry that has been dominated by men and big money since its inception, the advent of millennial women at the helm is a meaningful shift. In fact, a former product developer at a large multinational corporation shared with the founders of Conscious Period that his preference is to hire male engineers because, "when it comes to tampons, men aren't biased." The response? Bring on the bias.

No doubt the timing was a boon, too. "The Year of the Period" spurred the public's interest in and appetite for new products, which, in turn, fueled an uptick of reporting on the companies and entrepreneurs themselves—in every medium from the classic business heavies like *Forbes, Inc.*, and *Fortune*, to green-living entries like *MindBodyGreen*, to the style and even politics pages of nearly every major newspaper, women's magazine, and feminist blog. Discussion and innovation, in this case, created strong synergy. When people started talking openly about that which was once taboo, among the revelations were that the choices we have for managing our monthly bleeding are limited, to say the least.

Another key driver has been a vibrant and accessible crowdsourcing economy. By all accounts, the menstrual start-ups have kicked ass at the "kickstarter" stage, and then gone on to raise impressive amounts of funding—several securing well into the multimillions. Overall, in a field where women still struggle disproportionately to draw investors, conventional wisdom would suggest it might be doubly daunting to pitch anything period themed. Many of the entrepreneurs have chronicled stories of initial skepticism and outright rejection they encountered, largely by male prospects. In one example reported by *The New York Times*, a potential investor, visibly uncomfortable about the subject matter, was treated to seeing a tampon dunked in his water glass to illustrate product absorbency.[4]

With a combination of tenacity and determination, the surge of well-timed period publicity—and by sharing their own stories as everyday people who stepped up and took risks to create the products they want to see in the world and believe will improve lives—these entrepreneurs sparked a trend that investors couldn't ignore. And most succeeded not only in raising capital, but helping raise the bar for women-owned and -focused businesses writ large.

While the specific product offerings vary, among the start-ups there are many marked similarities. Most apparent is a deliberate emphasis on visual design as part of the overall branding, message, and appeal. Ads and presentation are artful and sophisticated, notably devoid of the traditional white leotards and flowery fields that have defined the marketing strategies of the twentieth century. Modesty has been replaced by mod. Some of the new tampons and pads come packaged in bright, candy-colored rows or in cool-blue wrappers; others are boxed in vintage-style sleek carry cases and display cubes. Even vagina inspired pouches are an option. A few of the major manufacturers have jumped into the game, too, with makeovers and hip new presentations of standard products, from jet-black boxes to neon-purple tampon wrappers.

Another welcome upgrade among the new companies: inclusive marketing as a discernible priority. Several products are explicitly marketed for the menstrual experience of transgender and gender nonconforming people, such as boxer-brief and boy short–style absorbent underwear. Gender neutral and welcoming language and imagery is increasingly common in ads and other consumer outreach, and use of the phrases "feminine hygiene" and "femcare" has been all but dropped from the lexicon.

There is star power at play, too, as celebrities join or invest in this burgeoning industry. Jessica Alba launched The Honest Company in 2015, which includes a line of organic tampons and pads. Whoopi Goldberg started promoting medicinal edible marijuana for menstrual cramps. In late 2016, Lena Dunham became a backer of LOLA, one of the latest all-natural organic tampon and pad subscription companies.

Innovation as Activism?

And then there's a connection many of the entrepreneurs are particularly proud to call out. That is, linking their products and mission to social action. The progressive business magazine *Fast Company* reported in the summer of 2016, "Startups are playing an activist role, helping break taboos," and that "as menstrual activism has heated up, these businesswomen have treated product innovation as a way to join the fight to destigmatize periods and improve women's quality of life."[5] A slightly more cynical roundup ran in *Bloomberg* around the same time, noting that each of the new period businesses have "adopted a similar marketing approach: rebrand menstruation as a symbol of strength, an opportunity for women to demonstrate—with their dollars, of course—a commitment to female empowerment."[6] The *Washington Post* splashed across the cover of its Sunday business section, "Why Your Daughter May Never Need to Buy a Tampon," reporting how "the market is ready [for innovation], largely because people are openly talking about periods," and then following with the rather blunt note: "The entrepreneurs are exploiting this conversation. . . ."[7]

It is true that companies with winning products, ambitious advertising budgets, loyal clientele, and engaging social media can be highly effective message bearers and conversation starters. But is branding menstruation—even if packaged in all the popular vernacular of feminism, autonomy, and girl power—a genuine, viable form of activism? It is a serious question, whether profit-seeking companies can be an honest broker for or the catalyst of sweeping social change. *Bloomberg* asked the question point-blank: "How authentic is your mission if you're trying to sell stuff?"

But what has emerged is a rather unusual phenomenon. The wave of activism and new menstrual policy agenda described in the previous chapters have unfolded simultaneously with highly publicized product campaigns. How best can—or even should—these respective narratives and priorities cohere?

On the one hand, unlike many other social movements, ours is one that truly relies on products, not only for the most basic of reasons—their actual, practical use—but also for the role they play in elevating public discussion and tackling menstrual stigma. Product advertising has been influential, pivotal really, in the perception of and discourse that has surrounded periods for the better part of the past century. It was the big companies, remember, that set the tone back in the mid-1900s and beyond about whether we were supposed to feel demure, secretive, or sassy about periods. And certainly innovation is at the heart of the quest for broader solutions and our fight to address lack of menstrual access for the poor—and lack of options for all.

But there is also a real and justified concern that what it takes to be a successful company—selling a product, achieving brand recognition, meeting shareholders' and consumers' demands, and minding a bottom line—can be incompatible, and perhaps at odds, with advancing a social agenda. The kind of competitive posturing that might be business as usual, even an asset, on *Shark Tank* can potentially hinder the cohesion that's so essential to coalescing a strong, aligned network of allies. It's not that I think profit is an inherently dirty word. Really, I don't. At the same time, though, I've maintained measured wariness, and have kept a vigilant eye on the ways in which profit making has the potential to clash with some of the bedrock principles of effective social organizing and advocacy—things like collaboration, coalition building, and coordination.

In her 2016 book, *We Were Feminists Once: From Riot Grrl to Cover Girl, The Buying and Selling of a Political Movement*, *Bitch Media* cofounder Andi Zeisler offers a deep dive into a related, critical dynamic also at play, a concept she defines as "marketplace feminism." Zeisler argues that a consumer-based approach is often too limited and self-serving to be the engine for achieving the deep, complex, and nuanced societal change that the fights for feminism entail. She worries that companies that latch on to glossy snippets and snapshots of feminism—a phenomenon she describes as "empowertising"—run the risk of watering down and cheapening the message, or worse, hindering real progress. "The diversity of voices, issues, approaches and processes required to make feminism work as an inclusive social movement," she writes, "is precisely the kind of knotty, unruly insurrection that just can't be smoothed into a neat brand."[8]

So where does that leave our corner of the movement and the role of menstrual products and marketing? Like Philip Morris's attempt to peddle Virginia Slims cigarettes in the 1960s as a symbol of women's liberation . . . have we come a long way, baby?

Most of the menstrual entrepreneurs go out of their way to display an unabashed and seemingly earnest feminist-minded approach, as well as an overt spirit of rebellion. Their companies—small, nimble, and largely women-led—purport to embed meaningful social values in their business plans and marketing strategies, whether via institutional ethos, brand promise, advertising copy and imagery, philanthropic endeavors, or all of the above. (Though one of the highest-profile of the pack, THINX, purveyors of period underwear, organic tampons, and reusable applicators, came under considerable fire in March 2017 after a series of scathing reports alleging an oppressive workplace that sexually objectified and undercompensated the largely female team. With headlines like, "THINX Promised a Feminist Utopia to Everyone but Its Employees" and "THINX Controversy Proves You Can't Sell Feminism," media and business pundits and disappointed customers alike were quick to point out the challenges of branding a business under the banner of feminism.)

Another marketing tactic has been the positioning of products and promotions as a form of political protest. One company, Cute Fruit Undies, sells custom-designed absorbent underwear with the image of a politician's face (the misogynist of your choice!) in the crotch, tempting purchasers to bleed on "the faces of politicians who have actively worked to pass legislation that will hinder women's access to abortions, birth control, and Planned Parenthood." Others jumped into the fray of the 2016 elections with social media and advertising campaigns to "Make Periods Great Again" or be "Patriarchy-Proof." While these slogans and concepts all make me smile, I'm prone to agree with *The New York Times* reporter Amanda Hess who posited that commercializing "the resistance" has its limits and cautioned that this "trend can draw attention to activist messaging, but it can also dilute, deflect, and distract from the cause, leading audiences away from the hard work of political action and civic organization and toward the easy comfort of a consumer choice."[9]

And we've seen that period feminism definitely seems to sell these days, too, both to consumers and investors alike.

Yet, despite the broad appeal, there's often a pretty hefty price tag attached—up to $38 for a pair of period underwear, and organic tampons as much as twice the price of standard—which means not all can afford to buy in. That's a challenge. Participation in social change movements should not ever be a "pay to play" proposition—which otherwise risks excluding those who are marginalized and whose perspectives are too often ignored (and most needed).

To be clear, my exploration of this question is not to catalogue, critique, or offer congratulations to any of the entrepreneurs and their products, in particular. The few companies I call out by name are for context only to highlight a particular strategy or noteworthy example. And I submit as a blanket statement that innovation and a spirit of do-good business in this space is an inherently positive thing. The more we have of safe, user-friendly, affordable menstrual products from which to choose, especially when they're created by women-led businesses that demonstrate high production and/or workplace standards, the better for society. Rather, I seek to consider the ways and extent to which emerging menstrual activism and advocacy have driven innovation and consumerism, and vice versa; to pose some caveats and red flags; and to offer potential best practices for how we all can effectively leverage the role of products in advancing the menstrual agenda.

These are the three areas where I believe the overlaps are most ripe:

The "greening" of periods.

One common thread among many of the start-ups is an explicit desire to offer and market products that are good for the body *and* good for the planet. For those selling reusables—from menstrual cups and discs, to cloth pads, to absorbent underwear—the environmental and health benefits stand far apart and above. There are numerous and meaningful reasons for consumers to feel compelled to purchase these products. And it's no gimmick. Consider just a few statistics about the waste that disposable menstrual products generate: on average, one person will use between ten thousand and sixteen thousand tampons or pads and amass three hundred pounds of related waste in a lifetime. A report out of Rochester Institute of Technology, along with many others who similarly cite the National Women's Health Network, estimates that twelve billion pads and seven billion tampons are used and disposed of annually in North America.[10] The number of years it takes for a single tampon or pad to break down is exponentially greater than the lifespan of the person who used it.[11] Chlorine bleaching of tampons, the pesticides used to grow cotton, and the reliance on plastic in menstrual products all have an adverse impact on air quality, oceans, and the environment. No doubt, disrupting the disposables industry and offering viable, eco-friendlier alternatives is in itself a radically important enterprise.

The tampon start-ups, too, profess to advance the greater, greener good. In addition to using natural, organic ingredients—forsaking rayon and synthetic fibers and exposure to chemicals—they demonstrate their commitment to consumer trust and corporate transparency by making public all their ingredients and processes. Across the board, their testing and disclosure practices go far beyond what is legally required of tampon providers by the government. (Since 1976, the FDA has classified tampons as midlevel medical devices—though, oddly, this categorization results in less stringent ingredient list-ing requirements than are imposed upon for cosmetics, how tampons were previously classified.)

Whether organic, cotton, or toxin-free tampons are safer and healthier than the commercial versions (given the dearth of test-ing, conflicting and inconclusive reports abound as to the risks and rewards of each), or whether reusable products are superior is not my point. Here is what *is* true: today's "green" start-ups play an activist role by addressing environmental concerns and calling attention to the feeble state of consumer protection when it comes to the safety of menstrual products. They shine a glaring light on that which our government and big business thus far have failed to do. We have the potential to force change in the industry if we reward a business model that reminds all of us that we deserve facts and science and honesty. At some future time, if and when the smaller companies assume a firmer hold on the market, their leverage may well create pressure for the major players to rise higher to compete for our dollars. For now, they at least give us the option to reject the status quo.

A recommendation: here is a place for the start-ups to lever-age their influence and resources to help advance the fight for policy change and, in particular, to urge the FDA to require more rigorous product testing and transparency. A popular online petition and campaign called #DetoxTheBox, launched by the nonprofit Women's Voices for the Earth, is supported by several of the natural menstrual companies. In 2015, these efforts succeeded in pressuring Procter & Gamble and Kimber-ly-Clark to begin disclosing some (though far from all) details about ingredients in their menstrual products; with no formal oversight or consistent guidelines, though, the information is too limited to amount to meaningful disclosure.[12] The cadre of new start-ups is in a unique position to deploy their already motivated and educated consumer base to join the fight, as well as, where feasible, to flex their own corporate lobbying muscle.

Doing well by doing good.

Nearly all of the recent brands are linked to a greater global good, and in most cases that equates to helping meet the menstrual needs of the poor and homeless at home and around the world. Many tout robust giveback programs that are integral to their business models, much in the footsteps of the "One For One" arrangement spearheaded by the TOMS Shoes company—a "model that helps a person in need with every product purchased," in the words of TOMS founder Blake Mycoskie; since its inception in 2006, TOMS has sold and subsequently given away seventy million pairs of shoes to children in need.[13] And it has inspired scores of businesses to follow its lead: Better World Books sells and donates new and used books; Bombas sells and provides free socks to homeless shelters; SoapBox Soaps donates a month of water, a bar of soap, or a year of vitamins for each soap product it sells; Warby Parker sells and distributes eyeglasses.

The typical menstrual giveback looks strikingly similar. For every product sold, a comparable donation is made to an organization, domestic or global, that helps address menstrual access and education. Many of the recipients are highlighted in this book—AFRIpads, Days for Girls International, Lava Mae, Support the Girls, among them. Some of the companies donate their own products; others make a financial contribution, usually a percentage of each sale.

Seems win-win, right? Mostly so. Overall, giveback programs appear to excite and align with consumers' interests.
From *Bloomberg*: "Social justice tends to be a winner among
female consumers, especially millennials. According to a 2015
study from Cone Communications on millennial attitudes
toward corporate social responsibility, 87 percent of women
age 18 to 34 say it's a key factor in purchasing decisions, and
75 percent say they're willing to spend more on a socially or
environmentally responsible product. Fully 90 percent say they
expect companies to actively address societal problems."[14]
That's heartening and a good harbinger for the future.

Generally, there have been broad critiques of the "One For
One" model and its potential for unintended consequences—
that it can inadvertently undermine local producers (for example, cobblers in the case of TOMS donations), or create a culture of dependency on donations instead of tackling systemic
roots of poverty. It is a complicated equation, of course, and
most proponents have been quite vocal about their desire to
effectively address and counter those concerns.

But, in any event, those limitations don't particularly apply
to the unique challenges, immediate and ongoing, posed by lack
of access to menstrual hygiene. First, raising awareness about
the reality of how periods impact the lives of the poor continues to be desperately important, given the silence that has surrounded the problem for so long. The more attention directed
to the issue, the better. And this niche consumer base has shown
to be quite responsive to messages about the global implications of menstrual access, judging by the testimonials posted on
social media directed at favorite start-ups. I've looked closely
at the various donation programs offered from company to

company, and the support does indeed appear to flow to recipients who are not only welcoming of the corporate partnership, but already operate in ways that are both locally appropriate and high impact.

A simple caveat is warranted. Start-ups must show extreme care and sensitivity not to overstate or co-opt the hard-earned reputation and mission of the organizations they support—and whose menstrual focus is so similar it can easily cause confusion for the consumer. Whereas one might think that the specialty product they're purchasing means they're subsidizing a girl's menstrual needs halfway across the world, they might find that those groups would get as much bang for their buck by a direct contribution. In other words, just a reminder that one doesn't have to buy a product to do good.

The politics of content.

The previously mentioned company that makes bleed-into-your-underwear, super-absorbent panties, THINX, has won the lion's share of media attention. From the start, this was partly due to the novelty and early strong reviews of the product (though it is not the first of its kind on the market; several other companies sell comparable versions), but also to a seriously shrewd advertising and promotional strategy. In a 2016 interview with *Fast Company*, THINX explained its philosophy as follows: "Every touchpoint that the consumer has with the brand, from the product to the website to the ads, needs to make a woman feel good about having her period. It has to hit the mark in terms of aesthetic design, product innovation and in accessible, relatable brand communication. [T]hese three prongs coming together can change culture."[15]

Change culture? Or sell a product? Are the two mutually exclusive? A real-time case study transpired back in October 2015 when THINX catapulted periods into the center of a highly publicized battle with the Metropolitan Transit Authority (MTA), the system that runs buses, trains, and subways in New York City. The controversy: a series of billboards for which THINX sought to purchase placement in the city's subway system—ads that would blanket the walls, turnstiles, and staircases of two of the busiest stations, one serving primarily suburban commuters (midtown's Grand Central Terminal) and another Brooklyn hipsters (Williamsburg's Bedford Avenue), as well as signage to be posted throughout the city's fleet of subway cars. The copy was simple, UNDERWEAR FOR WOMEN WITH PERIODS, and the imagery included a halved grapefruit with a decidedly vaginal look and a drippy raw egg. But both came under fire from the agency representing the MTA and were deemed "too suggestive." Ironically, the New York City subways are plastered with other grapefruit-specific imagery, including an ad that features a woman holding unpeeled fruits, double-fisted in front of her chest, to promote breast augmentation (clementines for before, grapefruits for after). And larger-than-life, scantily clad models with zoomed-in cleavage, promotions for everything from lingerie to *Fifty Shades of Grey*, are standard subway fare.

THINX took to the Internet to cry foul, calling out the MTA for penalizing periods. And the Internet, in turn, rallied to THINX's side. After *Mic* broke the story, and it was picked up by dozens of major national outlets, indignation flared on social media.[16] "Dear NYC Subway: There Will Be Blood!" The claims against the MTA may have come prematurely—transit officials responded in *The New York Times* that the ads were under review and had not been nor were ever going to be rejected. But soon enough that mattered little. Twitter and Facebook erupted in a flurry of discourse about whether the subway, or any public place, was a proper venue for period talk. The overwhelming majority answered: why shouldn't it be? It was an affirmative, satisfying win for the mainstreaming of menstruation, and certainly a highlight of "The Year of the Period." As for whether THINX sold more underwear as a result of the media hoopla, or of the subway campaign itself, once the ads were placed? *New York* magazine profiled the company a few months later in February 2016 and reported it had seen a significant revenue bump. Marketplace feminism doing its thing, perhaps. But it was also a broader win that smart, provocative discussion was instigated.

Here's where it gets tricky, though. Discussing THINX's overall strategy, the company's cofounder stated in an April 2016 post in *Contently*, a marketing blog, "We are a content company disguised as a period company." The blog posed an important question in response: "If this concept gives pause, it should. Can a for-profit, venture-backed company legitimately function as an outlet to discuss important social and political issues?"[17]

The controversy over the subway ads was indeed a lightning rod for the media and drummed up considerable publicity not just for the brand, but around issues of menstrual stigma. But consumers would be wise to think long and hard about sources of content and who is behind them. Today's start-ups may well espouse earnestly held beliefs in their products, and that is admirable. Even good business, which is exactly the point. But as activists and movement makers, we have the right and responsibility to ensure that public content fairly advances *all* aspects of a menstrual agenda, not just the message chosen by the brand that can afford to place the most (and most beautiful) ads, effective as they may be.

From the same *Contently* blog, the claim is further expanded, suggesting that ad content and purchase of products can even help spur policy change: "People are able to go to their politicians and say, 'Hey, I don't like the fact that we have a tampon tax,' or 'Hey, I don't like the fact that women in prison don't have easy access to feminine hygiene products.'" Following with the assertion, "It's not charity that is going to change the world's business." The company had claimed similarly a few months prior in February 2016, as reported by *New York* magazine: "If you *just* do good, you're a nonprofit. And they are just *shit,* the way they're designed, the way they're marketed. You have to have a level of motivation to make a big dent in the universe."[18] Those smacked of fighting words.

Now, at that point in time, advocacy campaigns were well underway to exempt menstrual products from sales tax and to ensure access to incarcerated women and others. Laws that directly, tangibly affect the lives of millions—so we're talking a seriously big dent. Among the many contributions necessary to advance the policy agenda—from rigorous budget crunching and tax code assessments, to legislative framing and messaging, to stakeholder engagement and mobilization—branded product ads and marketing materials and pithy press releases were not among them. And, quite frankly, never will be.

Which takes us back to the question of what role, if any, branding and content might play in achieving culture change. From the policy perspective, at least, I would strongly recommend that companies not conflate these with, and certainly not underplay or denigrate, the parallel change-making work of nonprofit advocacy. This will only stymie the path to achieving systemic policy change. That said, when approached strategically, coordinated public-private alliances can lend real value to the fights. For example, Conscious Period has made lobbying for sales tax bills both locally in California and nationally integral to its company mission and social media strategy; together with *Buzzfeed*, it produced a viral film short featuring free-bleeding women that reached more than six million viewers who got to see what lack of access to period products really looks like. LOLA, Lunapads, and Maxim, all of which provide natural, organic, and/or reusable menstrual products, work with advocates to offer extensive policy analyses through a regular blog series. Sustain and Cora, two more of the organic companies, have stepped up to coordinate product donations specifically for the purpose of incentivizing tampon tax and menstrual access legislation. And FLEX, the maker of a reusable menstrual disc, along with several of the menstrual cycle tracking apps, is charting an agenda to directly engage its customer base in national reproductive health policy.

We are fortunate to have an abundance of companies that desire to help advance policy reform for the greater social good. As we go forward, we should take advantage of this interest and aim to better define—and refine—how the mutual interests of activism, advocacy, and entrepreneurship can be best aligned. It makes for a unique, modern case study to offer other movements, too.

Corporate Engagement

Outside the realm of new product development and promotion, the for-profit sector has supported menstrual activism in another meaningful way. One of the original architects for this movement is digital marketing pioneer Nancy Kramer. Named one of the 100 Most Influential Women in Advertising by *Advertising Age* magazine, Kramer has been a transformative influence in the world of personal computers, dating all the way back to the evolution of Apple—her first client in 1981, then in its fledgling phase. Her commitment to the intersection of innovation and menstruation took root well before "The Year of the Period." In fact, the revelation came decades earlier when she first visited Apple's corporate headquarters in Cupertino. Stunned to see that its restrooms were fully stocked with free tampons and pads, she began to question why all workplace and public facilities didn't routinely do this—a gesture, she believed, that could dramatically improve employees' ability to do their jobs.

Since then, Kramer has been an outspoken national champion for menstrual access—namely, the provision of free products in the workplace, schools, and other public facilities. By her calculations, it costs only $4.67 per person, per year for a midsized company to offer employees enough tampons and pads to get through the workday. (She knows because she did this herself.) She launched a nonprofit organization called Free the Tampons, delivered a rousing TEDx Talk on the topic in 2013, and commissioned new research by Harris Interactive, polling more than one thousand US women age eighteen and over, so she could better understand the impact of periods in the workplace.[19] The polling results were hardly shocking: 86

percent of women have been caught off guard by their period and without the supplies they need; and when periods come unexpectedly, workers can experience humiliation and are less productive. Her research is bolstered by that of the cycle-tracking app called Clue, which conducted a far-reaching survey of ninety thousand of its users worldwide in 2015. Among its findings, 18 percent of American respondents reported to have missed work due to anxiety around menstruation—and this doesn't even account for the accumulated hours and energy expended on dealing with an unexpected period, from scavenging for needed supplies to hiding stains.[20]

Among the innovations Kramer has conceptualized and overseen is the creation of a new, modernized product dispenser for restrooms that releases free tampons and pads triggered by a timed motion sensor. The machine is being used by the New York City agencies now mandated by law to provide free menstrual products and by all reports they are especially beloved in the schools. And she has successfully lobbied universities and other major companies—including the John Glenn Columbus International Airport—to use it and provide free supplies to their employees and patrons. Some much-needed next steps include taking this same approach to the employers of low-wage workers, for whom a period can mean missed days of work, and therefore lost income and compromised job security.

Beyond Kramer's vast business acumen and leadership, she's the parent of six and, quite honestly, knowing her is as close to being in the presence of Wonder Woman as I may ever come. In her "Free the Tampons" TEDx Talk, and to everyone she meets, she regales the promise she made to her daughters: "Before I die, I want to help change the social norm around this issue."

I THINK IT IS FAIR to say that this movement is undeniably changing the social norm—and that we've come a far way in the short time since we've started taking periods public. How will all of the players in this movement keep leveraging the momentum generated in "The Year of the Period"? I can hardly wait to see what's next when it comes to activism and innovation.

From my perch, the time is now to chart an even broader, more meaningful menstrual policy agenda. Onward.

TAKING A STAND FOR MENSTRUAL EQUITY

chapter seven

PARTiNG THE RED SEA

AGAINST ALL ODDS, "THE YEAR of the Period" morphed into a vital, vibrant era. The world got woke to periods thanks to a groundswell of activism and innovation and enterprise and advocacy. As for our first policy missive—beginning to take down the tampon tax and ensure free access to products via public agencies—we proved that not only was a menstrual agenda viable but absolutely winnable. Our work is now cut out for us to replicate those legislative victories in more cities and states across the country, and around the world.

But, really, there's so much more still that can be achieved by fully harnessing this new momentum. Certainly that includes advancing policies that prioritize the immediate needs of those who menstruate—access, affordability, safety. But I propose that we commit to something even more far-reaching. That is, to elevating menstruation as an actual catalyst, a core focal point, for how we consider *all* of the laws and rules by which we live, and how we evaluate whether they are just, practical, and equitable.

So far, in calling out the societal norms that have enabled the powers-that-be to disregard menstruation or deem it unworthy of accommodation, we've begun to make a case for *equality*. The arguments that have been most successful are those that make the case that periods should be treated the same as other analogous bodily functions. But what I'd like to next explore is a shift in our thinking to the broader concept of genuine *equity*— what we stand to gain by making menstruation an affirmative measure of full, fair societal participation.

Because the truth is, when it comes to periods, there is not really such a thing as "equal" treatment. In the case of the tampon tax, for example, the equality frame only gets us so far as to ensure that menstrual products are regarded identically as products used by men or the whole population. I often find myself arguing *ad nauseum* where tampons rank on the scale of necessity as compared to toilet paper . . . or razors . . . or Rogaine . . . or Viagra. But why do we need to harken to other bodily functions to validate our needs at all? Shouldn't it be enough to state that menstruation stands apart and requires its own, unique set of interventions? In crafting the case for equity, we can do just that and establish a whole new baseline. The tampon tax argument might then be made as follows: exempting menstrual products from sales tax produces an affirmative public good—that is, increased health benefits and economic empowerment for half the population that, ultimately, yields benefits for us all.

Which, of course, brings us back to the very concept first introduced more than a year ago to the skeptical *Chicago Sun Times* reporter: that of menstrual equity. It is the heart of the next policy agenda for this movement and the focus of the proposals set forth in this section. In each one, I imagine what our laws and lives might look like if we put the theory to the true test. Or, in practical policy speak, I've applied a "lens" through which I examine various rules and laws and expectations. This is a fairly common exercise, though more typically reserved for health or racial or gender reflection. Here we'll call it the menstrual lens.

What follows is a selection of nine areas of public life and policy, considered first from the perspective of the societal objectives each seeks to address—for example, whether to afford educational opportunity, a safety net for the poor, or hygiene protocol in prison—and then followed by specific implications for menstruation. As a practical matter, applying the menstrual lens simply would call upon policy makers, employers, educators, and the like to do the same and ask themselves the question: if we were looking at those affected by this rule or policy and judging its efficacy by how it addresses the fact that their bodies menstruate, what might we find? And then, what might we do differently?

It is a telling exercise. How might public benefits be calculated or distributed more rationally? Could workplace rules be more accommodating of menstruation and if so, what advantage might that yield for employees and employers, alike? Might politicians view laws that impact reproductive decisions or the lives of transgender people differently if they were prone to better understand or empathize with menstruation? Would philanthropy focused on programs that support vulnerable populations be more effective if there was an overt menstrual component? And so forth.

Yes, it sounds a little far-fetched. But my aim is not to argue for a new world order, a menstrual utopia (or . . . menstrutopia!). Rather, it is simply meant to push the boundaries on envisioning the ways our policy making can do better by all of us.

What is exciting about these proposals is that they encompass a diverse range of individuals and interests and contextual applications. Introduction need not be linear: they could be plotted and paced, unveiled in different scenarios and circumstances. Each also provides a building block for any future advocacy that may emerge as menstrual stigma is further eradicated. One policy change helps clear the path and open a dialogue for the next . . . and the next one after that.

Of course, in the interim we still may need to rely on quick fixes and scoring points on the board. Scrapping the tampon tax isn't our most far-reaching goal, but the more states that make it happen, the stronger position we will be in to fight for higher impact change. And we also must recognize that some of the proposals are incomplete, or conflict and run counter to one another. For example, promoting the provision of disposable tampons and pads for the homeless does not address the fact that these products are woefully unregulated, potentially dangerous to our health, or wreak havoc on the environment. My advice here is patience. We have to accept that there's no immediate catch-all solution or set of alternatives—at least not yet. Consider this a blueprint, not a battle plan.

In the end, of course, the ideal is to achieve policies that acknowledge, appreciate, even celebrate how menstruating bodies function. When it comes to equity, our periods, suddenly and amazingly, are a rich starting place.

Making Menstrual Ends Meet: Public Benefits Policies

Poverty in America is inextricably intertwined with gender. A few key statistics drive home the profound impact. The National Women's Law Center reports that across all races and ethnicities, nearly six in ten poor adults are women, and nearly six in ten poor children live in single-parent families headed by women. Poverty rates are especially high among certain women: those who head families (36.5 percent); African American women (23.1 percent); Hispanic women (20.9 percent); and millennials (21.7 percent).[1] Women are 35 percent more likely to be poor than their male counterparts, according to Legal Momentum.[2] And, by sheer numbers, recall the Shriver Center statistic that one in every three American women—42 million, in total—lives in poverty or right on the brink of it.[3]

It follows logically, then, that women are also primary participants in many of our nation's largest public assistance programs. Yet the very fact that those participants menstruate, and the ensuing financial burden it causes for them and their families, has been conspicuously absent from policy making. Using the menstrual lens to examine a selection of federal nutritional and health benefits demonstrates just how out of touch with the reality of periods our lawmakers have been. It also offers creative ways to push for adjustments that acknowledge the costs and intersecting health and economic impacts of menstruation.

Nutrition programs.

Women are about twice as likely as men to be among the 45 million recipients of food-stamps benefits, formally named the

Supplemental Nutrition Assistance Program, or SNAP.[4] As a historical matter, food stamps weren't ever created to serve as a safety net primarily for poor women and their families or to address the realities of their lives and budgets—menstrual or otherwise. Established as part of a pilot in 1933 in the midst of the Great Depression, the program's original impetus was to support rural farmers struggling to sell their surplus crops when prices crashed. It enabled funding for the federal government to buy the harvest at a discount and distribute it among hunger relief agencies in states and local communities. Farmers got paid, the masses were fed. As the nation's focus later shifted to addressing poverty and nutrition, as well as improving the agricultural economy, food stamps became a permanent legislative fixture in 1964. The program has contended with countless modifications, restrictions, and rollbacks in the decades that followed. And now, nearly a century after its introduction, food stamps certainly are as much about helping to ensure the working poor can simply, sanely make it through the checkout aisle of the supermarket with the staples they need. On average, a food-stamps allowance is $255 per month for a family of three with an income of $26,000 per year.[5]

And women and children are the exclusive recipients of the Special Supplemental Nutrition Program for Women, Infants, and Children—better known as WIC—which was established in 1972 exclusively for impoverished new mothers. Initially designed as a series of nutritional programs for pregnant women, today WIC's more broadly stated goal is to improve health outcomes of the nation's poorest families. It serves a far smaller population than food stamps, around eight million women, babies, and children, and offers supplemental food packages and other health and nutrition resources.

Both SNAP and WIC are administered by the US Department of Agriculture and provide participants monthly subsidies in the form of checks, vouchers, or debit-style cards to purchase specific food and nutritional products. WIC also provides health-care referrals, nutrition counseling, and an array of breast-feeding resources (and, more recently, incentives to breast-feed that come in the form of extended benefits and a more diverse range of covered food options for those who fully or partially forego formula).

But, of course, the kicker: neither of these federal assistance programs have allowances for the purchase of menstrual products. Food stamps, incidentally, lumps tampons and pads in the same category as pet food, cigarettes, and alcohol. All of which are off-limits.

Despite these programs' agricultural and business roots, given the current demographics of the recipients of these benefits, the continued exclusion of menstrual products is almost incomprehensible.

Let's start with WIC users—all of whom are soon-to-be or new moms and their children. Anyone who has ever given birth knows that the weeks that follow the blessed event are among the messiest and leakiest imaginable. Tampons are to be strictly avoided, and even the most bulky overnight pads are barely sufficient for absorbing the postpartum flow known as lochia. In the immediate postdelivery days, lochia can gush quite dramatically. (The first time I stood up after giving birth I was stunned by its magnitude and intensity. I remember describing it to a friend like an elevator plummeting down a shaft, doors opening *The Shining*–style.) All told, the need for a steady supply of pads can last for as long as six weeks. Pads are medically necessary for the immediate physical and emotional well-being of postpartum women—and among WIC recipients especially, who bear sole responsibility (no night nannies, no doulas) for ensuring that their newborns are healthy and thriving.

Consider also the fact that the mothers who receive WIC benefits traditionally have had among the nation's lowest breast-feeding rates. WIC has worked to reverse this trend, adding resources, counseling, and support, and constructing a tiered system of benefits to incentivize breast-feeding. But the formula-focused programs it offers still attract the majority of users. Breast-feeding exclusively delays the return of menstruation after giving birth (along with a long list of other potential health benefits . . . but that's not this book), so as long as there are WIC participants who rely on formula, fully or partially, they are also likely to have a need for menstrual products.

Those who use food stamps bear the burden of the exclusion, too. Smart, cost-effective grocery shopping entails balancing a budget and aligning nutritional needs with overall health; it's all inextricably connected. And menstruation implicates nutrition, whether it is foods to avoid (or that are craved) during the menstrual cycle, or the need for medication and products. For food-stamps recipients with more than one person who menstruates—families with teenage daughters, for example—the financial pinch is felt exponentially. Statistically, lesbian couples are twice as likely as straight couples to depend on food stamps; the need for menstrual products is also dire (and doubled).[6]

The need is real. Why is it so routinely ignored by programs that serve more who menstruate than who don't?

It is time to shift gears. Here are some ways the menstrual lens could be used to influence policy change: making menstrual products eligible for purchase with food stamps, as a pragmatic matter, could be a fairly simple expansion. The problem, of course, is the cascade effect. Without increasing the overall allowance, the same meager benefits would then only be stretched further or compete with funding for food items.

The SNAP program is reauthorized by Congress every five years as part of what's known as the Farm Bill, though food stamps now account for 80 percent of that funding. The Farm Bill's last reauthorization was in 2014 and included some draconian cuts. When it next goes back to Congress we must make the case for the inclusion of menstrual products. It will be an uphill battle, and it isn't likely we'll see much in the way of empathy for the plight of poor families overall or additional dollars made available; if anything, even deeper cuts are to be expected given the record of the current Congress. Arguing for larger allowances that include menstrual products doesn't stand to yield immediate success. But it's a public platform and messaging campaign well worth undertaking. Women's and families' firsthand testimony would be powerful, as would a series of their stories reported in political publications and mainstream newspapers. With the potential momentum of other period policies, and especially the success of the tampon tax campaigns in states, the time is ripe to plant that seed and start the conversation in the Farm Bill reauthorization. At a future time and in a more receptive Congress, menstruation should and could absolutely qualify to be part of the products eligible for purchase with food stamps.

WIC, on the other hand, is regulated by the Department of Agriculture's child nutrition legislation, not the Farm Bill. The case to make there is much more straightforward and not constrained by the same formal timing limits of the reauthorization process. Members of Congress need to hear loud and clear the realities and needs of new mothers, and why pads especially are a necessary part of their health and wellness and ability to parent.

Another incidental benefit would ensue if both programs included menstrual products: that is, all purchases made with food stamps and WIC are already exempt by law from state sales tax. This would mean effectively eliminating the tampon tax for the poorest women—a double win.

Arguments focused on the scope of both programs—and WIC, in particular—might also be wisely waged by joining with the parallel campaign for the inclusion of baby diapers as a public benefit (which are also, unconscionably if you ask me, excluded). Like menstrual products, diapers are flat-out expensive and used with greater frequency, costing parents on average a whopping $80 a month, per child. A third of the babies in this country are raised by parents who struggle to afford diapers.[7] Like menstrual products, failure to have an adequate supply can lead to incidental harms. In the case of diapers, this often means being shut out of day care and early childhood education programs that require participants to bring their own supply.

There have been a few state and federal legislative attempts to provide diapers as a public benefit. California has tried for several years to advance a bill to provide a monthly voucher for diapers; the city of San Francisco began including diapers in its provision of welfare benefits. In 2014, a federal bill was introduced to allow states to create pilot programs to either give low-income families a subsidy to buy diapers or distribute them directly. President Obama spoke up about it too in 2016, announcing a partnership that would pair up private industry with nonprofits to create effective distribution channels. None of these, though, has led to anything close to meaningful, systemic change.

We should work to elevate this dialogue together. This is especially important given that, like menstrual products, diapers are largely an expense borne by women. At first blush, it might even seem that diapers could generate a more sympathetic audience. Who could argue that babies don't need them for good health? Babies are cute, vulnerable, innocent . . . right? Not so much. Sadly, the argument for diapers may invoke even more vociferous disdain than tampons. Notably, Rush Limbaugh went off on a tirade in 2014 over the federal legislative proposal for diaper subsidies. It goes back to all the self-righteous fury directed at poor women, the insidious myth of the welfare queen having babies just to collect benefits. The gist of it: "If you can't afford the kid, don't ask me to diaper it." Our respective movements, together, would address many of the prevalent stereotypes that harm women and perpetuate the cycle of poverty.

Now, Limbaugh also made the case that he was raised on cloth diapers and there's no case to be made for subsidizing disposable products for anyone. That argument has similarly been made about menstrual products. But let's just take that off the table. Until we are providing viable options in all corners of

American life—jobs, housing, health care, even access to laundry facilities—cloth diapers are not a realistic option for all, and neither are reusable menstrual products.

Health-care programs.

Over the past two decades, Medicaid has expanded dramatically from its welfare roots and now operates as the primary health coverage program for more than thirty million low-income children, women, and families. Women continue to rely more heavily on Medicaid coverage than men. But, as is almost expected at this point, the costs of menstrual products aren't covered. Creating a subsidy for menstrual products—or at least making allowances for reduced costs—would help ensure that the millions of the poorest Americans have greater access. As a matter of practicality, it would not be difficult. Users could present a Medicaid card at purchase much like is done to pick up other qualifying items and prescription drugs.

Making the case for Medicaid coverage would likely entail reclassifying menstrual products as a medical necessity under the program. Other federal agencies already deem them as such; the Food and Drug Administration does explicitly so in its classification of tampons and pads as "medical devices."

There already exists plenty of evidence that reusing products or using tampons and pads for too long—or not using them at all—leads to higher rates of infection and other conditions for which patients are likely to require medical intervention. That is data that has been readily collected in parts of the developing world. Arguments about the physical effects could be further reinforced by showing if or how lack of menstrual products causes psychological stress; comparable studies have demonstrated the impact of being unable to afford diapers on the mental health of parents. And the fact that periods involve bodily fluids create potential implications for public health, hygiene, and sanitation.

Extending this classification to Medicaid would implicate and benefit other proposed reforms, especially state sales tax exemptions and possibly federal programs, too, like Flexible Spending Account (FSA) allowances and other federally run health reimbursement programs. FSAs enable employees to place up to $2,550 of pretax income in an account dedicated for certain medical expenses. Currently, tampons and pads are not eligible for reimbursement. According to the federal government's website:

Why aren't tampons eligible for reimbursement?

Tampons are feminine hygiene products made with soft, absorbent materials that are designed to control the flow of menstrual blood by being inserted into the vagina during the menstrual period. Although these products were classified as "cosmetics" for much of the 20th century, in 1976, the US Food and Drug Administration (FDA) reclassified them as medical products as they are "intended to affect the structure or any function of the body of man or other animals, and which [a product] does not achieve any of its primary intended purposes through chemical action within or on the body of man or other animals and which is not dependent upon being metabolized for the achievement of any of its primary intended purposes."

While the FDA classifies tampons as a medical product that must be tightly regulated and stringently tested before being allowed to be sold, the IRS views tampons differently in determining whether they are deemed eligible for reimbursement. Tampons have been deemed products that are for "general health" purposes, and not to treat a specific medical condition. Because these items do not play a role in alleviating or aiding in the treatment plan of a specific illness, they are not covered under any circumstance with consumer spending accounts.[8]

There is so much here with which to take exception, it is hard to know where to start. But the main takeaway: the FDA deems tampons medical devices (though "tightly regulated and stringently tested" is a tremendous overstatement, as we'll soon explore) but the good folks at the IRS have their own view—as the *doctors* and *health specialists* that tax experts are known to be—and have decided that menstruation is not a specific medical condition but rather a matter of "general health." Never mind that the products we use are the very thing that keep menstruation *from* causing medical conditions. (It is hard to write this without sarcasm dripping from my keyboard the same way blood drips down my legs when I go without a tampon.) This is perhaps even more outrageous than the silent exclusion of menstruation in other programs. It is the tax man playing doctor—and a doctor who willfully ignores the reality of the need to manage periods, at that.

As discussed earlier, US Congresswoman Grace Meng already has introduced federal legislation to make menstrual products eligible for coverage via FSAs. Calling out the absurdity of this IRS rule, securing more support for her federal bill, and rallying a Senate sponsor for it are direct action steps we can take. So too is forcing a debate in Congress over the inconsistency of the classification of menstrual products as medical devices across various federal agencies and programs.

THESE EXAMPLES AND PROPOSALS ARE not intended to be comprehensive—but rather to jump-start broader and more creative thinking about public benefits and aiding menstrual access. There are numerous state and locally administered programs across the country that could develop comparable initiatives. But the goal is the same: demanding recognition that advancing healthy lives necessarily includes ensuring menstrual needs are met.

Bleeding on the Job: Workplace Policies

Even though women now make up just about half the US work-force—and are expected to become the majority (51 percent) of workers in this country by 2018—it is still a man's world. Women are grossly underrepresented at the very top, holding a mere 5.8 percent of CEO positions in Fortune 500 companies,[9] but overflowing the ranks of the nation's lowest paying jobs.[10] Two-thirds of American workers who earn minimum wage are women; women also comprise two-thirds of those paid by tips.[11] Income disparity persists. Overall, women earn 78 cents on average for every dollar a white man makes; the gap is even greater for women of color, with black women at 63 cents and Latinas 54 cents for every dollar earned by a white man.[12]

For sure, there are countless statistics and narratives and accounts that shed light on the myriad challenges women face in their working lives, from inadequate family leave policy and the pernicious prevalence of sexual harassment, to glass ceilings, sticky floors, and everything in between. But for the purpose of this section, I daresay it is sufficient to simply agree that women are working, and that managing menstruation in the workplace is but a small facet of the avalanche of biases and disadvantages women face. Yet there are simple policies for which we could advocate now not only to bring about immediate relief but also to help spur long-term culture shifts.

Access to menstrual products.

Employers should make tampons and pads available for free in employee restrooms as a best practice, a way to maximize employee output, and an acknowledgment that it is what's best for workers' health, well-being, attendance, and productivity. In the case of the nation's low-wage workers—who are most likely to be women and who are least likely to be able to afford the menstrual products they need at the moment they need them—something as simple as free tampons and pads on the job could be a consequential shift.

Let's use Walmart as a case study, given that 57 percent of its nationwide workforce (1.5 million employees in total) are female. From Walmart's own corporate diversity report, women appear to be among the company's lowest ranked and lowest paid workers, woefully sparse at the senior management and executive level.[13] Couple that with a startling reality: a 2014 study by Americans for Tax Fairness reports that Walmart employees at the bottom of its pay scale earn so little they qualify for and must rely on food stamps and other public assistance, to the tune of a national cost to taxpayers of $6.2 billion dollars.[14]

When it comes to paid time off, Walmart's policy for sick leave in particular has been the subject of widespread public criticism, both for being opaque and draconian. Up until 2015, a mandated one-day wait-to-use earned sick time was enforced.[15]

Overall, not a pretty picture for its rank-and-file employees, especially those who menstruate while working there.

But what if research could be undertaken that made the case to Walmart and similarly situated employers that providing menstrual products would be a boost to employee productivity? And that a workforce that is more punctual and more present is also more profitable? We know from Nancy Kramer's analysis that the annual aggregate cost of providing free tampons and pads for her much smaller company is minimal ($4.67 per person retail). In the case of Walmart's size and scale, the return on investment could be exponential. Even using Kramer's retail pricing, the cost to Walmart would amount to $3.9 million per year—and likely much less, given its wholesale purchasing power. A drop in the bucket compared to its 2017 annual revenue of $485 billion and profit of $124 billion.[16] But the relative expense would be irrelevant if it turned out that there were measurable benefits to the bottom line. I would urge that this is just the kind of research our movement desperately needs to champion and commission, and that could be the ammunition that could incentivize big business to act.

While low-wage earners have the most pressing need for freely available menstrual products, providing them for all simply amounts to good business. Even for well-compensated employees with the resources to purchase and use products at will—meaning having the dollars in one's wallet and the ability to dash away or punch off the clock to make a quick purchase or bathroom break—the added bit of security that comes with a reliable stash goes a long way toward peace of mind. I know I've been late for meetings due to a midday emergency drugstore run; I've even stained an office chair or two. The price of a tampon is a small investment in having employees who feel supported and on their best game. (And, I might add, a wiser expense than subsidizing said employee's time spent scrubbing blood off a conference room seat.)

And thanks to Alyssa Mastromonaco, former deputy chief of staff for operations to President Obama, even the White House got with the program and began providing tampons to employees. In her 2017 book, *Who Thought This Was a Good Idea?: And Other Questions You Should Have Answers to When You Work in the White House*, Mastromonaco shared how she "made it her mission" to spearhead the installation of the first-ever tampon dispenser in the West Wing restroom. "If we were truly serious about running a diverse operation and bringing more women into politics, we should give the office a basic level of comfort for them," she writes. "It would be better than menstruating all over the Oval."[17] In an interview with *ThinkProgress* about why employers overlook this necessity she shared, "My view is, they don't give it any thought. I don't think it's malice. But not considering an entire sex that needs tampons and maxi pads, it's like, is not thinking about it some form of malice unto itself?"[18]

Somehow, the novelty of free menstrual products manages to simultaneously raise awareness and generate goodwill, too. (Trust me, every time a friend finds herself in a restroom where this is the practice, I find a smiling tampon selfie in my inbox.) We should use that as an opportunity to expand impact—in particular, by coupling free product provision with information about how lack of access can cause harm to poor women at home and around the world. I've already borne witness to the domino effect of this strategy. Employees have gone on to advocate for free products in their kids' schools, their town halls, and other venues, and others have engaged their employers and colleagues in large-scale donation drives and charity initiatives. It is important momentum to tap.

And it's not just about persuading the Walmarts of the world to get on board for their own bottom line. There's a viable public policy strategy to undertake, too. Most workplace restrooms are under the purview of the US Department of Labor's Occupational Safety and Health Administration agency (OSHA), whose mission is to "assure safe and healthful working conditions for working men and women by setting and enforcing standards and by providing training, outreach, education, and assistance." OSHA mandates that employers provide all workers with safe, sanitary, and immediately available toilet facilities; its sanitation standard "is intended to ensure that . . . workers do not suffer adverse health effects that can result if toilets are not sanitary and/or not available when needed."[19]

In addition to toilets, most of the various products found in workplace restrooms—for wiping, washing, and drying—are all there as a matter of regulation. And yet somehow, menstrual products never made the list of necessities.

It isn't that OSHA is unaware of this particular bodily function or the fact that restrooms are the place where we take care of menstrual needs. While the agency "does not generally consider discarded feminine hygiene products, used to absorb menstrual flow, to fall within the definition of regulated waste,"[20] it is the case that the small bins in toilet stalls for tossing used tampons and pads, for example, are there as a matter of OSHA policy, which dictates that they "be discarded into waste containers which are lined in such a way as to prevent contact with the contents."[21] OSHA notes that 5.6 million employees in the United States are at risk of exposure to bloodborne pathogens. But might OSHA regulators have also considered the hygienic impact of blood running down the legs of workers?

We should lobby members of Congress and call upon OSHA to mandate the provision of menstrual products as it does all other aspects of restroom functions. No one clamors that big government wastes our tax dollars providing free hand soap and dryers. We must argue the same for tampons and pads as a matter of both personal hygiene and public health.

There is already a federal bill we can get behind. US Congresswoman Meng's Menstrual Equity for All Act of 2017 includes a provision that would direct the Secretary of Labor to promulgate regulations that mandate large employers (with one hundred or more employees) to provide free tampons and pads in workplace restrooms along with other already mandated supplies.

Period leave.

There's an even more fundamental concept playing out around the world—paid days off from work for menstruation.

Nike is the first-ever global brand to officially include menstrual leave in its code of conduct and has offered it to employees since 2007. But Japan can lay claim to the inaugural nationwide policy that allows sick days explicitly on account of menstruation; under its 1947 Labor Standards Law, those who suffer from painful periods or whose job might exacerbate period pain are allowed *seirikyuuka* (literally, *physiological leave*). Over the years, several other Asian countries—South Korea (2001), Indonesia (2003), Taiwan (2014), and even parts of China (the Anhui, Shanxi, and Hebei provinces)—have followed Japan's lead. When the policy was most recently debated in Taiwan, a coalition of politicians went the distance affirmatively claiming that failure to provide menstrual leave, above and beyond regular sick days, amounted to a violation of women's basic rights.

Despite the sweeping Taiwanese tribute, many of the Asian policies come with a hefty dose of paternalism. Women are often required to present a doctor's note or even submit to a physical exam at the employer's behest. And the endgame is often less about women's productivity and more about advancing and protecting traditional beliefs regarding the delicacy of female workers and their reproductive futures. As the author Emily Matchar framed it for the *Atlantic* in 2014, these policies are based on "the scientifically dubious notion that women who don't rest during their menses will have difficulty in childbirth later. Some say the laws are therefore more about treating women as future baby-vessels than valued employees."[22]

Period leave started gaining mainstream attention in the spring of 2016 when an upscale British-based start-up called Co-Resist—woman-led with a predominantly female workforce—announced that it was implementing a corporate policy to allow employees to take days off while menstruating.

A few months later, the Zambian government unveiled a national menstrual leave policy, the first of its kind in Africa. Named the "Mother's Day" law, it guarantees women one day off from work per month. The rule applies equally to those without children, despite the limited name—a purposeful designation, intended to acknowledge and celebrate women's caregiving role. In that spirit, and unlike comparable Asian policies, workers need not report their cycles to their employers but are only asked to call in to say they are taking Mother's Day. Zambia's Labour Minister Joyce Nonde-Simukoko, a former trade union activist, notes that the practice has been informally observed since the 1990s.[23] Given the prevalence of stigma and taboo throughout Africa, any positive cultural recognition of menstruation is heartening. It has also inspired debate and activism in other parts of Africa, including Nigeria.

And then in March 2017, a new bill was presented in the Italian Parliament that would mandate companies to grant three days of paid period leave each month—the first of its kind in Europe and the western world.[24]

A spate of raucous "Year of the Period"–style media coverage and debate ensued following each announcement, demonstrating that there's little agreement and lots of discord about whether menstrual leave policies are a win. With regard to the proposal in Italy, many critics express concern that it will only worsen workplace inequality—and justify discrimination against women, as has been a reported outcome of expanded maternity policies there. And whereas some argue period leave improves women's opportunities to compete in the workplace, most believe it implies impairment—that women are weak, hormonal, and unfit to lead with a built-in, biological monthly lapse in judgment.

Disregarding the absurdity of the last statement, it is important to acknowledge that menstruation is indeed debilitating for many, though certainly not all. For the vast majority, cramps and leaks and stains are the extent of monthly discomfort. But for as many as one in five women who experience severe period pain, particularly those with conditions like uterine fibroids and endometriosis, a chronic disorder in which the tissue that lines the uterus spreads throughout the pelvis, the need for accommodation is real and not insignificant. Actress Lena Dunham spoke out in 2015 in her newsletter, *Lenny Letter*, and again in 2017 in a *New York Times* op-ed about the excruciating physical and psychological pain of living with endometriosis, which prompted a slew of reporting and personal storytelling. All told, there are an estimated 2 to 10 percent of American women between the ages of twenty-five and forty suffering from this incurable condition.[25]

As a matter of workplace policy, is their pain our collective fight?

Here's what an application of the menstrual lens would suggest. First, the notion that menstruation makes women less competent should be firmly rejected and shut down. We certainly do need to educate how and why it is that periods are incapacitating for many and stand behind the assertion that even this is not a sign of weakness. And we must simultaneously keep up the drumbeat that the ability to manage menstruation in the workplace is part of having healthy, productive employees writ large.

Rather than focus exclusively on menstrual leave now, a policy America isn't likely ready to embrace on a grand scale, a smart opportunity instead would be for menstrual advocacy to encompass the fight for paid sick leave, which is as much a women's issue as pay equity, family leave, and other related policies. We can lend our voices to those who are leading federal and state campaigns for ample paid sick leave, especially for low-wage workers, groups like Make It Work, Family Values @ Work, and the National Women's Law Center. Worth exploring, too, are the pros and cons of including menstrual health under the federal Family and Medical Leave Act, which applies to certain-sized employers (fifty or more employees in a 75-mile radius), and Americans with Disabilities Act and related state laws.

In so doing, we can be clear in making the case that managing menstruation is an essential part of our regular health, care, and keeping—as well as the reality that, for some, menstrual pain is as valid an ailment as the flu.

The Red School model.

Now, for some real menstrutopia: the rather incredible, intensely holistic model of the Red School movement and its founder, Alexandra Pope. Pope is at the fore of the concept called "menstruality" in the workplace and has conceptualized a "cycle awareness" program designed to take business to a whole new lunar level. Her primary tenet suggests the ideal community, including and especially the workplace, is one that enables all employees to take a positive, open, interactive approach to menstruation. Treating the menstrual cycle as a force to be leveraged and harnessed, she advises, promises greater effectiveness, efficiency, and satisfaction for both men and women.[26]

Pope partnered with the above-mentioned British company, Co-Resist, to formulate its period leave policy. Co-Resist simultaneously announced its participation in Pope's seminar entitled, *The Pioneering Period Policy: Valuing Natural Cycles in the Workplace*, through which she coaches employees in how to "create a positive approach to menstruation and the menstrual cycle that empowers women and men and supports the effectiveness and well-being of the organisation. To restore the menstrual cycle as the asset it is."

From Pope's promotional materials:

The menstrual cycle is a stress management and self-care tool that also offers a clear model of the creative process and sustainable living for women and men. When a woman is aware of the energy dynamic of her cycle and values and works with it, she has a more effective and efficient means of managing her energy and time for personal well-being and optimum creativity and productivity in the workplace. In short, cycle awareness is a mindfulness tool for women.

This resource in women is unrecognised and unvalued. For centuries women have endured shame, ridicule and embarrassment and been deprived of education and positions of power because of the cycle. While this historical worldwide disempowerment has shifted to some degree today for many women in the world, until women everywhere can comfortably talk about their cycles as healthy and positive we are all in some way diminished.

While this conversation is focused on the menstrual cycle, it forms part of a larger debate about honouring cycles in general—circadian, ultradian, seasonal etc., and cyclical consciousness as a model of sustainability—individual and organisational.

Can I start by saying how intrigued and motivated I am by this idea? It is the essence of the menstrual lens in so many ways. This is what life might look like if we had the freedom to accept and then extol the sheer power of our bodies. This is a far cry from period leave—the view of menstruation as an illness or condition—and instead offers a fuller picture of the natural ebbs and flows that guide our bodies and lives.

Here is what I can envision. First, employees are offered an opportunity to chart their cycles. After doing so, they consider their observations and assess its impact on work habits and best practices. Personal anecdotes like: "I am lethargic and irritable for two days before my period. My flow is heaviest days 1 to 3 of my period, and I prefer to be sedentary at that time. My energy level peaks on day 4 as my flow lightens and ceases, and lasts at that level for two weeks, through ovulation, when it rises again." (For the record, this is basically my own experience. If it is nothing like your cycle, well, all the more reason to start tracking for yourself.) This could then provide guidance for customizing scheduling and assignments, at least where there is the flexibility to do so (not always possible, I know), with those assets and liabilities in mind. Another riveting opportunity could be to gauge group dynamics, and how to harness and maximize the cycles of members of teams.

I spoke with Holly Grigg-Spall, author of the 2013 book *Sweetening the Pill: Or How We Got Hooked on Hormonal Birth Control* about the benefits and detriments of using the menstrual cycle as an affirmative work and life-coaching tool. On the one hand, she emphasizes that there is clear value to women's physical health and overall wellness when we have the tools to understand our cycle and its potential to enhance our lives, both personally and professionally, rather than be viewed as an obstacle to success. (She cites, for example, why "the ovulation phase is the best time for giving a presentation, the luteal phase is the best time for doing your taxes, the follicular phase is the best time to learn a new skill."[27]) But on the other hand, she warns that we still need to take into account how sharing information about our menstrual cycles can be used against us, potentially as a means for exploitation and abuse.

And the concerns go further than that: use of such information could amount to privacy intrusions that run afoul of key antidiscrimination protections afforded to employees, especially with regard to conditions ranging from pregnancy to mental health—a dangerous step backward.

Now, of course, the pragmatist in me knows full well that this concept would be a national nonstarter in any event. (Can you imagine the *Breitbart* outcry? Ouch.) I wouldn't even think of proposing it on any wide scale. (Yet.) But small-scale, employer-by-employer? For open-minded, progressive work-places? I'm so curious. It would be exciting to see how compa-nies might engage in the process and report on their findings. Someday we just may be ready for it.

Periods Behind Bars: Correction Policies

Women have entered the criminal justice system in staggering numbers over the past two decades. Between 1980 and 2014, the number of incarcerated women increased by more than 700 percent—a by-product of the War on Drugs and the stiffer, more sweeping sentencing laws ushered in during the 1990s. Today there are more than two hundred thousand women in prison— and another million otherwise entangled in the vast web that is the American criminal justice system.[28]

Of course, the depth of the crises plaguing female inmates, including the denial and deprivation of basic health and hygiene, hardly starts with menstruation. And it certainly doesn't stop there either. But, in an establishment that simultaneously ignores and abhors women, periods often amount to yet another opportunity for degradation and punishment.

As we discussed in chapter three, "The Year of the Period" started to raise awareness of the harsh realities surrounding incarceration and menstruation—from Chandra Bozelko's first-hand account in the *Guardian*, to episodes of *Orange Is the New Black*. Over the past two years, articles made the rounds with titles like, "What It's Like to Have Your Period in a Women's Prison" (*Mic*); "Providing Free Tampons and Pads to Incarcerated Women is About More Than Hygiene" (*Huffington Post*); "Menstruation Can Become Humiliation in Prisons" (*New York* magazine); and "In Jail, Pads and Tampons as Bargaining Chips" (*The New York Times*). Yet periods in prison remain widely, systematically unaddressed.

As a matter of formal oversight, menstruation is not specifically mentioned in the United Nations Standard Minimum Rules for the Treatment of Prisoners. In 2010, the United Nation's Bangkok Rules—to which the United States is a signatory—specified, "The accommodation of women prisoners shall have facilities and materials required to meet women's specific hygiene needs, including sanitary towels provided free of charge and a regular supply of water to be made available for the personal care of children and women, in particular women involved in cooking and those who are pregnant, breastfeeding, or menstruating."[29] But without specific rules for how, and how many, products are allocated and distributed, the guidelines are ineffective and women too often are denied what they need.

That is partly why applying the menstrual lens to this topic is so important. It not only helps to identify discreet, direct actions that can be taken with regard to menstruation management but also sheds light on the impact of lack of access to self-care and hygiene more generally, including basic necessities like showers, working toilets, and toilet paper, which is exacerbated by monthly bleeding.

An especially important point to emphasize here: those who are incarcerated are, by very definition, in the government's direct custody. Neither tampons nor toilet paper is a bonus, a reward, an entitlement, or a favor to be considered or bargained for. These core human needs are fully the responsibility of the public sector. And should be treated as such. Period.

Access to menstrual products.

Denial of tampons and pads to inmates either by withholding them or failing to provide adequate access is the heart of the problem. The new legislation passed in New York City in 2016 mandating the provision of menstrual products in its correctional facilities is an important victory and a good starting place for establishing baseline rules.

By law, the New York City Department of Correction is now required to give tampons and pads to inmates (and those under arrest or otherwise detained) who request them "as soon as practicable upon request." Certainly this beats the city's prior protocol, which amounted to a faulty distribution formula that was both overly subjective (a person could be selectively denied their weekly allotment by whomever was passing out the pads that day) and insufficient in number (recall it was eleven pads per month, on average). Some states, such as California, similarly require that incarcerated women have access to menstrual products on an "as-needed" basis.[30] Others make no formal statement at all.

How might these policies be improved? First, by removing menstruation from any form of social interaction among or between inmates and staff—especially where the ability to exert dominance or reinforce stigma looms. At New York City Council hearings about the proposal prior to its passage, activists testified that for pads to truly be freely accessible, they must be centrally placed near toilets or in a common location so inmates can simply take what's needed without having to seek permission or intervention. Putting women in a situation where they have to make the request at all—and then not mandating that products be provided immediately (but only, subjectively, when "practicable" or "as needed")—reinforces a power imbalance. The risk for abuse is great. It is a dynamic that should be avoided.

Policies also need to explicitly address the quality of products, which is a frequent complaint and reported cause of distribution shortages (and relatedly, infection). Cheap products do not necessarily amount to cheaper government costs, especially when pads themselves are reportedly so shoddy and thin that inmates have to double and triple them up in order to be usable or when *any* quantity is insufficient.

Wherever possible, facilities should make as wide an array of options as possible available—both tampons and pads, in different sizes and absorbencies. Having access to the most comfortable and right-sized products is simply more effective and hygienic. Menstrual products, like our bodies, are not one-size-fits-all. In January 2017, Los Angeles County addressed this issue when it approved an ordinance to provide access to tampons for girls in juvenile detention. Previously, they were provided only with poor-quality maxi pads; one girl reported that it was like "sitting in your own blood all day." In allowing a variety of options for detainees, the county supervisor stated, "Incarceration and removal from their families and communities can be a traumatic experience," and that providing a choice of menstrual products would help girls "maintain a sense of dignity . . . and focus on their education, self-sufficiency, and rehabilitation."[31]

As for commissaries, correction officials often point out that women have the opportunity to purchase their own supply. But that is hardly a realistic option for most, who don't have the means to do so. Even women who can afford it face obstacles like products not always being in stock or available and often needing to be ordered in advance. Commissaries must not be a cop-out for bad policy and practice.

Menstrual medicine.

When inmates require additional pads or simple over-the-counter remedies for menstrual cramps like hot water bottles or heating pads, they're frequently required to undergo interrogation or a medical examination. As a matter of correction policy, periods must be understood and regarded as a normal bodily function that simply requires basic products—not a condition warranting supervision or suspicion. Managing basic menstrual needs or discomfort should not require red tape, delays, and intervention—unless the inmate truly needs medical assistance. (And some certainly may. Using pads for too long can lead to reproductive and urinary tract infections, and too infrequent changing of tampons is a risk for toxic shock syndrome.)

Access to basic hygiene.

Toilets and showers are especially critical during menstruation for those in close quarters. A related necessity is proper disposal for tampons and pads so they don't get flushed, causing toilets to back up and overflow. Recall the concerns OSHA leveled about the risks of exposure to bloodborne pathogens. Why would we not aim to similarly ensure comparable conditions for those who live and work in prisons? Paper for wrapping used products and a secure dispenser for containing them is a simple, sanitary addition.

Toilet paper allocation is directly related to menstruation, too. According to *Reproductive Injustice*, the report from New York State, the overwhelming consensus of prisoners is that the standard toilet paper ration does not meet their needs. Not surprisingly, women and men receive equal amounts of toilet paper each month, even though biology dictates that women need more overall and especially during menstruation. Without disposal bags, toilet paper is also used to wrap used tampons and pads. And the catch-22, of course, is that when denied menstrual products, inmates craft their own makeshift pads with . . . toilet paper.

The menstrual lens here calls for a revised hygiene distribution formula that includes more access to toilets and showers for female inmates, at least during menstruation, and a supply of toilet paper that takes into account that menstruating bodies require more coverage.

The same is true for laundry facilities. Menstrual leaks are common for those of us in the best of circumstances, let alone those living under the conditions of incarceration. Even when the necessary menstrual products are provided, clothing and bedsheets can still wind up soaked and stained with blood. As a matter of basic dignity for inmates, and certainly for the safety for the entire living facility, temporary replacements should be promptly provided, regardless of the laundry schedule.

Menstrual products and their default uses.

Just a quick note on this. If *Orange Is the New Black* gets it right, inmates use pads for all kinds of purposes: to quiet squeaky doors, craft earplugs, steady uneven tables and chairs, and scrub cells. Bozelko corroborates this does indeed happen. And it warrants a simple solution. Address those problems, too! Seriously, silence the squeaks, provide a sponge. But don't curb menstrual dignity.

Strip searches.

US Supreme Court Justice Stephen Breyer wrote in 2012: "A strip search that involves a stranger peering without consent at a naked individual, and in particular at the most private portions of that person's body, is a serious invasion of privacy . . . such searches are inherently harmful, humiliating, and degrading."[32] His was one of the four dissenting votes in a case called *Florence v. Board of Chosen Freeholders of County of Burlington* that cemented the legality of routine strip searches, even for those arrested for minor offenses.

Menstruation clearly is an exacerbating circumstance. Given that strip searches can't be avoided, at a minimum our activism should include a watchdog stance and overt arguments that those who are menstruating be afforded as much privacy and dignity as is humanly possible.

The intersection of strip searches and menstruation received some attention in 2015 when a Tennessee prison owned by the nation's largest private prison operator, CoreCivic, was sued for requiring a visitor who had tampons in her purse to submit to a full body search; several other women came forward to claim they were subject to the same demand. In order to prove they were menstruating, each testified she was forced to remove a tampon or change a pad in the presence of a female guard. Refusal to consent to the search meant being banned from all future visits. It is an unusual case, perhaps an outlier, and it settled quietly in March 2017.[33] Even though it involved outsiders rather than inmates, I raise it here as a red flag for future potential abuses and, if needed, subsequent policy advocacy.

So who exactly is able to carry out this agenda to ensure menstrual hygiene and dignity for those behind bars? Given the wide reach of our criminal justice system, there are officials at every level of government who can demonstrate leadership. Policies can be advanced and implemented via federal guidelines by the US Department of Justice and Bureau of Prisons;

through state and municipal legislation; and/or as a matter of local, site-specific protocol and procedure.

I do worry that these proposals and ideas, while fairly simple and objective on paper, do not fully get to the heart of the matter: the inherent power imbalance and rampant misogyny to which women behind bars are frequently subject. Says Bozelko in an interview with *Women's Health* magazine, "The real problem in the lack of [menstrual] supplies for women is lack of empathy. A law or regulation would help in some places, I'm sure, but the problem with how people are treated in prison can't be cured with statutes. It has to be solved by training guards to be humane."[34] Certainly, enforcement will always be a challenge. In every proposed policy, the more clear-cut the rules are the better, ideally leaving as little room as possible for subjectivity and discretion as to the manner in which products are distributed.

There are small signs the issue is being taken more seriously. In December 2016, staff at the Federal Correctional Institution in Dublin, California, incorrectly announced that inmates would have to pay for menstrual products and toilet paper—wreaking havoc and causing widespread panic. Two inmates wrote a letter to regional officials at the US Department of Justice to express their concerns and received a prompt personal reply with assurances that facility policy is to stock and distribute these products.[35] A heartening response that these concerns were handled respectfully.

This is a dialogue and a protocol shift that we must continue to pursue and publicize, despite the obstacles, if we are serious about tackling menstrual equity for all. Incarcerated women are among the least regarded and most vulnerable in our society. Our agenda must not exclude their needs.

Period Poverty: Policies Addressing Hygiene and Homelessness

With upward of 550,000 people in the United States experiencing homelessness on any given day, the fastest growing segment of this population is women—who account for nearly 40 percent of shelter residents nationwide (another 20 percent are children, often accompanied by their mothers).[36]

And, then, not all women who are homeless are able to or even choose to seek shelter. Quality and safety of facilities vary wildly. Some have untenable restrictions, for example, like curfews that conflict with other responsibilities, especially challenging for those holding down jobs with odd hours or who have children going to school. Many shelters are too chaotic and risky for families, from overcrowding to vermin infestation to rampant drug use. And fears for personal safety, from sexual assault to theft, are of real concern, especially given that among women-led families who are homeless most have already suffered abuse and trauma; nearly two-thirds are domestic-violence survivors.

Given all the media coverage during "The Year of the Period," the stories that evoked the most interest and compassion were those that highlighted the perils of managing menstruation under the circumstances of homelessness. As described already, a proliferation of collection drives and fundraising campaigns ensued—a trend that still has yet to subside. And as gratifying a response as that has been, all the care packages in the world will not single-handedly solve the problem—not of poverty, not even of periods. The systemic issues run deep. The solutions must as well.

Shelters.

At the very minimum, public shelter budgets must include funding to ensure menstrual products are available for residents, as well as nonresidents who request them whenever possible. Certainly one model ripe for replication is legislation like New York City's, which now requires this provision. Federal homelessness prevention and shelter programs—including those run by the US Department of Housing and Urban Development, Department of Health and Human Services, and Federal Emergency Management Agency—should all do the same, a proposal already put in motion by US Congresswoman Meng.

Direct partnerships between shelters and the growing army of donation drives are essential, too. Search the Internet and conflicting conventional wisdom abounds regarding the homeless and menstrual needs. Some argue that tampons are most sought, others claim pads are preferable. Prepacked period kits or a yearlong supply—is either too much to carry or at risk of being stolen? Is a quick emergency stash preferable—or do one-offs not offer enough for consistent health and peace of mind? There is no one-size-fits-all answer. Shelters know their clients' needs best and can help guide collection efforts to ensure that large-scale donations are appropriately tailored to the realities of those being served.

Beyond distributing tampons and pads, we should also consider ways to promote the benefits and help incentivize the usage of menstrual cups and other reusable products. Certainly these are more cost-effective, environmentally conscious, and possibly healthier than disposables. Still, they're not a simple fix since they require specific amenities that are challenging to come by on the streets or even in shelters: clean water, soap for washing cups and cloth pads (and hands), a private space for drying pads, and, for most, a tutorial in how to use each option properly and safely.

Leading the charge to help low-income women break the cycle of reliance on disposable products has been a New York City–based nonprofit, UnTabooed. Through on-site educational workshops held at shelters and support agencies that serve homeless and poor women, it developed a curriculum that offers basic information about menstrual health and instruction in the use of menstrual cups and cloth pads. As part of the model, participants are provided with materials and a kit for making their own pads; those who are game are given a free menstrual cup. According to founder Diandra Kalish, women who make the switch from disposables appreciate not only the cost savings but benefit psychologically from the autonomy and its subsequent empowerment. Advocating for further study and support of such initiatives and potential replication and expansion of this kind of program—with both public funds and private philanthropy—could have an exponentially far-reaching impact.

Similarly, it is important for shelters to offer adequate support for self-care during menstruation. Very simple interventions range from easing restrictions on usage of sinks and showers (for example, not limiting it to certain times of day or days of the week), to ensuring heightened diligence about restroom privacy and safety. Even things like working locks on a door can help one feel less vulnerable or in danger of unwelcome intrusion when changing a tampon or cleaning menstrual blood.

Public facilities.

Outside the shelter system, public restrooms are one of the few available options for using a toilet or sink. But access isn't always guaranteed, especially for those facilities where paying clientele share the space. For companies that are catering to customers, many of whom are low-income themselves, simultaneously trying to maintain restrooms that are safe for all is no small challenge. Efforts to lock out the homeless are common— quite literally, by keeping the facilities under lock and key or plastered with "customers only" signs.

A good starting place would be for restrooms in public buildings, such as government agencies, libraries, train and bus stations, to include menstrual products in their budgets and provide tampons and pads free of charge in the interest of public health and hygiene. These facilities should also strive to maintain hours that are as extensive and flexible as possible. Even better, some could be designated public "safe spaces" for the homeless and offer additional resources, information, and interventions specific to their health and needs, menstrual and otherwise. Cities from Miami to Sacramento are even investing in mobile restrooms for the homeless to address issues of public defecation and related health concerns.[37] Managing menstruation could easily be considered as part of these programs.

As for private restroom facilities used by the public, some progressive companies are leading by example. A notable model was spearheaded in Australia in 2016 by a citizen-led donation project, Share the Dignity, and supported by a unique combination of players: a partnership with a local McDonald's franchise, bolstered by participation and funding from Australia's Department of Housing and Public Works. Known as Project

Pink Box, the initiative consists of specially designed restroom vending machines that deliver free "period packs," including a cycle's worth of tampons and pads. The machine has an automatic timer, and is set to wait ten minutes between each package it dispenses (to deter any one person from trying to empty the entire machine).[38]

The project specifically is targeted toward women fleeing domestic abuse, so the dispensers and packs are labeled with safety information, including a directory of local resources and support groups. That's also part of the wisdom of having McDonald's as a host partner. For many women in domestic crisis, the "golden arches" is a frequent destination, with high police presence, clean space for children to eat and play, and accessible restrooms. The Pink Box team issued a statement in December 2016: "While we work toward longer term solutions, projects like these . . . (ensure) women who need hygiene products can access them easily and discreetly, without having to feel awkward about it. They're in control of the whole process."

This model may be one of the truest exemplifications of the menstrual lens: an initiative focused first on women's safety that still acknowledges the likelihood of the need to manage menstruation. And an understanding that by removing periods from a woman's list of worries—and doing so in a dignified way—it enables those who are in crisis to exert their energy where it is most needed. I'd love to see more private companies adapt and replicate this approach—other fast-food joints, yes, but also places that low-income and homeless people frequent such as grocery and big-box stores—as well as to cull research about the efficacy of the three-way partnership between private enterprises, charities, and governmental bodies.

Another similarly multifaceted partnership was launched in the United Kingdom in December 2016. As mentioned in chapter three, the group of activists and lawmakers who spearheaded the tampon tax petition and legislative agenda, together with #TheHomelessPeriod campaign, announced they'd be teaming up with Britain's biggest pharmacy chain to create a large-scale donation and public education campaign.[39] A few more details on what makes that program unique: pharmacy customers, primarily women, were offered a chance at checkout to gift menstrual product donations that were then matched by the company. The structure of the model ensured that every customer learned of the issue, as well as the corresponding legislative agenda in Parliament, in addition to being asked to contribute. Financial support, public education, political action for menstruation: a win-win-win model.

Here's one slightly more radical idea. One route out of homelessness is a stable income. But given that poor women are most likely to lack the education and skills necessary to find employment, programs that offer job training are critical. Might this be a chance to try replicating the "Make-Your-Own-Pads" model from India on a small American scale? Conscious Period is one of the organizations that has begun to explore the feasibility of initiating micro pad-production sites to be housed at shelters and other homeless resource agencies. Like the "popular innovation" model, it would meet multiple needs including job training, a small earning potential, and a steady supply of pads for the host shelters.

Menstruation Generation: Best Practices and Policies for Schools

Schools are a uniquely potent setting for initiating and establishing healthy practices and attitudes around menstruation. How we equip our children to understand, empathize, appreciate, and manage periods—personally, and as members of a community—matters as much as anything else we do. Eradicating stigma starts with the ways we raise and communicate with the next generation.

From the day five-year-olds first arrive for kindergarten, through the decade-plus that follows, school is the place where all of us establish our basic and best sensibilities of good civic life. And, as it happens, it is also the first public and communal environment in which just about everyone learns to navigate menstruation. So much of the embarrassment surrounding periods—being sent to the nurse to request a pad, quietly coping with cramps, stashing a tampon up a sleeve, scrambling to cover leaks and stains—take root during those early social experiences, in class and between the bells. Honestly, I don't know anyone who does not have a story—menstrual mishaps and messes, ranging from the mildly embarrassing to the mortifying. My 1980s memories take me back to bloodied white Sassoon jeans and tampons that accidentally spilled out of backpacks.

But there's no reason why embarrassment or shame have to be universal rites of passage. Quite the opposite, we can reverse that tide. The primary and secondary school experience is as ideal a place as any for a creative application of the menstrual lens.

Classroom culture.

Americans today reach puberty at much younger ages than in generations past. On average, first periods now happen at around age twelve, though it is not unusual for nine- or ten-year-olds to menstruate. Scientists have offered a variety of potential reasons for this shift, ranging from environmental toxins to childhood obesity to family stress. But regardless of *why*, it certainly calls for changing *when* we begin talking and teaching about menstruation. Simply stated, kids' bodies and brains are ready for it much earlier than ever before.

And when you factor in our current culture of information saturation—Kimberly-Clark hardly corners the market anymore with its Kotex-peddling, pastel-covered informational booklets—much of what is now available is quite excellent: from refreshingly frank Q&A books and young adult fiction to magazines, chat rooms, and blogs to product ads and their corresponding social media and web presence. But the barrage of resources often comes without context or instruction, a challenge for young, hungry minds. Even the best information requires a real-life (as the kids would say, IRL) social and educational component that is equally supportive.

Columbia University's Marni Sommer, whose global expertise in menstrual hygiene management among school girls was discussed in chapter two, has also researched the American educational landscape. In an April 2017 study, Sommer and her colleagues detailed their findings about the experiences of low-income teens in the United States—how they understand and cope with puberty, and particularly how they manage menstruation.[40] Among the top lines: girls reported feeling scared or embarrassed about first periods, that they hadn't received enough information about it in advance—and what they did receive was too little, too late.

Something has to change.

The good news is teaching about menstruation in school and creating a welcoming, open environment for managing and discussing periods need not necessitate a full or immediate leap into the thorny and bureaucratic battle over American sex education. (Which, as a matter of national policy, is scattershot and inadequate to say the very least. Fewer than half of the states require it at all and of those that do, most focus narrowly, and often ineffectively, on minimizing the risk of pregnancy and sexually transmitted diseases.[41] As much as I'd love to advocate for comprehensive and accurate sexuality, health, and respect curricula here, my main focus is on making sure menstruation isn't the proverbial baby that gets thrown out with the bathwater.) Rather, there are some simple shifts that could help transform schools into places that foster a healthier and more supportive atmosphere.

The reality is that kids are having periods whether or not they're sexually active. It is to all of our detriment, but most especially theirs, if we miss the opportunity to afford them the tools and knowledge they need to manage this basic aspect of their health and disentangle it from all the other aspects of sex ed that make some squirm. Just as we address other lessons in hygiene in pragmatic, practical ways—insisting on handwashing after using the toilet, blowing noses into tissues instead of sleeves—menstruation could be as simply addressed, too.

When should schools start the process? As early as possible, even kindergarten. This is not an outlier idea. Since 2013, the city of Chicago's public schools have offered three hundred minutes of related health education from kindergarten through fourth grade, for boys and girls alike, tailored to each age and stage. The youngest children learn the proper names of body parts, including the basic idea of reproduction. In Florida, Miami-Dade County does so too, including focusing on issues like body image and social media. Young minds aren't yet swayed by stigma. No shame, no blame, no taboo.

By the time students are eight and nine years old, talking openly about simple puberty basics is key and should include the specifics they need to know about changing bodies and how to care for themselves. As for periods, comic and coloring books are a smart option for this age group. Products like India's *Menstrupedia*, ZanaAfrica's *Nia Teen* magazine, and UNICEF's Indonesian comic for boys and girls, all highlighted in chapter two, are excellent models. The latest entry on the US market is the whimsical *Adventures of Toni the Tampon: A Period Coloring Book*, which was created for children by Cass Clemmer in a gender studies course at American University.[42] Part of the book's charm is its cute Sponge Bob–esque characters—in addition to Toni, there's Marina the Menstrual Cup and Patrice the Pad—all of whom make appearances on a companion Instagram account, too. Yet another friend, Sebastian the Sponge, offers a gentle way to include boys, and even gender nonconforming audiences in the discussion. (Yes, this idea surely rattles conservatives. As reported by the *Christian Post*, and echoed in right-wing blogs, these cartoons are cause for umbrage. Jennifer Roback Morse, PhD, founder of the Ruth Institute, an organization that seeks "Christ-like solutions to the problems of family breakdown," referred to the *Toni* coloring book as "scientific malpractice and child abuse" for its inclusion of a male-named character.[43])

For middle and high school students, when more formal sexual health and hygiene curricula kick in, class discussion should be supplemented quite simply with a supportive atmosphere—one that reminds all students that their bodies are healthy and normal, and that their comfort and confidence matters. Among some recommended practices: keep classrooms and restrooms fully stocked with menstrual products and offer easy ways to dispose of them as well as to clean reusables. Save trips to the nurse for when periods are painful, not for access to products and basic care. Offer sessions with health education projects like The Fifth Vital Sign and #periodpositive, which can address practical health concerns and provide guidance on body literacy and cycle charting information. Avoid using branded health curricula (in other words, marketing materials) offered by major product manufacturers. Encourage teenage boys to carry and offer supplies to classmates in need. Most of all, keep the dialogue respectful and positive.

Creative curriculum.

Beyond teaching about menstruation in a traditional health and personal hygiene context, periods can play a supporting role across all subjects and be easily incorporated into lessons about literature and language, social studies and world history, math and science. Let's get creative! Some options in literature appropriate for high school students: Anne Frank's *The Diary of a Young Girl*; Harper Lee's *Go Set a Watchman*; Stephen King's *Carrie*; Toni Morrison's *The Bluest Eye*; Margaret Atwood's *The Handmaid's Tale*; and Anita Diamant's *The Red Tent*. Cycle tracking could be factored into math lessons. As for an innovative science lab, Rebecca Alvandi, "Chief Flow Rider" for the New York–based Maxim Hygiene Products, a manufacturer of organic, natural products, has developed a roster of (unbranded) interactive menstrual product experiments and offers lesson plans for middle and high school projects—like "the absorbent core test," to test the differences between cotton and wood pulp fibers, the main ingredient of most commercial pads.[44] Students learn about the materials that are in menstrual products and the effects they have on our bodies and the planet. Alvandi reports that schools that use the curriculum create a space to explore not only the science of menstrual products but also to respond to basic health and hygiene questions.[45]

Another opportunity for creative, critical learning is instruction focused on the plight of menstrual stigma and lack of access, both as a global and domestic matter. Such lessons offer even more value when paired with opportunities for students to get involved with related activism and service projects. Whether designed to be part of the school day, as a social studies or current events assignment, or an extracurricular activity, there are numerous quality resources to adequately inform and educate. Schools that help harness such engagement can achieve multiple positive outcomes: helping to destigmatize discussion about menstruation while facilitating students to become innovators, organizers, or philanthropists themselves.

IN ADDITION TO WHAT WE'VE already discussed about why it is important to ensure that menstrual products are readily accessible and provided for free in schools, there are a few additional considerations to note about best (and most simple) practices.

First, local town councils, school boards, principals, even PTAs all can be called upon to take this on, one facility at a time; it need not entail a massive legislative campaign.

Another essential caveat for the provision of free products in schools: product dispensers absolutely need to be marked with vital information about safe usage, such as how often tampons and pads should be changed, the dangers of not changing them frequently enough, and proper disposal. This should be supplemented in any health-related class or curricula.

Finally, schools should be encouraged to collect as much feedback as possible—are the products helping with attendance rates? Improving classroom productivity?—to help fuel new research to better understand how supporting students during their periods enhances their ability to learn. As this is becoming better understood in the developing world, Americans' investment in comparable research can help ensure the best outcomes for students.

All Who Bleed:
Policies That Transcend Gender

Gloria Steinem's 1978 essay, "If Men Could Menstruate," pondered what the world would look like if suddenly it were men doing the monthly bleeding. In 2016, Twitter fired back: some men already do. That September, after a male physician tried to "mansplain" ovulation to her, Dr. Jennifer Gunter, a practicing OB/GYN, kicked off a flurry of tweets using the hashtag #IfMenHadPeriods. She intended to spark conversation about the ways menstruation is often trivialized. But she got an unexpected response: an outcry that, in fact, menstruating men are not a hypothetical. A heated, compelling discussion emerged about transgender and gender nonconforming people—men who have periods, women who don't—and how the exclusion of those experiences from public discourse exacerbates the invisibility and erasure this already marginalized population faces.

Though it is nearly impossible to get a formal count, there are an estimated 1.4 million adults who identify as transgender living in America today.[46] Menstruation aside, the challenges to leading a safe and healthy life are staggering. Harassment, discrimination, and intimidation are rampant. Fifteen percent earn less than $10,000 a year (compared to 4 percent of the general population).[47] The poverty rate for transgender people of color is even higher.[48] One in five transgender people has experienced homelessness—and, of those, nearly one in three (29 percent) report that gender identity has caused them to be turned away from a shelter.[49] Rates are higher for incarceration, HIV infection, smoking, drug and alcohol use, and suicide attempts than in the general population.[50] Barriers to health care range from insurance companies and state health systems resistant to accommodating trans needs, to uninformed, even hostile doctors who refuse to provide care, many of whom have not received trans-specific training.[51]

And then, of course, there's the issue of bodies that menstruate. In the midst of the #IfMenHadPeriods Tweetstorm, Zoyander Street, a transgender man, wrote a riveting essay for *The Daily Beast*, "Yes, Men Can Have Periods and We Need to Talk About Them." Street reflected on a complicated relationship with menstruation: "I remember being congratulated when my period started, because 'it meant I was becoming a woman.' This felt like cold comfort when I was in physical agony and psychological distress because the entire experience seemed like it was fundamentally wrong. It wasn't until later that I made sense of that 'fundamentally wrong' feeling as part the pervasive gender dysphoria that would not change until I transitioned. The idea that my period 'made me a woman' was echoed every time I sought support for debilitating menstrual pain."[52]

ACLU attorney and trans activist Chase Strangio responded in a Twitter message reported by *Upworthy*, "The refusal to accept and recognize that there are men who menstruate and get pregnant and there are women who have penises and don't, contributes to the relentless assault on trans people in courts, legislatures and on the streets."[53]

And, from *Upworthy*'s Parker Molloy, a transgender woman and reporter: "Everything bad that happens to women who have periods happens to trans men, but in a more shameful way, if that's even possible." Reminding us that not all women have periods either: those who are transgender, who have gone through menopause, or who have amenorrhea (when periods suddenly stop); some choose to voluntarily cease menstruation with chemical contraceptives and hormones.

Even in framing this book, my focus has been on a historical exploration of menstruation and the more recent policy agenda—the vast majority of which pertains to cisgender women and girls. As an advocate and writer, I've struggled with how to reconcile a fuller array of perspectives, doing my best to employ gender neutral language—using "menstrual products" instead of "feminine hygiene," for example; in my advocacy, I urge policy makers and other influencers to do the same. I've found that swapping the more inclusive phrase "people who menstruate" for "women and girls," however, only works in small doses. It hasn't always been feasible or easy to do consistently, especially in the policy arena. (Or quite honestly, for anything more than an explanatory conversation or short essay.) The very same week as the #IfMenHadPeriods debate blew up Twitter, Planned Parenthood used the term *menstruator* in an unrelated tweet about the tampon tax, igniting a simultaneous round of discussion on social media as to whether that frame was dehumanizing or inclusive. (Or just a little clinical and clunky.)

As we muddle through the linguistics, there are policy moves we can make to ensure we're forging a movement that speaks not just to—but *for*—all of us. A holistic agenda for menstrual access must include trans people who are dealing with periods in some of the most difficult and dangerous circumstances. And, no question, achieving better menstrual policies means pushing back on the patriarchal norms and stigmas that hurt us all.

Proposals pertaining generally to the economics of menstruation—federal benefits, the workplace, correction facilities, homelessness, school—necessarily apply to the trans community as well and can be refined and tailored as needed. Here I offer three additional areas where practical applications of the menstrual lens can help lend support to trans-specific advocacy and ensure a more inclusive menstrual agenda.

Bathroom access.

In a 2013 survey from UCLA's Williams Institute on Sexual Orientation and Gender Identity Law, 70 percent of transgender and gender nonconforming participants reported having had a negative experience in a public restroom—ranging from menacing glares to physical violence.[54] And from a 2016 survey by the National Center for Transgender Equality, half of its respondents avoided using a public restroom for fear of confrontation, with a third admitting that they had resorted to restricting food or liquid consumption specifically to avoid having to use a toilet.[55]

For trans men, on the most pragmatic level, dealing with periods adds an additional layer of danger. Among the panic triggers: the potential for stains on clothes, floors, and toilets; the sound of tearing a wrapper or peeling an adhesive strip; an accidental dropping of a tampon or pad; the need for disposal of used products and wrappers. Some report just giving in and using the women's restroom for the week—temporary discomfort winning out over potential harm.

The latest battle over transgender rights, access to public restrooms, has upped the ante. In March 2016, bigotry materialized into law in North Carolina via House Bill 2 (HB2), known as the "bathroom bill" and formally named the Public Facilities Privacy & Security Act. (While the law was repealed in March

2017, a new, equally detrimental proposal is slated to take its place.) Under the pretense of public safety concerns for women and children, the law restricted individuals to restrooms and changing facilities that correspond to the gender on their birth records. And, if the bill does not seem severe enough, in North Carolina, only gender-affirming surgery warrants changes to one's birth certificate. Since 2013, at least twenty-four states have considered comparable bills, some with even more draconian requirements like the 2017 Alabama Privacy Act, which stipulates that an attendant be stationed at the door of each restroom to monitor its use and answer any questions or concerns posed by users.

It was heartening to see swift blowback in North Carolina. Celebrities including Bruce Springsteen and Ringo Starr called off all concerts there; the NBA moved its All-Star game and the NCAA remained vocal about avoiding the state. Many businesses canceled expansion plans, and groups pulled conferences and conventions. It came with a hefty economic price—$630 million in lost business in 2016.[56] And an estimated $3.76 *billion* in lost opportunities predicted over the next dozen years.[57] It does seem likely that this could deter some states from fully following through with similarly discriminatory agendas. Big-box retailer Target took a stand, too, announcing a policy that welcomed trans people to use bathrooms and fitting rooms that correspond with their gender identity. (This also led to backlash—a petition launched by the conservative American Family Association and signed by 1.4 million who pledged to stop shopping at Target—which the store faced down.)

But it is the sentiment behind these drives—the dreadful rhetoric, the intolerance in which they are rooted, the animosity and fear they stoke, and misconceptions they invite of trans bodies—that make the already uncomfortable experience of using a public restroom all the more undignified and dangerous.

Menstrual advocacy can lend a voice to the fight against bigotry. Inclusive language is a start. So too are policies for managing menstruation in public restrooms, though this requires some care and dexterity. Conservatives had a field day on Twitter mocking and expressing revulsion over the #IfMenHad Periods debate. It might necessitate starting in friendlier territory, such as the eighteen states and hundreds of cities and school districts that affirmatively protect transgender people's right to access restrooms, with some small but meaningful changes to help lessen the potential for period shame. Simple interventions that implicate menstruation include adding disposal receptacles inside all individual stalls, women's and men's, and offering private gender neutral facilities.

Are bathrooms that big of a deal? I'd argue, yes. Consider this analogy about how they can influence social change: A recent federal law now requires all restrooms in publicly accessible government buildings to be equipped with baby changing tables, not just the women's rooms. The 2016 Bathrooms Accessible in Every Situation Act (very cute, the BABIES Act) does more than give men their equal shot to change dirty diapers. It offers a visual reflection of an evolving societal narrative, whether that's recognizing the importance of fathers playing a proactive role in child rearing, an acknowledgment of same-sex parents and single fathers, or all of the above. And while in this case the growing acceptance of shifting familial dynamics preceded and likely fueled the law, it is also the case that the very sight of changing tables and diapers in men's restrooms will help cement a new image of modern parenting. Yes, bathrooms can be part of the march toward social change and shifts in public perspective.

Brown University was one of several campuses that acknowledged trans people who menstruate, when its student government began offering free tampons and pads in all campus facilities in September 2016—including those designated for women, men, and all/any gender.[58] While it is hard to imagine this becoming common practice in any other venue, colleges are a ripe starting place. Across the country, higher education institutions are demonstrating a considerable commitment to trans-inclusivity policies, and an open acknowledgment that transgender students often arrive with distinct economic disadvantages. When it comes to financial aid and scholarships, for example, built-in bureaucratic details create obstacles and inconsistencies across government records, which can result in delayed applications, reduction in aid, or outright rejection. The practice of providing free menstrual products on campus is an excellent display of compassion, a response to financial insecurity, and show of commitment to visibility, health, and dignity.

Health care for all.

Access to quality medical care is not just a matter of social justice, but a public health imperative. Insurance companies and state health systems are prone to deny coverage for trans health care. Physicians and office staff often lack trans-specific training—to the tune that one in five trans men in the United States has been refused care due to gender identity; half have postponed doctor's visits due to discrimination; and one in four report having been harassed during a medical situation.[59]

Regardless of whether one undergoes sexual reassignment surgery or hormonal therapy, there is an array of gynecological issues specific to trans men. Among these: the hormonal changes and the physical and emotional dissonance caused by menstruation can be disruptive; failure to address reproductive and menstrual pains can result in undetected, and thus, untreated cases of reproductive cancers, infections, and endometriosis; trans men who use chemical birth control to suppress periods require prescriptions and regular health appointments. Insurance protocol often creates complications, too: a trans man who has legally changed gender from female to male might be denied coverage for a Pap smear, which is covered only as part of a "woman's wellness" visit. When these issues go ignored or are undermined by the medical establishment, the consequences can be disastrous.

Health-care disparity has been high on the trans movement's advocacy agenda with fights ranging from the call to raise awareness and education within the medical field to expansion of health-care coverage toward medical procedures prevalent within the transgender community. Among the most simple and immediate ways to bolster these efforts is by making the broad case that menstrual access and care are among the health-care rights that we deem necessary—for all.

Menstrual marketing.

With increased representation in popular culture of fictional transgender characters, such as Jeffrey Tambor's Maura in Amazon's acclaimed show *Transparent*, and rising stars like actress Laverne Cox, former Olympian and reality TV star Caitlyn Jenner, and spokeswoman and former staff editor of

People magazine, Janet Mock, companies are seeing opportunities to expand their market base. It could potentially be a keen business move; the extended LGBT community reached a buying power of $917 billion in 2015.[60]

It is noteworthy that the menstrual start-up market has been a prominent leader and offers a unique platform for acknowledging and normalizing the biology of trans bodies. Several companies sell trans-friendly products and offer mail subscription services that provide extra privacy in making purchases. Most are extremely cognizant of and sensitive about inclusivity in outreach and marketing. One of the menstrual calculator apps, Clue, offers a fully gender-neutral experience; so, too, does the company Lunapads. THINX, the company that tussled with the MTA in 2015 over grapefruits and raw eggs in its period underwear ads, launched a 2016 series of New York City subway billboard ads starring a transgender model, Sawyer DeVuyst, sporting boy short underwear. Perhaps the most high-profile of the menstrual marketing efforts, THINX also edited its tagline to "For People Who Menstruate"—an adjustment from a prior slogan, "For Women with Periods," for which it had come under critique.

As part of the ad campaign, a testimonial published by DeVuyst sought, among other things, to educate the public about the differences between sexual orientation and identity. He explained, "Gender and sexuality are two separate things. Gender is who you go to bed *as*, and sexuality is who you go to bed *with*."[61]

A powerful, clarifying message for us all, menstruators or not.

THE INTERPLAY BETWEEN GENDER IDENTITY and menstruation is one I imagine we'll be further fleshing out for a long time still to come. As I indicated earlier, I am still struggling to find my own footing, even the vocabulary and voice to help advance inclusive, productive policy. But the areas for advocacy spelled out here are among many of the ripest right now, and also a starting place from which we can aim to chart out forward-looking agendas—together.

Green Days: Product Safety Policies

Given the vast amounts of information about nearly everything we consume in modern society—pesticides in our foods, chemicals in cosmetics and cleaning products, the plastics our water bottles are made of—the void when it comes to the details we are afforded about the ingredients in menstrual products is almost unfathomable. The average American will bleed through between ten thousand and sixteen thousand tampons and pads over a lifetime of periods. Assuming an average of sixty menstruating days per year multiplied by forty years, per person that's a cumulative six-plus years of flow.

And there are special considerations with regard to this particular bodily function—namely, vaginas. More sensitive and porous than the skin or the mouth, the vagina is known to be among the most permeable membranes of the body; substances absorbed by the vagina pass directly into the bloodstream. Which means the menstrual products we wad inside our bodies should matter to us as much, if not more, as all the foods, lotions, sprays, and liquid containers in our lives. And of course, this is not to discount the reality that our vaginas exist on this beautiful planet. Disposable menstrual products bear environmental costs that impact us all, from overflowing landfills to coastlines dotted with tampon applicators. The manufacturing processes for conventional cotton and plastic take a toll, too.

When it comes to approving and disclosing what's in tampons and pads, the federal government bears responsibility for rules and oversight via the Food and Drug Administration. And what the FDA requires of manufacturers, from testing to public disclosures, is downright minimal. As we know, these products are classified as "medical devices," which sounds good on paper. Clinical. Rigorous. Right? Not exactly. There are three classifications of medical devices, and menstrual products (including tampons and some pads) fall in Class II, in the company of contact lenses, condoms, and pregnancy test kits. Just under half (43 percent) of the products the FDA classifies as medical devices fall into Class II. Items in the most stringent category, Class III, include breast implants and female condoms; the least rigorous classification, Class I, is for goods like dental floss and elastic bandages.[62]

The only affirmative obligations required of manufacturers of Class II medical devices are that they provide basic instructional labeling on packaging and keep records of adverse events caused by their products. Companies do have to assert their products are safe, but since they don't have to share internal studies or research with anyone outside the FDA, we've got no recourse for getting a second opinion.

Tampons, in particular, are subject to two additional regulations, both of which were initiated after the spate of deaths caused by toxic shock syndrome in the 1980s. Manufacturers must print information on packaging warning about the signs of toxic shock syndrome and how to minimize risk. And measurement of tampon absorbency requires industry-wide standardized methods and terminology. The words printed on boxes—*junior*, *regular*, *super*, and *super-plus*—equate to an actual scale ranging from six to fifteen grams of absorbency. To test said absorbency, the FDA concocted a special contraption, called a "syngyna," which simulates all the physical conditions of how tampons work inside the vagina.[63]

Labeling or detailed disclosure about product ingredients on packaging is not required of medical devices in any FDA class. Though, worth noting, ingredient listings are mandatory for cosmetics manufacturers, meaning we're afforded more details about what's in lip gloss and shampoo than tampons.[64]

Here is the basic information that we are able to know about the ingredients—namely, bleached rayon, cotton, and plastic—in conventional tampons. Up until around ten years ago, the bleaching agents for rayon were a dioxin-producing chlorine gas that is now considered toxic; methods have since gone chlorine-free, and the FDA asserts the presence of dioxin has diminished to trace levels. On its website, the agency states, "this exposure is many times less than normally present in the body from other environmental sources, so small that any risk of adverse health effects is considered negligible." As for non-organic cotton, it is generally considered the dirtiest of all crops due to the high level of pesticide use.[65] Plastic tampon applicators contain endocrine disrupting phthalates. Among the potential long-term health implications: cancer, hormonal and endocrine system disruption, reproductive illness, and infertility.

How alarmed should we be? The research is limited, and even the experts disagree on the risks. And, quite honestly, the answer requires an in-depth investigative study that goes far beyond the scope of this book and explores not only the medical perspectives but also the vast monetary and corporate interests at stake. There are many competing agendas, which, in itself, is disturbing. But given what we *do* know—that the evidence on which the FDA relies is severely lacking in transparency—my focus here is to advise on the kinds of activism we can employ to help fight the regulatory battle. And to consider how concurrent advocacy efforts to provide access to menstrual products for the poor—which, to date, mostly presses for conventional disposable tampons and pads—might be adjusted to account for health and safety concerns.

#DetoxTheBox.

Because the FDA has exclusive oversight of the menstrual product industry, federal advocacy is our primary avenue for making systemic change. To be clear, the issue hasn't gone wholly unnoticed, though it has been routinely ignored when raised. As we've discussed, for a full two decades US Congresswoman Carolyn Maloney repeatedly has proposed legislation that would direct the government to address and rectify the current lack of research and transparency that makes it impossible to know what, if any, diseases—she calls out cervical cancer, endometriosis, infertility ovarian cancer—may be linked to the ingredients in tampons. First known as The Tampon Safety and Research Act of 1997, Maloney crafted the bill in response to a woman named Robin Danielson who had contracted toxic shock syndrome. Danielson died a year later at age forty-four and the bill was renamed in her memory. Over twenty years, The Robin Danielson Feminine Hygiene Product Safety Act has never even gotten out of committee. Relentless, Congresswoman Maloney has reintroduced the legislation ten times since first proposing it in 1997, most recently in 2017.[66]

Among the bill's principal requirements, the National Institutes of Health would be required to allocate resources for independent research into the potential hazards posed by various ingredients and chemical processes used in many menstrual products. It would also call for companion research to confirm data submitted to the FDA by manufacturers. There is a transparency and accessibility provision, as well, requiring that the results of all future independent studies submitted to the FDA also be shared with Congress, the Environmental Protection Agency, and the Consumer Product Safety Commission, and be made available to the public.

Given the momentum of "The Year of the Period," we must leverage and direct energy toward garnering support for this legislation. For a movement that has focused so emphatically on revving up public discourse, I'm not sure why it has been a challenge to reconcile all the new activism with environmental and product safety advocacy. It is due time to make sure this is part of the collective focus.

One positive step: US Congresswoman Meng joined the cause and introduced The Menstrual Hygiene Product Right to Know Act of 2017 (H.R. 2416), a more limited bill that would simply require listing of ingredients on packaging. In the immediate term, it may be a more practical, winnable step and a way to lay the groundwork for the sweeping and much-needed Robin Danielson Act.

There is a small but long-standing national activist base in this arena with which to partner. It includes Women's Voices for the Earth, the Society for Menstrual Cycle Research, as well as the National Latina Institute for Reproductive Health and others. Although the federal legislative fights have languished, the coalition's organizing campaign, called #DetoxTheBox, has successfully pressured some of the major manufacturers. In 2015, both Procter & Gamble and Kimberly-Clark agreed to start posting online the ingredients in their products. Procter & Gamble also expanded the information it offers about the inclusion of synthetic materials; Kimberly-Clark disclosed ingredients in its tampon applicators. But since there is no uniform set of rules for the presentation of this information, what's listed still may be incomplete and therefore misleading.

Joining and publicizing these efforts, and serving as both catalyst and watchdog, should be a key priority for the menstrual equity agenda.

Step by step.

Until we achieve greater transparency regarding product testing and disclosures, and therefore more knowledge about the safety of tampons and pads, one near-term solution would appear to be seemingly simple: aim to use fewer conventional and disposable products and incentivize reusable options. And yet, the vast majority of Americans do not. There is no resounding endorsement of any of these products by the medical establishment, and they tend to require more of an investment, whether of finances, education, or time. Even with online and other support communities for alternative options, these are dwarfed by the power of immediate influencers—and most of us are quietly, subconsciously prone to simply follow the lead of our mothers/sisters/best friends (family brand loyalty and all that). While I am not in the game of recommending particular menstrual brands or supplies—I'm no expert, and this book does not offer conclusions about the safety or efficacy of any of them—we all do have the right to make informed choices. I find it unlikely, unfortunately, that there are any policy avenues for bolstering or rewarding companies whose products or standards exceed the federal minimum. Our lobbying efforts are better spent focusing on transparency for all.

Instead, we can choose to flex our spending power as consumers. Even if going totally green isn't an option, for costs or convenience, changing up product usage may be. Just as there is wisdom in diversifying one's financial investments, the same holds true for our health. Be "brand disloyal." When any product, tampons included, is recalled or called into question, it's best to not have been using it exclusively.

What about those who can't afford the luxury of product choice? Or basic products at all? So much of the advocacy that's led to the distribution of free tampons and pads—and most of the proposals presented in this section—is focused on mass market disposables, primarily for their ease of use. How should we address this? Government can be called upon to facilitate distribution of organic disposable products to low-income consumers, as well as encourage donations to shelters and schools with tax breaks and other incentives to the companies that provide them—and to support programs that make it easier for low-income people to use menstrual cups and other reusables.

As we fight for transparency, we must be sure that those who are low income or otherwise lack agency or ability to obtain menstrual products aren't left behind. Healthy, safe products can't only be for those who can afford them.

Pro-Choice Periods:
Reproductive Freedom Policies

The mechanics of menstrual equity are interwoven with so many of the colossal fights now being waged to protect access to reproductive health care and decision making. And on all fronts, our rights, our bodies, our choices—our lives—are under attack.

In the nation's capital, the 2016 elections swept in a staunch conservative stronghold, to say the least. On day one in the Oval Office, President Trump set the tone for his administration when he not only reinstated but also drastically expanded the scope of the "Global Gag Rule"—the Reagan-era ban on US aid for international health programs that provide abortions (using other nongovernment funds) or even utter the word. Vice President Mike Pence earned his stripes as chief anti–women's health crusader over a decade ago. During his tenure in Congress from 2000–2011, Pence introduced the first federal measure to block funds from going to Planned Parenthood and cosponsored a bill that insisted on differentiating "forcible" rape as criteria for public funding for abortion. (Differentiating it from what? Non-forcible or consensual rape? No such thing.) As governor of Indiana, he signed eight antiabortion bills in four years and was catapulted to Twitter infamy as the subject of the viral #PeriodsForPence campaign after he signed a restrictive package of laws that included a "fetal funeral" provision requiring all remains from abortions, and even miscarriages, to be buried or cremated.

In Congress, federal funding for Planned Parenthood and access to contraception, prenatal care, and other core health services all are in the firing line. And in the states, emboldened lawmakers across the country have introduced a spate of harsh and restrictive laws ranging from "heartbeat bills"—that would ban abortions when a fetal heartbeat is detected, as early as at six weeks and before many women are aware they're pregnant—to twenty-week bans, and even the outright criminalization of abortion at any stage of pregnancy, with threats of felony charges for both women and doctors.

But quite frankly, the pro-choice landscape was already rather bleak, even before November 8, 2016. Yes, it was a monumental victory when the US Supreme Court ruled 5–3 back in June 2016 to strike down a harsh abortion law from Texas and uphold the core tenets of *Roe v. Wade*. But now the composition of the Court hangs in the balance, with conservatives in the driver's seat and a potential majority hell-bent on overturning *Roe*. And new state restrictions just keep on coming. In 2016, eighteen states enacted fifty new abortion laws; since 2011, a total of 338 restrictions have gone into effect.[67] By the close of the first quarter of 2017, another five states had adopted ten new abortion restrictions.[68]

How might the menstrual lens help advance the broader fight for reproductive freedom? I've identified three ways our frame can offer a strategic supporting role.

Periods as bridge builder.

Now that periods have gone public—and political—are they also primed to go pro-choice? In making the case for menstrual access policies, it has been my position that it is to both movements' benefits to keep periods cabined, at least for now, and make the menstrual discourse as nonpolarizing as possible.

My observation and experience is that when menstruation is stripped of its reproductive purpose, and framed solely as a basic bodily function—right up there with nosebleeds—legislators from both sides of the aisle are more willing to engage. This defies the core goal of the equity argument, I know. But it is pragmatic. Once more conservatives are on board and become comfortable with making and endorsing menstrual arguments, we can then try to move ahead to draw reproductive connections. To me, this is a worthwhile trade-off and really just a matter of pacing and patience.

Already, there are some early opportunities to test this idea. Consider Texas, for example, which has introduced many of the most far-reaching and punitive abortion restrictions in the country over the past decade. Yet there is also growing, even bipartisan, support there for the eliminating the tampon tax. Among the sponsors of a 2017 bill to exempt menstrual products from sales tax is State Representative Drew Springer, an unlikely champion for anything progressive or pro-woman. On his website he describes himself as a "lifelong conservative Republican" and a strong supporter of "all measures to limit or eliminate abortion." And he touts endorsements from Texas Right to Life, Alliance for Life, Conservative Republicans of Texas, Young Conservatives of Texas, and Texas Conservative Coalition. And yet, his response to constituents who contacted him about the tampon tax is almost stunning: "We have the ability to say, 'I'm going to buy a Coke.' I make that choice freely. Ladies don't have the same option. [Tampons] can easily be classified as a medical property item."[69] Ladies . . . choice . . . freely? That all sounds familiar. While I can't imagine a shift in his thinking on abortion, there may well be other aspects of women's health and economic equity that enable us to forge some common ground.

Periods as proof of bad legislating.

There is a visible disconnect between recognition of how the menstrual cycle works and the technical rules relevant to certain abortion restrictions. Those fetal "heartbeat" bills, I mentioned, for example, fail to acknowledge that many women don't yet even know they are pregnant by the six-week mark. Pregnancy is measured by the date of the last menstrual period, (also called "LMP," this is actually a medical term of art, not just a circled day on the calendar), and not the date of conception. This means that by the day she misses her period, the earliest indicator that a woman may realize she is pregnant, she is already considered four weeks along. That would allow two weeks to obtain an abortion, an almost impossible window even for the most resourced among us. For those who are poor and adversely affected by other restrictions—from long travel times, to faraway clinics, to mandatory delays—the time frame is quite literally impossible. "Fetal funeral" provisions similarly incorporate truly deleterious menstrual misunderstanding. Many are worded such that they do not just implicate clinical abortions but also spontaneous miscarriages, some of which are never even detected by women. Yet technically, one would be subject to criminal penalties for what was otherwise thought to be a late or heavy period.

These misunderstandings may well be deliberately calculated or part of the punitive intent of these laws. But our ability to call out such misguided menstrual science and math is an imperative advocacy strategy and may even sway some minds. Heartbeats may pull heartstrings but facts matter, too. And, in this case, it may just be that a menstrual expert as messenger rather than a traditional pro-choice voice can make the case more neutrally, and therefore convincingly.

Periods as protest.

Menstrual activists have shown exceptional capacity (and crude humor!) as creative organizers, notably when linking periods to a broad array of reproductive issues. In addition to #Periods ForPence, similar campaigns calling out onerous abortion restrictions include #AskBevinAboutMyVag and #AskDrKasich, responses to antiabortion laws passed in Kentucky and Ohio respectively. In 2016, Texas activists took it up a notch and called on activists to send "used tampons, panty liners, or indefinitely ruined underpants" to Governor Greg Abbott.[70] I'm not particularly a fan of that practice (bloodborne pathogens and all), but I appreciate the spirit of the gesture. If the Lone Star State is going to deign to legislate the fertilized status of women's eggs, some of which may emerge in their menstrual blood, they should let the powers that be see what they're asking women to examine themselves.

In early 2017, the menstrual protest message landed the highest profile platform of all. Actress Ashley Judd spoke period truth to power at the Women's March on January 21, 2017, the largest mobilization of its kind. Across the globe, millions took to the streets to stand up for the rights and lives of women and the case for social justice for all. In Washington, DC, Judd performed an ode, written by nineteen-year-old Nina Donovan, to all the "nasty women"—a reference to yet another insult that Trump hurled out during the presidential campaign, which has since become a mobilizing rallying cry—and she fueled the audience when the talk turned to periods: "I'm nasty, like my blood stains on my bedsheets. We don't actually choose when and where to have our periods. We do not like throwing away our favorite pairs of underpants. Why are pads and tampons still taxed when Viagra and Rogaine are not? Is your erection really more than protecting the sacred, messy part of my womanhood? Is the blood stain on my jeans more embarrassing than the thinning of your hair?"[71]

By catapulting menstruation and linking it so vividly to the movement for reproductive justice and freedom, Judd cemented periods as a fierce connector, and placed them at the heart of a global vision and the belief that women's rights are human rights.

HOW MUCH FURTHER THE MENSTRUAL movement might go in being a partner to and strong ally of the broader reproductive rights community—beyond what's proposed here—is a strategy question for both sides. As for me, it should not come as a surprise that I am ardently pro-choice and am committed to advancing these twin ideals. But as I indicated earlier, as a menstrual policy advocate I am wary of the policy pitfalls of fully aligning the issues too closely, too soon. I'd urge that we keep a healthy distance until more wins are scored, especially on basic proposals like the tampon tax, and we've further garnered neutral, nonpartisan support. Perhaps then will we be able to weave in the full reproductive experience.

Dollars that Do Good: Periods and Philanthropy

When envisioning the quintessential philanthropist, lofty images often come to mind: wealthy patrons of the arts; successful tycoons who emblazon their family name on hospital wings and ivy-covered university buildings; Silicon Valley trailblazers who drive social investments in global health and education; or the likes of Warren Buffett and Andrew Carnegie, business magnates who dedicate their fortunes to foundations that champion human rights and social justice.

But it is actually the charitable donations made by everyday citizens that fuel our national philanthropic tradition and support the vast array of organizations that improve lives, strengthen communities, and respond to crises at local, national, and global levels. In 2015, individuals led the way in charitable giving, collectively making contributions that totaled a whopping $264.58 billion.[72] By comparison, total foundation funds awarded to charitable organizations that year was $58.46 billion and corporate giving just $18.45 billion.

More and more, those dollars are being donated and directed by women. Regardless of education, age, or income, women are shown not only to contribute more generously than men but also to be more diligent and hands-on in assessing the impact of their charities of choice, serving as active, integral participants in the quest for social change. And at the top tier, women are increasingly likely to earn and manage their own fortune, or be the deciders of how wealth accumulated by a spouse or earlier generations is given away. Of the nation's top ten grant-making foundations, half are headed by women.

Nevertheless, a glaring gender gap persists in how those funds are spent. According to the Women's Philanthropy Institute, only 15 percent of all the philanthropic contributions raised in the United States go toward initiatives that aim to directly impact the lives of women and girls. *All In For Her: A Call To Action,* a 2014 report issued by Women Moving Millions, a group created to catalyze women's philanthropy, calls upon donors to apply an explicit gender lens to their giving.[73] Jacki Zehner, the group's chief engagement officer, explained to *Forbes,* "One example I love to use in explaining why applying a gender lens is so important is heart disease. When scientists were studying heart disease they tended to study men's hearts. Men were the default. It was only after studies specifically took in to account the sex of the patient, as well as other factors, that is was discovered that heart disease in women is very different than for men. All of a sudden, huge strides were made in treatment."[74]

This is my cue to argue that we go a step further and apply the menstrual lens to philanthropic giving. This means, first, supporting more programs that aim to empower vulnerable populations, especially women and girls; and second, making clear that their empowerment includes having the means to properly manage menstruation. Here, we can drive home the point with our wallets and elevate the menstrual equity agenda via the dollars we donate.

Think global, act local.

The most important force for change is each and every one of us. There are multiple ways to lend support and be philanthropists. First, collection drives. Among the many that have multiplied across the country, some are raising modest sums of money, but most are focused on amassing products to donate. That's one urgent, immediate need. Anyone can make a financial contribution, donate products, host a drive.

But let's take it further than that. For every single charitable program that involves or includes women—whether it is a local soup kitchen, domestic abuse shelter, "Dress for Success" collection drive—chances are it serves those who desperately need menstrual products. The same is true for contributions to your house of worship or alma mater. My own synagogue now makes a call for tampons and pads among the congregants, thanks to "Girls Helping Girls. Period." Bring donations to public libraries, schools, or the town hall. Consideration of menstruation in every donation, every interaction, is surely a simple and effective step.

Especially when supporting local projects, it is critical to always be mindful of the importance of bringing the populations served into the process. The more that stakeholders are involved in shaping and implementing the very programs designed to support them, the more likely it is their needs will be adequately reflected and met. In the menstrual context, this means asking first about what kinds of products are most used, tampons or pads. Or offering workshops if there's a desire to try something new, like reusables. Or holding focus groups to find out what kinds of cultural ideas or dynamics may be at play that are holding students back in school.

When donating money or raising funds, we can't afford to be shy about getting on a soapbox about menstruation. The stories have been hidden for far too long. The reality of what it means to manage menstruation while poor is truly shocking to most people. Menstruation is the great equalizer, and anyone who has ever had a period knows what it feels like to face a menstrual emergency. The more we sound that common chord, the more philanthropic champions we will rally to this cause.

Influence the influencers.

Even though major foundations—the Fords and MacArthurs of the world—represent only a quarter of the philanthropic giving in the United States, the largest ones wield extraordinary influence, not only as incubators and drivers of innovation, direct service models, research and reform agendas, but as a force for shaping the very priorities of civil society.

At the most basic level, more of these institutions must be systematic in prioritizing and expanding the rights and agency of girls and women, because when we ensure that girls are healthy and educated, and able to live their full potential as women, *all* of society rises. From the Clinton Global Foundation: "Even one extra year of schooling beyond the average can increase women's wages by about 10 percent, and studies suggest that raising the share of women with secondary education is linked to increases in economic growth. When women participate in the economy, poverty decreases and gross domestic product (GDP) grows. It is estimated that as much as $28 trillion, or 26 percent, could be added to the global GDP by 2025 if women played an identical role in formal labor markets to that of men."[75]

In an April 2017 essay for the blog *Well + Good*, it was heartening to see Chelsea Clinton weigh in on the importance of considering menstruation in a holistic philanthropic agenda: "When was the last time you heard menstruation talked about in a conversation about economic development? Or economic justice? In a conversation about health care in the developing world or health care for refugees? Or in a conversation about education here in the US? We need to support menstruating girls and women of all ages to erase the stigma and the access barriers that too often go hand-in-hand with 'that time of the month.'"[76]

Taking this further, those foundations that focus on women and girls must explicitly commit to incorporating and embedding menstruation management into the grants they award, the research they make possible, the solutions they forge. This has the potential to be a tremendous catalyst for elevating the understanding of the relevance of menstruation to advancing the lives of women and girls.

Currently, there are only a small handful of foundations that focus explicitly on menstruation for its own sake, almost exclusively in the global health and development area. There is no domestic effort among foundations to support programs or research that address menstrual access in the United States. *Inside Philanthropy*, an industry newspaper, attributes the dearth of interest to stigma and reports, "even the most pragmatic global health and development experts can get a little bit uncomfortable whenever the conversation turns to periods."[77] That is not acceptable.

Among those rare funders, the most well-known is the Bill & Melinda Gates Foundation, which has invested in research initiatives to improve the understanding of menstrual education and products for girls in Kenya (including that of ZanaAfrica, and its work described in chapter two). The Illinois-based Caterpillar Foundation concentrates on the root causes of global poverty and includes menstrual hygiene as an integral part of its funding strategy. A few others—the UK-based Waterloo Foundation and Grand Challenges Canada—recently awarded substantial six- and seven-figure grants in support of global projects that specifically seek to address menstrual hygiene management.[78]

It's true that our individual dollars go a long way. But they must be joined by the powerful organizations that influence the policies that guide us all. Foundations should follow the lead of global health advocate Lisa Schechtman, who wrote for the Gates Foundation, "If we get menstrual hygiene right, what else will have changed in the process?"[79] *Inside Philanthropy* gets it right: "The short answer is *everything*—from improving gender parity to breaking generational cycles of poverty."[80]

Tony Award–winning playwright, performer, and activist Eve Ensler, author of *The Vagina Monologues* and creator of V-Day, the global activist movement to stop violence against women and girls, once said, "Money doesn't make you special, it makes you lucky. Be generous, be crazy, be outrageous."[81]

That is a call to action for all of us—to put our money where our vaginas are and take a stand for menstrual equity with every dollar we donate.

FINAL THOUGHTS

WHAT I'VE FOUND SO UNIQUELY inspirational and motivating about this burgeoning menstrual movement is that it truly offers a home for everyone. Fellow activist Kiran Gandhi wrote in an essay for *TIME* describing how viable, vibrant social organizing comes to life through four critical components—activism, education, innovation, and policy advocacy.[1] And, without a doubt, each of these are at the heart of our collective accomplishments to date.

Think about it: since 2015, we've seen support for menstrual access, acceptance, and pride expressed through a colorful array of music, poetry, visual art, recreation, athletic displays—and have had more than our fair share of news headlines, social media trends, and pop culture moments. Collection drives and social enterprise have not only provided a direct service, but they've doubled as education and an alert to the very problem itself. Advocating for policy reform is more user-friendly than ever with online petitions and email as an essential organizing tool; one need not trek all the way to the nation's capital to demand change. Effective rules for ensuring access can be implemented locally—in schools and libraries and town halls—and impact just as many lives. But by all means, take the fight as far as you can: we the menstruators are half the population. Let's not let any of our leaders—from the White House on down—ever forget that.

So if after reading about all that's fueled "The Year of the Period" thus far, you're eager to help be part of writing its next chapter, please consider any or all of these action steps:

Speak out and speak up.

Talk about the dangers of not talking about periods. Talk about your own period! Share the testimonies you've now heard about those who have challenges managing or affording their periods. The louder and prouder we *all* are about claiming these stories, the harder they will be to ignore and the further we will go toward eradicating stigma. The world is our stage.

The pen (and the tampon) is mightier than the sword.

Cement those words in writing. It's one thing to hear them—but memorializing them in print is quite another. Write op-eds and letters to your local paper, school paper, and on sharing websites. Write poetry. Write action plans. Write to your representatives. Codify your words and extend their reach.

#HashtagIt.

Get on social media platforms where your voice can be amplified exponentially. Push back against period shaming and online bullies. Make it safe for everyone to speak their truth.

Be an educated and conscious consumer.

Do your homework and aim to buy from companies that go above and beyond what's required when it comes to product transparency—menstrual or otherwise—and that adhere to the highest standards in the products they sell and the values they embody and represent.

Host or donate to a collection drive.

Connect with the various menstrual projects named in this book or do a quick online search to see if there are local groups doing the same near you. Start your own drive—at work or at school—or link up with your house of worship, local businesses, or any other community organizations to extend your reach. Talk to the staff at the shelters and food pantries in your neighborhood and ask what they need. Spend time with, be a friend to, and get to know those clients yourselves. Their stories will motivate you. (And then, see above. Share those stories!)

Make the personal political.

Petition your lawmakers to make menstrual products affordable and available. Sign the national tampon tax petition, "Stop Taxing Our Periods! Period." Raise the issue of access with your local government representatives and agencies, and ask them to consider menstrual needs in the facilities they oversee. Demand the same of your state legislators and Congress members. Tweet at them, too. (After the #TweetTheReceipt campaign in New York, I know it really works!)

Become a citizen of the world.

Keep up with and follow all the efforts to ensure periods aren't a barrier for anyone, anywhere. Support the organizations around the globe that are addressing the problem—the groups called out in this book and others—with your dollars and time. Remember that these same issues exist in our own backyard, so always lend a hand locally, too.

And this bonus tip is for good measure . . .

Get Wet!

Yes, do a polar bear swim! There is nothing quite like the feeling of diving into icy cold water on an icy cold day. It rejuvenates the body, mind, and soul. It turns New Year's resolutions into . . . well, revolutions. (All the better if you've got a Wonder Woman costume.)

ACKNOWLEDGMENTS

EVER SINCE I STARTED THIS project, I've daydreamed about this section. Partly because I've been on the ride of a lifetime and am extraordinarily grateful to so many people. But mostly because it would mean that this book would actually be completed! Being an author and having this platform to share the details about a movement that matters so much to me has been equal parts exhilarating and terrifying. Like all the best things in life, I suppose, it is that grand mix of emotion that makes it all worthwhile.

Since the very heart of *Periods Gone Public* is the story of my obsession with all things menstrual, I'll start with the moment the madness was born—January 1, 2015, a.k.a. Wonder Woman on the Beach. My first debt of thanks rightfully belongs to my fellow Coney Island Polar Bear swimmers on that fateful day: Lisa, Peggy, and Jen. The secret to all the magic is the gold glitter. Don't ever forget that.

And then my next life-altering New Year's Day encounter—Elise, Emma, and Quinn Joy, and "Girls Helping Girls. Period." Thank you for your magnificent project and spirit of volunteerism and for all you've done to send my brain spinning and spiraling. It still hasn't stopped. I know you all haven't either.

To my fellow menstrual activists, flung far across the globe, and some of the most creative, compassionate, and generous people with whom I've ever had the pleasure to collaborate. Every one of you has influenced me—and this book—with your vision: Rebecca Alvandi, Caroline Angell, Shyam Bedekar, Swati Bedekar, Chris Bobel, Chandra Bozelko, Cass Clemmer, Aanjalie Collure, Laura Coryton, Becca Freeman, Alexandra Friedman, Pablo Freund, Kiran Gandhi, Ganga Gautam, Holly Grigg-Spall, Molly Hayward, Rachael Heger, Meika Hollander, Diandra Kalish, Danielle Keiser, Jordana Kier, Nancy Kramer, Margo Lang, Annie Lascoe, Connie Lewin, David Linton, Jaydeep Mandal, Dana Marlowe, Megan White Mukuria, Arunachalam Muruganantham, Alison Nakamura Netter, Nadya Okamoto, Sabrina Rubli, Elizabeth Scharpf, Lauren Schulte, Margo Seibert, Holly Seibold, Laura Shanley, Madeleine Shaw, Kylyssa Shay, Suzanne Siemens, Diana Sierra, Marni Sommer, Elissa Stein, Alisa Vitti, Agnieszka Wilson, and Camilla Wirseen.

Thank you especially to those who read and weighed in so thoughtfully on drafts of the manuscript. All my beloved Lauras—Laura Strausfeld, Laura Fischer, Laura Epstein-Norris. And double thanks for Laura Strausfeld's critical insight and research on environmental concerns and unending support and partnership; for Laura Fischer's glorious worldview; and for Laura Epstein-Norris's photographic genius. Lisa De Bode, your feedback has been my fuel—and your reporting has changed the world. Annie Lascoe, your perception and insight astound, and you are my heart and soul. Kiran Gandhi, you embody #TheFutureIsFemale—magnificent, epic, and so very dope. Elissa Stein, you got here well before I did! Thank you for your colorful insights and energy. Marni Sommer, the rigorous scholarship and deep compassion you bring to this work is remarkable; I am grateful to have you in my corner. Madeleine Shaw and Suzanne Siemens, I relish your perspective on the overlaps and intersections among business, feminism, and activism; the world is fortunate to have you at the forefront of all three. Danielle Keiser, you are truly "The Hub"—the eyes, ears, and pulse of the movement! Holly Grigg-Spall, your wealth of knowledge about the interplay of hormonal contraceptives and menstrual stigma and health offers much nuance to this discussion. Jeanine Plant-Chirlin, your timeless and certain understanding of . . . well, everything never ceases to amaze me. Your input is on point every single time. Michael Waldman, your advice about how to pace and frame this story has been an invaluable contribution—you earned each and every "I told you so"—as has your tremendous encouragement and support. Thank you also to Alyson Krueger, fact checker extraordinaire.

My partners at Hearst who, as much as anyone, took to heart the mission to make periods go public, powerful, and political: Danielle McNally, Sara Austin, Lori Fradkin, and Joanna Coles.

Bold, inspiring women who lead the nation and have been the champions of US menstrual equity policy: New York City Council Member Julissa Ferreras-Copeland, truly my other half, and her dynamic team, Ivan Acosta and Lillian Zepeda; California Assembly Member Cristina Garcia; Connecticut

Representative Kelly Luxenberg; Wisconsin Representative Melissa Sargent; and US Congresswoman Grace Meng, along with the wonderful Rachana Shah.

Among the reporters, writers, and editors who have given such a powerful platform to the issue and provided personal inspiration, I'm especially thankful for the work, wisdom, and partnership of Zoe Greenberg, Liriel Higa, and Nicholas Kristof at the *The New York Times*; Abigail Jones at *Newsweek*; and Carmen Rios at *Ms*. And I am forever grateful to *Teen Vogue*'s Alli Maloney—ahhh, the creation of our inspired *Lenny Letter* interview!—and Taryn Hillin for *Fusion*'s definitive tampon tax map.

Chelsey Emmelhainz and Arcade Publishing, my gratitude goes to you for finding me and for trusting me to take on this book! Your humor, kindness, patience, generosity of spirit, pragmatism, sagacity, and unbelievably keen editing are a true gift. I will be forever appreciative.

My colleagues at the Brennan Center for Justice: I owe you all kinds of thanks. And then some. Writing a book during one of the most intense and trying times for our nation's democracy was not without its challenges. Thank you for making it possible for me to lead a double life—especially the amazing development team: Anna Coe, John Donahue, Diana Kasdan, Jaemin Kim, Pia Levin, Charles Ombwa, and Carson Whitelemons. Beatriz Aldereguia, you provided me with sustenance (quite literally, all those late-night takeout dinners!) and so much vision and perspective; your thoughtful, careful research and writing, especially on policies that transcend gender, have been essential contributions. And to Bob Atkins, Patricia Bauman, Nancy Brennan, Inimai Chettiar, Mike German, Tom Jorde, Myrna

Perez, Kimberly Thomas, Vivien Watts, and Wendy Weiser—thank you for your ideas and enthusiasm and moral support along the way. Thank you also to Elisa Miller for lending a legal eye; Dorothy Samuels, for the early, influential edits; and L. B. Eisen for being my partner in crime and sharing in all the pain and glory.

To my family: You tolerate my crazy ways more than I deserve, especially Mom, Dad, and Hali. Harry and Wendi (and Echo Love), you saved my sanity with a well-timed Florida writing retreat. Irwin, Nina, and Sharon, I'll be free of writing deadlines by the next Hanukkah party, I promise.

Nathaniel, Rebecca, and Sarah: I hope you're proud and have come to believe there's nothing you can't achieve. It is never too late (or too early!) to find your passion. I recognize that having a tampon crusader for a mom can't be easy. But let that be a lesson. Life sometimes leads you to your purpose in wholly unexpected ways. Run with it. Revel in it. And . . . always know, I love you more.

And last but never least, it has to be Alan Wolf. My love, my life. Nothing I do would be possible without you. Thank you for believing in me, for putting up with me, for inspiring me, for laughing with (or at) me, for nourishing me, for finishing my sentences when I can't find the words myself. Even for becoming a vicarious menstrual enthusiast and policy aficionado. And, maybe most importantly, for making sure Finch didn't hold a grudge or forget me. (He'll miss these days, I think.)

ENDNOTES

Introduction

1. "Talking About Periods: An International Investigation," HelloClue.com, accessed April 8, 2017, http://www.helloclue.com/survey.html.
2. "Every Woman's Right to Water, Sanitation and Hygiene," United Nations Human Rights Office of the High Commissioner, March 14, 2014, http://www.ohchr.org/EN/NewsEvents/Pages/Everywomans righttowatersanitationandhygiene.aspx.
3. Jessica Valenti, "The Case for Free Tampons," *The Guardian*, August 14, 2014, https://www.theguardian.com/commentisfree/2014/aug/11/free-tampons-cost-feminine-hygiene-products.
4. Milo Yiannopoulos, "*Guardian*: World Needs Taxpayer Subsidized Tampons," *Breitbart*, August 12, 2014, http://www.breitbart.com/london/2014/08/12/guardianistas-are-demanding-free-tampons-on-the-taxpayer-where-do-i-send-my-wish-list/.
5. Susan Rinkunas, "One NYC High School Now Offers Free Tampons," *New York* magazine, September 22, 2015, http://nymag.com/thecut/2015/09/free-tampons-new-york-city-high-school.html.
6. Gina Florio, "7 Badass Menstrual Activists You Need to Know About," *Bustle*, April 4, 2016, https://www.bustle.com/articles/150117-7-badass-menstrual-activists-you-need-to-know-about.

7. Fran Spielman, "Finance Committee Approves 'Tampon Tax' Exemption," *Chicago Sun Times*, March 11, 2016, http://chicago.suntimes.com/news/finance-committee-approves-tampon-tax-exemption/.

8. Holly Yan, "Donald Trump's 'Blood' Comment about Megyn Kelly Draws Outrage," CNN.com, August 8, 2015, http://www.cnn.com/2015/08/08/politics/donald-trump-cnn-megyn-kelly-comment/.

Chapter One: Surfing the Crimson Wave

1. Abigail Jones, "The Fight to End Period Shaming is Going Mainstream," *Newsweek*, April 20, 2016, http://www.newsweek.com/2016/04/29/womens-periods-menstruation-tampons-pads-449833.html.

2. TimesMachine, NYTimes.com, accessed March 8, 2017, https://timesmachine.nytimes.com/browser.

3. Malaka Gharib, "Why 2015 Was The Year of The Period, and We Don't Mean Punctuation," National Public Radio, December 31, 2015, http://www.npr.org/sections/health-shots/2015/12/31/460726461/why-2015-was-the-year-of-the-period-and-we-dont-mean-punctuation.

4. Sara Austin, "How These 3 Women Are Working to Make Menstrual Equity a Reality," *Cosmopolitan*, November 17, 2016, http://www.cosmopolitan.com/sex-love/a8287266/periods-menstrual-equity-tampon-tax/.

5. Jones, "The Fight to End Period Shaming is Going Mainstream."

6. Aristotle, *On Dreams*, trans. J. I. Beare, 350 BCE, The Internet Classics Archive, accessed March 25, 2017, http://classics.mit.edu/Aristotle/dreams.html.

7. Judy Grahn, *Blood, Bread and Roses: How Menstruation Created the World* (Boston: Beacon Press, 1994), 4-6.

8. *The Moon and Menstruation: A Taboo Subject; Selected extracts from Robert Briffault's The Mothers*, ed. Hillary Alton (London: East London University, London Radical Anthropology Group, 2011), http://radicalanthropologygroup.org/sites/default/files/pdf/pub_the%20mothers.pdf.

9. Mary Lane, "Why Can't Women Be Sushi Makers," *Wall Street Journal*, February 18, 2011, http://blogs.wsj.com/scene/2011/02/18/why-cant-women-be-sushi-masters/.

10. Julie Weigaard Kjaer, "From Menstrual Huts to Drinking Blood: The Weird and Wacky World of Cultural Attitudes to Menstruation. Pt.1," RubyCup, April 17, 2013, http://rubycup.com/blog/from-menstrual-huts-to-drinking-blood-the-weird-and-wacky-world-of-cultural-attitu0des-to-menstruation-pt-1/.

11. Gloria Steinem, email message to author, December 11, 2016.

12. Julie Zeilinger, "12 Women of All Ages Share the Incredible Stories of Their First Periods," *Mic*, September 15, 2015, https://mic.com/articles/125297/12-women-of-all-ages-share-the-incredible-stories-of-their-first-periods#.eCl7ttGUr.

13. "Kimberly-Clark Historical Journey: An Interactive Timeline," Kimberly-Clark.com, accessed March 12, 2017, http://www.kimberly-clark.com/Timeline.aspx.

14. Sir Almroth Wright, "Feminism Behind the Suffrage War," *New York Times*, March 28, 1912, accessed April 21, 2017, https://timesmachine.nytimes.com/timesmachine/1912/03/28/104847109.html?pageNumber=3.

15. JR Thorpe, "The History of the Tampon—Because They Haven't Always Been for Periods," *Bustle*, November 19, 2015, https://www.bustle.com/articles/124929-the-history-of-the-tampon-because-they-havent-always-been-for-periods.

16. Margaret Gurowitz, "The Product That Dared Not Speak Its Name," in Kilmer House (Johnson & Johnson Services, 2008), accessed March 12, 2017, http://www.kilmerhouse.com/2008/02/the-product-that-dared-not-speak-its-name/.

17. Lara Freidenfelds, *The Modern Period: Menstruation in Twentieth-Century America* (Baltimore: Johns Hopkins University Press, 2009).

18. Sharra Vostral, *Under Wraps: A History of Menstrual Hygiene Technology* (Maryland: Rowman & Littlefield, 2008), 122.

19. Germaine Greer, *The Female Eunuch* (New York: Harper Perennial, 1991).

20. "Global Network Partners & Projects" *Our Bodies Ourselves*, accessed March 8, 2016, http://www.ourbodiesourselves.org/global-projects/.

21. Ellen Barry, "Judy Blume for President: Meet the Woman who Invented American Adolescence," *The Boston Phoenix*, May 28,

1998, http://www.bostonphoenix.com/archive/features/98/05/21/ JUDY_BLUME.html.

22. Rebecca Traister, "God to Margaret: Always with Wings!" *Salon*, March 2, 2006, http://www.salon.com/2006/03/02/blume/.

23. Perri Klass, "The Banned Books Your Child Should Read," *New York Times*, January 16, 2017, https://www.nytimes.com/2017/01/16/well/family/the-banned-books-your-child-should-read.html?_r=0.

24. David G. Goodman, *Jews in the Japanese Mind: The History and Uses of a Cultural Stereotype* (Maryland: Lexington Books, 2000), 168.

25. Gloria Steinem, "If Men Could Menstruate," *Ms.*, October 1978.

26. "Introducing: The Manpon," WaterAid, accessed March 12, 2017, http://www.wateraid.org/uk/learn-more/manpons.

27. Vostral, *Under Wraps*, 149.

28. Ashley Fetters, "The Tampon: A History," *The Atlantic*, June 1, 2015, https://www.theatlantic.com/health/archive/2015/06/history-of-the-tampon/394334/.

29. Ann Friedman, "Astronaut Sally Ride and the Burden of Being First," *The American Prospect*, June 19, 2014, http://prospect.org/article/astronaut-sally-ride-and-burden-being-first.

30. Fetters, "The Tampon: A History."

31. Ibid.

32. TimesMachine, NYTimes.com, accessed March 8, 2017, https://timesmachine.nytimes.com/browser.

33. "Statement by Congresswoman Carolyn B. Maloney upon Introduction of 'The Tampon Safety and Research Act of 1997,'" Maloney.house.gov, accessed March 12, 2017, https://maloney.house.gov/media-center/press-releases/statement-congresswoman-carolyn-b-maloney-upon-introduction-tampon-safety-and-research.

34. Karen Houppert, *The Curse: Confronting the Last Unmentionable Taboo: Menstruation* (New York: Farrar, Straus and Giroux, 2000).

35. Lia Kvatum, "A Period Comes to an End: 100 Years of Menstruation Products," *Washington Post*, April 25, 2016, https://www.washingtonpost.com/national/health-science/a-period-comes-to-an-end-100-years-of-menstruation-products/2016/04/25/1afe

3898-057e-11e6-bdcb-0133da18418d_story.html?utm_term=.
ad6f6242558d.

36. "Museum of Menstruation and Women's Health," accessed
March 12, 2017, http://www.mum.org/.

37. Susan Kim and Elissa Stein, *Flow: The Cultural History of Menstruation* (New York: St. Martin's Press, 2009).

38. Freidenfelds, *The Modern Period*.

39. Rachel Kauder Nalebuff, *My Little Red Book* (New York: Twelve, 2009).

40. Chris Bobel, *New Blood: Third-Wave Feminism and the Politics of Menstruation* (New Jersey, Rutgers University Press, 2009).

41. Amanda Fortini, "First Blood: Introducing 'Menstrual Activism,'" *Salon*, October 6, 2009, http://www.salon.com/2009/10/06/menstruation_moment/.

42. Gharib, "Why 2015 Was the Year of The Period."

43. Jones, "The Fight to End Period Shaming is Going Mainstream."

Chapter Two: Code Red

1. Nurith Aizenman, "People Are Finally Talking About The Thing Nobody Wants to Talk About," All Things Considered (National Public Radio), June 16, 2015, http://www.npr.org/sections/goatsandsoda/2015/06/16/414724767/people-are-finally-talking-about-the-thing-nobody-wants-to-talk-about.

2. Laurel Wentz, "P&G Whisper's 'Touch the Pickle' Wins Glass Grand Prix," *AdvertisingAge*, June 23, 2015, http://adage.com/article/special-report-cannes-lions/p-g-whisper-s-touch-pickle-wins-glass-grand-prix/299182/.

3. A.C. Nielsen, "Sanitary Protection: Every Woman's Health Right" (2010), a survey undertaken by A.C. Nielsen and Plan India.

4. Rose George, "The Taboo of Menstruation," *New York Times*, December 28, 2012, http://www.nytimes.com/2012/12/29/opinion/the-taboo-of-menstruation.html.

5. *25 Years: Progress on Sanitation and Drinking Water, 2015 Update and MDG Assessment* (New York: UNICEF and World Health Organization, 2015), http://files.unicef.org/publications/files/Progress_on_Sanitation_and_Drinking_Water_2015_Update_.pdf.

6. Bethany A. Caruso, Alexandra Fehr, Kazumi Inden, Murat Sahin, Anna Ellis, Karen L. Andes, and Matthew C. Freeman, *WASH in Schools Empowers Girls' Education in Freetown, Sierra Leone: An Assessment of Menstrual Hygiene Management in Schools* (New York: United Nations Children's Fund, November 2013), https://www.unicef.org/wash/schools/files/Sierra_Leone_MHM_Booklet_DM_15_Nov_1020_single-Sierra_Leone.pdf.

7. Marni Sommer, Emily Vasquez, Nancy Worthington, and Murat Sahin, *WASH in Schools Empowers Girls' Education: Proceedings of the Menstrual Hygiene Management in Schools Virtual Conference 2012* (New York: United Nations Children's Fund and Columbia University, 2013), https://www.unicef.org/wash/schools/files/WASH_in_Schools_Empowers_Girls_Education_Proceedings_of_Virtual_MHM_conference.pdf.

8. Sommer et al., *WASH in Schools Empowers Girls' Education.*

9. Marni Sommer, Emily Vasquez, Nancy Worthington, and Murat Sahin, *WASH in Schools Empowers Girls' Education in Rural Cochabamba, Bolivia: An Assessment of Menstrual Hygiene Management in Schools* (New York: United Nations Children's Fund, November 2013), https://www.unicef.org/wash/schools/files/Bolivia_MHM_Booklet_DM_15_Nov_single_0940_Bolivia.pdf.

10. Freshta Karim, "How Social Stigma and Lack of Access to Sanitary Pads Make Menstrual Cycle a Nightmare for Women in Afghanistan," *Afghan Zariza*, December 28, 2014, http://www.afghanzariza.com/2014/12/28/how-social-stigma-and-lack-of-access-to-sanitary-pads-make-menstrual-cycle-a-nightmare-for-women-in-afghanistan.

11. Penelope A. Phillips-Howard, George Otieno, Barbara Burmen, Frederick Otieno, Frederick Odongo, Cliffor Odour, Elizabeth Nyothach, Nyanguara Amek, Emily Zielinski-Gutierrez, Frank Odhiambo, Clement Zeh, Daniel Kwaro, Lisa A. Mills, and Kayla Laserson, "Menstrual Needs and Associations with Sexual and Reproductive Risks in Rural Kenyan Females: A Cross-Sectional Survey Linked with HIV Prevalence," *Journal of Women's Health* 24, 10 (2015): 801-811, https://www.ncbi.nlm.nih.gov/pmc/articles/PMC4624246/.

12. Sarah House, Thérèse Mahon, and Sue Cavill, *Menstrual Hygiene Matters: A Resource for Improving Menstrual Hygiene around the World* (New York: WaterAid, 2012), http://www.wateraid. org/what-we-do/our-approach/research-and-publications/view-publication?id=02309d73-8e41-4d04-b2ef-6641f6616a4f.

13. Danielle Priess, "15-Year-Old Girl Found Dead in a Menstrual Hut," National Public Radio, December 20, 2016, http://www. npr.org/sections/goatsandsoda/2016/12/20/506306964/15-year-old-girl-found-dead-in-a-menstrual-hut-in-nepal.

14. Yudhijit Bhattacharjee, "Launch Pad: How an Indian Engineer Reverse-Engineered the Making of Sanitary Pads," *New York Times Magazine*, November 10, 2016, https://www.nytimes. com/interactive/2016/11/13/magazine/design-issue-sanitary-pads-india.html?_r=0.

15. Vibeke Venema, "The Indian Sanitary Pad Revolutionary," BBC, March 4, 2014, http://www.bbc.com/news/magazine-26260978.

16. Vibeke Venema, "The Unlikely Sanitary Pad Missionary," BBC, December 3, 2015, http://www.bbc.com/news/magazine-34925238.

17. Marni Sommer, Margaret L. Schmitt, David Clatworthy, Gina Bramucci, Erin Wheeler, and Ruwan Ratnayake, "What Is the Scope for Addressing Menstrual Hygiene Management in Complex Humanitarian Emergencies? A Global Review," *Waterlines* 35, 3 (July 2016), 246.

18. Anna Pujol-Mazzini, "For Refugee Women, Periods a Dangerous, Shameful Time," Thomson Reuters Foundation, March 8, 2017, http://news.trust.org/item/20170308150652-db2y1/.

19. Siana Jannesari, "Banana Pads in Rwanda: Interview with Elizabeth Scharpf, CEO of Sustainable Health Enterprises," *Euromonitor International*, January 8, 2017, http://blog.euromonitor. com/2017/01/banana-pads-in-rwanda-interview-with-elizabeth-scharpf-ceo-of-sustainable-health-enterprises-she.html.

20. "Menstrupedia," accessed March 12, 2017, https://www. menstrupedia.com/.

21. Priti Salian, "Menstrupedia is Destroying Taboos and Improving Health in India," *TakePart World*, September 9, 2014, http://

www.takepart.com/article/2014/09/09/menstrupedia-destroying-taboos-and-improving-health-india.

22. Dayo Olopade, "Comic Book Convinces Kenyans to Dye Their ChickensPink," *New Republic*, March 7, 2014, https://newrepublic.com/article/116916/shujaaz-kenyan-comic-book-transforming-education-africa.

23. Fran Kritz, "Menstruation 101 for Boys: A Comic Book Is Their Guide," National Public Radio, March 4, 2017, http://www.npr.org/sections/goatsandsoda/2017/03/04/516628738/menstruation-101-for-boys-a-comic-book-is-their-guide.

24. "Project Jeune Leader," accessed March 8, 2017, http://www.projet jeuneleader.org/.

25. Alexandra Geertz, Lakshmi Iyer, Perri Kasen, Francesca Mazzola, and Kyle Peterson, *An Opportunity to Address Menstrual Health and Gender Equity* (FSG, May 2016), http://www.fsg.org/publications/opportunity-address-menstrual-health-and-gender-equity.

26. "Marni Sommer, Associate Professor, Sociomedical Sciences" Columbia University, Mailman School of Public Health, accessed March 12, 2017, https://www.mailman.columbia.edu/people/our-faculty/ms2778.

27. Amy Stopford, "Why Adolescent Girls Miss School in Rural Kenya," Duke Global Health Institute, January 24, 2012, https://globalhealth.duke.edu/media/news/why-adolescent-girls-miss-school-rural-kenya.

28. Emily Oster and Rebecca Thornton, "Menstruation and Education in Nepal" (working paper, National Bureau of Economic Research, Cambridge, MA, April 2009), http://www.nber.org/papers/w14853.

29. Paul Montgomery, Caitlin R. Ryus, Catherine S. Dolan, Sue Dopson, Linda M. Scott, "Sanitary Pad Interventions for Girls' Education in Ghana: A Pilot Study," *PLOS ONE*, October 2012, http://journals.plos.org/plosone/article?id=10.1371/journal.pone.0048274.

30. Paul Montgomery, Julie Hennegan, Catherine Dolan, Maryalice Wu, Laurel Steinfield, Linda Scott, "Menstruation and the Cycle of Poverty: A Cluster Quasi-Randomised Control Trial of Sanitary Pad and Puberty Education Provision in Uganda," *PLOS*

ONE, December 21, 2016, http://journals.plos.org/plosone/article ?id=10.1371/journal.pone.0166122.

Chapter Three: Aunt Flo and Uncle Sam

1. Kylyssa Shay, "Homeless Periods: A Problem of Poverty, Dignity, and Feminine Hygiene," *Soapboxie*, November 19, 2016, https://soapboxie.com/social-issues/Homeless-Periods-Suck.

2. Maria Shriver and the Center for American Progress, *A Woman's Nation Pushes Back from the Brink, The Shriver Report—Special Editions*, January 12, 2014, http://shriverreport.org/special-report/a-womans-nation-pushes-back-from-the-brink/.

3. Laura Epstein-Norris and Jennifer Weiss-Wolf, "Blood in the Streets: Coping with Menstruation while Homeless," *Medium*, January 12, 2016, https://byrslf.co/blood-in-the-streets-bf578a1b9634 #.89yjgwbqh.

4. Meghan Henry, Rian Watt, Lily Rosenthal, and Azim Shivji, *The 2016 Annual Homeless Assessment Report to Congress* (Washington, DC: US Department of Housing and Urban Development, November 2016), https://www.hudexchange.info/resources/documents/ 2016-AHAR-Part-1.pdf.

5. Tristia Bauman, *No Safe Place: The Criminalization of Homelessness in U.S. Cities* (Washington, DC: National Law Center on Homelessness and Poverty 2014), https://www.nlchp.org/ documents/No_Safe_Place.

6. Rachel Stevens, "SPGIA Students Testify to NY City Council About Importance of Access to Menstrual Hygiene Products," The New School Milano, June 10, 2016, http://www.milanoschool.org/in-testimony-at-new-york-city-council-sgpia-students-explain-importance-of-access-to-menstrual-hygiene-products/.

7. Lisa De Bode, "Hygiene and Heartache: Homeless Women's Daily Struggle to Keep Clean," *Al Jazeera America*, January 13, 2015, http://america.aljazeera.com/articles/2015/1/13/-scared-to-walk-thestreet.html.

8. "#The Homeless Period," accessed March 12, 2017, http://the homelessperiod.com/.

9. Libby Brooks, "Boots to Support Campaign to End 'Period Poverty,'" *The Guardian*, December 16, 2016, https://www.theguardian.

com/society/2016/dec/16/boots-support-campaign-end-period-poverty-paula-sherriff-tampons.

10. Lisa De Bode, "More Pads for Homeless Women on Their Periods," Al Jazeera America, April 15, 2015, http://america.aljazeera.com/articles/2015/4/15/more-pads-for-homeless-women-help.html.

11. Applied Survey Research, *San Francisco Point-In-Time Homeless Count & Survey: Comprehensive Report 2015* (Watsonville, CA: ASR, 2015), https://sfgov.org/lhcb/sites/default/files/2015%20San%20Francisco%20Homeless%20Count%20%20Report_0.pdf.

12. Janet Upadhye, "This Is How Homeless Women Cope with Their Periods," *Bustle*, October 18, 2016, https://www.bustle.com/articles/190092-this-is-how-homeless-women-cope-with-their-periods.

13. Eliazabeth Swavola, Kristine Riley, and Ram Subramanian, *Overlooked: Women and Jails in an Era of Reform* (New York: Vera Institute for Justice and Safety and Justice Challenge, supported by John D. and Catherine T. MacArthur Foundation, 2016), 14.

14. ACLU Reproductive Freedom Project and National Prison Project, "ACLU Briefing Paper: The Shackling of Pregnant Women & Girls in U.S. Prisons, Jails & Youth Detention Centers," ACLU, https://www.aclu.org/files/assets/anti-shackling_briefing_paper_stand_alone.pdf.

15. Tamar Kraft-Stolar, *Reproductive Injustice: The State of Reproductive Health Care for Women in New York State Prisons*, (New York: Women in Prison Project of the Correctional Association of New York, January 2015), http://www.correctionalassociation.org/wp-content/uploads/2015/03/Reproductive-Injustice-FULL-REPORT-FINAL-2-11-15.pdf.

16. Alex Brook Lynn, "The Unspoken Rape Crisis at Rikers," *Vice*, September 24, 2015, https://broadly.vice.com/en_us/article/the-unspoken-rape-crisis-at-rikers-island.

17. Zoe Greenberg, "In Jail, Pads and Tampons as Bargaining Chips," *New York Times*, April 20, 2017, https://www.nytimes.com/2017/04/20/nyregion/pads-tampons-new-york-womens-prisons.html.

18. Semelbauer et al. v. Muskegon County, 1:14, No. 01245-JTN, (W. D. Mich., S. Div. September 11, 2015), accessed March 24, 2017, http://www.aclumich.org/sites/default/files/054%20Opinion %20and%20Order.pdf.

19. Melissa Goodman, Ruth Dawson, and Phyllida Burlingame, *Reproductive Health Behind Bars in California* (San Francisco: ACLU of California, January 2016), www.aclunc.org/Reproductive HealthBehindBars_Report.

20. Sirin Kale, "Judge Outraged After Female Inmate Brought to Court with No Pants," *Vice*, August 1, 2016, https://broadly.vice. com/en_us/article/judge-outraged-after-female-inmate-brought-to-court-with-no-pants.

21. "Department of Justice, Federal Bureau of Prisons, MCC, New York, July 2015 Commissary Price List," Federal Bureau of Prisons, accessed March 25, 2017, https://www.bop.gov/locations/ institutions/nym/NYM_CommList.pdf.

22. "Muskegon County Commissary Menu," Canteen Services, accessed March 25, 2017, http://www.canteenservices.com/ wp-content/uploads/2017/02/Muskegon-Menu.pdf.

23. Kraft-Stolar, *Reproductive Injustice*, 67.

24. Catrin Smith, "A Period in Custody: Menstruation and the Imprisoned Body," *Internet Journal of Criminology* (2009), https://www. researchgate.net/profile/Catrin_Smith/publication/40670406_A_ Period_in_Custody_Menstruation_and_the_Imprisoned_Body/ links/55775cf308ae7521586e1718.pdf.

25. KteeO, "Letter from KteeO: Menstruation and Incarceration," Committee Against Political Repression, Monthly Archives: November 2012, accessed March 25, 2017, https://nopolitical repression.wordpress.com/2012/11/.

26. Chandra Bozelko, "Prisons That Withhold Menstrual Pads Humiliate Women and Violate Basic Rights," *The Guardian*, June 12, 2015, https://www.theguardian.com/commentisfree/2015/ jun/12/prisons-menstrual-pads-humiliate-women-violate-rights.

27. "Women in the Criminal Justice System: Briefing Sheets, The Sentencing Project," May 2007, accessed April 8, 2017, http://www. sentencingproject.org/wp-content/uploads/2016/01/Women-in-the-Criminal-Justice-System-Briefing-Sheets.pdf.

28. Steve Suitts, *A New Majority: Low Income Students Now a Majority in the Nation's Public Schools* (Atlanta, GA: Southern Education Foundation, January 2015), http://www.southerneducation. org/getattachment/4ac62e27-5260-47a5-9d02-14896ec3a531/A-New-Majority-2015-Update-Low-Income-Students-Now.aspx.

29. Sophia Addy, William Engelhardt, and Curtis Skinner, *Basic Facts About Low-Income Children* (New York: National Center for Children in Poverty, January 2013), http://www.nccp.org/publications/pub_1074.html.

30. US Department of Health and Human Services, "Poverty Guidelines," Office of the Assistant Secretary for Planning and Evaluation, accessed March 25, 2017, https://aspe.hhs.gov/poverty-guidelines.

31. "Girls 'too poor' to Buy Sanitary Protection Missing School," BBC, March 17, 2017, http://www.bbc.com/news/uk-39266056.

32. Kirk Carapezza, "The Number of Hungry and Homeless Students Rises along with College Costs," National Public Radio, February 8, 2017, http://www.npr.org/sections/ed/2017/02/08/513902272/the-number-of-hungry-and-homeless-students-rises-along-with-college-costs.

33. Kathleen Megan, "Connecticut College Student Fighting Menstruation Stigma with Free Tampons, Pads," *Hartford Courant*, November 8, 2016, http://www.courant.com/education/hc-connecticut-college-menstruation-pilot-1108-20161107-story.html.

34. Abigail Jones, "Free Tampons and Pads are Making Their Way to U.S. Colleges, High Schools and Middle Schools," *Newsweek*, September 6, 2016, http://www.newsweek.com/free-tampons-pads-us-schools-496083.

35. Courtney Couillard, "Columbia Should Pay for My Period," *Columbia Spectator*, February 19, 2016, http://spc.columbiaspectator.com/opinion/2016/02/19/columbia-should-pay-my-period.

36. Rebekah Rennick, "This One Feminist Decided to Pick Locks. Here's Why." *Grinnell Underground Magazine*, September 11, 2015, http://gumag.net/this-one-feminist-decided-to-pick-locks-heres-why/.

37. Jake New, "If Condoms Are Free, Why Aren't Tampons?" *Inside Higher Ed*, March 11, 2016, https://www.insidehighered.com/news/2016/03/11/students-demand-free-tampons-campus.

Chapter Four: Carrie at the Prom

1. Kiran Gandhi, "Going with the Flow: Blood & Sisterhood at the London Marathon," Medium, July 20, 2015, https://medium.com/endless/going-with-the-flow-blood-sisterhood-at-the-london-marathon-f719b98713e7#.q6gpgh1xr.
2. Gandhi, "Blood & Sisterhood at the London Marathon."
3. Amy Jo Clark and Miriam Weaver, "Chicks on the Right: Progressive Feminism Taken to the Absurd," *USA TODAY*, August 20, 2015, http://www.usatoday.com/story/opinion/2015/08/20/chicks-right-progressive-feminism-taken-absurd/32047403/.
4. Oliver JJ Lane, "'Free-Bleeding' Feminist Runs Marathon During Period Without Tampons . . . Bleeds All Over Herself," *Breitbart*, August 10, 2015, http://www.breitbart.com/london/2015/08/10/apparently-free-bleeding-is-a-thing-now-and-social-justice-warriors-want-you-to-know-all-about-it/.
5. Noreen Malone, "Panty Raid," *New York* magazine, February 2, 2016, http://nymag.com/thecut/2016/01/thinx-miki-agrawal-c-v-r.html.
6. Emma Gray, "The Removal of Rupi Kaur's Instagram Photos Shows How Terrified We Are of Periods," *Huffington Post*, March 27, 2015, http://www.huffingtonpost.com/2015/03/27/rupi-kaur-period-instagram_n_6954898.html.
7. Meghan Markle, "How Periods Affect Potential," *TIME*, March 8, 2017, http://time.com/4694568/meghan-markle-period-stigma/.
8. Simon Briggs, "Martina Navratilova Offers Support to Heather Watson after Brit Complains of Period Pains at Australian Open," *The Telegraph*, January 22, 2015, http://www.telegraph.co.uk/sport/tennis/australianopen/11361893/Martina-Navratilova-offers-support-to-Heather-Watson-after-Brit-complains-of-period-pains-at-Australian-Open.html.
9. Martha Cliff, "Sport's Last Taboo? Czech Star Petra Kvitova Admits It's 'difficult' for Female Players to Compete While Having Their Period," *Daily Mail*, June 30, 2015, http://www.dailymail.co.uk/femail/article-3144279/Czech-star-Petra-Kvitova-admits-s-difficult-female-players-competing-having-period.html.
10. Emily Feng, "Uninhibited Chinese Swimmer, Discussing Her Period, Shatters Another Barrier," *New York Times*, August 16,

2016, https://www.nytimes.com/2016/08/17/world/asia/china-fu-yuanhui-period-olympics.html.

11. Soraya Nadia McDonald, "Larry Wilmore Hosted a Refreshingly Frank Discussion about Menstruation on the 'Nightly Show,'" *Washington Post*, May 7, 2015, https://www.washingtonpost.com/news/arts-and-entertainment/wp/2015/05/07/larry-wilmore-hosted-a-refreshingly-frank-discussion-about-menstruation-on-the-nightly-show/?utm_term=.16182af9870b.

12. Eliana Dockerman, "These Girls are Fighting Sexism with a Video Game about Tampons," *TIME*, September 15, 2014, http://time.com/3319562/tampon-run-girls-who-code/.

13. Jenny Kutner, "Salon Talks with Gaming Girl Wonders Andy Gonzalez & Sophie Houser," *Salon*, February 18, 2015, http://www.salon.com/2015/02/18/i_don%E2%80%99t_think_a_guy_would_have_made_tampon_run_salon_talks_with_gaming_girl_wonders_andy_gonzalez_sophie_houser/.

14. Christina Cauterucci, "Girls Should Learn About Their Periods from This Cutesy Board Game," *Slate*, September 13, 2016, http://www.slate.com/blogs/xx_factor/2016/09/13/the_period_game_aims_to_teach_girls_about_menstruation_in_a_fun_new_way.html.

15. "Child's Play: Millennial Women Drive Sales of Adult Coloring Books," Nielsen, July 1, 2016, accessed April 7, 2017, http://www.nielsen.com/us/en/insights/news/2016/childs-play-millennial-women-drive-sales-of-adult-coloring-books.html.

16. Alli Maloney, "See the First Period-Themed Coloring Book," *Teen Vogue*, November 2, 2016, http://www.teenvogue.com/story/first-period-coloring-book-images.

17. "Kiyama Movement," accessed March 12, 2017, http://www.kiyamamovement.com/.

18. "The Murphy's Law of Menstruation," FreetheTampons.org, http://www.freethetampons.org/uploads/4/6/0/3/46036337/ftt_infographic.pdf.

19. "Menstrual Hygiene Day," accessed March 12, 2017, http://menstrualhygieneday.org/.

Chapter Five: Lady's Days

1. Eve Hartley, "Stella Creasy Perfectly Sums Up Why Tampons Are Not 'Luxury' Items," *Huffington Post*, October 27, 2015, http://www.huffingtonpost.co.uk/2015/10/27/stella-creasy-perfectly-sums-up-why-tampons-are-not-luxury-items_n_8399402.html.

2. Anna Bessendorf, *From Cradle to Cane: The Cost of Being a Female Consumer: A Study of Gender Pricing in New York City* (New York: New York City Department of Consumer Affairs, December 2015), https://www1.nyc.gov/assets/dca/downloads/pdf/partners/Study-of-Gender-Pricing-in-NYC.pdf.

3. Libby Brooks, "Period Poverty: Call to Tackle the Hidden Side of Inequality," *The Guardian*, December 12, 2016, https://www.theguardian.com/society/2016/dec/12/period-poverty-call-to-tackle-the-hidden-side-of-inequality.

4. Vicky Hallett, "What Kenya Can Teach the U.S. About Menstrual Pads," National Public Radio, May 10, 2016, http://www.npr.org/sections/goatsandsoda/2016/05/10/476741805/what-kenya-can-teach-the-u-s-about-menstrual-pads.

5. Neville Okwaro, Sailas Nyareza, Jenny Karlsen, and Inga Winkler, *First National Training of Trainers on Menstrual Hygiene Management—Kenya: Workshop Report* (Geneva: Water Supply and Sanitation Collaborative Council, 2016), http://wsscc.org/2016/08/10/wsscc-menstrual-hygiene-management-training-kenya-breaks-silence-menstruation/.

6. American Medical Association, "AMA Adopts New Policies on Final Days of Annual Meeting," AMA-ASSN.org, June 15, 2016, accessed March 25, 2017, https://www.ama-assn.org/ama-adopts-new-policies-final-day-annual-meeting.

7. Erwin Chemerinsky, "In Tampon Tax, a Discriminatory California Policy Lives On," *Los Angeles Daily News*, September 21, 2016, http://www.dailynews.com/opinion/20160921/in-tampon-tax-a-discriminatory-california-policy-lives-on-erwin-chemerinsky.

8. Kira Davis, "Menstrual Equity, or What Happens When Government Officials Have Too Much Time on Their Hands," *The Resurgent*, February 21, 2017, http://theresurgent.com/menstrual-

equity-or-what-happens-when-government-officials-have-too-much-time-on-their-hands/.

9. Evan Siegfried, "What Republicans Have to Learn from the Women's March," *New York Times*, January 23, 2017, https://www.nytimes.com/2017/01/23/opinion/what-republicans-have-to-learn-from-the-womens-march.html.

10. Catherine Rampell, "The 'Tampon Tax' Fraud," *Washington Post*, January 25, 2016, https://www.washingtonpost.com/opinions/the-tampon-tax-fraud/2016/01/25/fb9c7e68-c3a8-11e5-8965-0607e0e265ce_story.html?utm_term=.8219bad6ea4c.

11. Samantha Allen, "The 'Tampon Tax' Outrage is Overblown," *The Daily Beast*, October 22, 2015, http://www.thedailybeast.com/articles/2015/10/22/the-tampon-tax-outrage-is-overblown.html.

12. The *Times* Editorial Board, "Editorial: Keep Taxing Diapers and Tampons," *Los Angeles Times*, February 29, 2016, http://www.latimes.com/opinion/editorials/la-ed-sales-tax-20160229-story.html.

13. Prachi Gupta, "Why the Hell Are Tampons Still Taxed?" *Cosmopolitan*, October 15, 2015, http://www.cosmopolitan.com/politics/news/a47780/abolish-tampon-tax-america/.

14. Yiannapoulos, "*Guardian*: World Needs Taxpayer Subsidised Tampons."

15. "Mayor de Blasio Signs Legislation Increasing Access to Feminine Hygiene Products for Students, Shelter Residents and Inmates," NYC.gov, July 13, 2016, accessed March 25, 2017, http://www1.nyc.gov/office-of-the-mayor/news/611-16/mayor-de-blasio-signs-legislation-increasing-access-feminine-hygiene-products-students-.

16. Menstrual Equity for All Act of 2017, H.R. 972, 115th Cong. (2017), accessed March 26, 2017, https://www.congress.gov/bill/115th-congress/house-bill/972.

Chapter Six: Shark Week

1. Clare O'Connor, "Why 2016 Was the Year of the Women-Led Period Startup," *Forbes*, December 22, 2016, https://www.forbes.com/sites/clareoconnor/2016/12/22/why-2016-was-the-year-of-the-women-led-period-startup/.

2. "Global Market Study on Feminine Hygiene Products: Increasing Awareness of Female Health and Hygiene and Changing Lifestyle to Boost Demand During Forecast Period," August 2016, accessed March 25, 2017. http://www.persistencemarketresearch.com/market-research/feminine-hygiene-product-market.asp.
3. Mona Chalabi, "How Many Women Don't Use Tampons?" *FiveThirtyEight*, October 1, 2015, https://fivethirtyeight.com/datalab/how-many-women-dont-use-tampons/.
4. Hiroko Tabuchi, "Menstruation Joins the Economic Conversation," *New York Times*, April 21, 2016, https://www.nytimes.com/2016/04/22/business/menstruation-joins-the-economic-conversation.html?_r=0.
5. Elizabeth Segran, "Bleeding on the Job: A Menstruation Investigation," *Fast Company*, July 25, 2016, https://www.fastcompany.com/3061417/bleeding-on-the-job-a-menstruation-investigation.
6. Jennifer Miller, "A New Crop of Companies Want to Make Your Period Empowering," *BloombergBusinessweek*, May 18, 2016, https://www.bloomberg.com/news/articles/2016-05-18/a-new-crop-of-companies-want-to-make-your-period-empowering.
7. Danielle Paquette, "Why Your Daughter May Never Need to Buy a Tampon," *Washington Post*, October 22, 2016, https://www.washingtonpost.com/news/wonk/wp/2016/10/22/its-liberating-the-revolutionary-products-transforming-the-way-women-think-about-their-periods/.
8. Andi Zeisler, *We Were Feminists Once: From Riot Grrl to Cover Girl, The Buying and Selling of a Political Movement* (New York: Public Affairs, 2016).
9. Amanda Hess, "The Trump Resistance Will Be Commercialized," *New York Times*, March 17, 2017, https://www.nytimes.com/2017/03/17/arts/the-trump-resistance-will-be-commercialized.html?_r=0.
10. Ann Borowski, "Are American Women Turning to Reusable and Greener Menstrual Products Due to Health and Environmental Pollution Concerns?" (thesis, RIT, 2011), http://scholarworks.rit.edu/cgi/viewcontent.cgi?article=1547&context=theses.
11. Rosie Spinks, "Disposable Tampons Aren't Sustainable, But Do Women Want to Talk about It?" *The Guardian*, April 27, 2015,

https://www.theguardian.com/sustainable-business/2015/apr/27/disposable-tampons-arent-sustainable-but-do-women-want-to-talk-about-it.

12. Rachel Abrams, "Under Pressure, Feminine Product Makers Disclose Ingredients," *New York Times*, October 26, 2015, https://www.nytimes.com/2015/10/27/business/under-pressure-feminine-product-makers-disclose-ingredients.html.

13. "TOMS," accessed March 12, 2017, http://www.toms.com/.

14. Miller, "A New Crop of Companies Want to Make Your Period Empowering."

15. Segran, "Bleeding on the Job: A Menstruation Investigation."

16. Jenny Kutner, "Will the New York City Subway Ban These Ads for Using the Word Period?" *Mic*, October 20, 2015, https://mic.com/articles/127022/will-the-new-york-city-subway-ban-these-thinx-ads-for-using-the-word-period.

17. Erin Nelson, "How Feminist Brands are Using Storytelling to Upend Age-Old Taboos," *Contently*, April 22, 2016, https://contently.com/strategist/2016/04/22/period-piece/.

18. Malone, "Panty Raid."

19. "Free the Tampons," accessed March 12, 2017, http://www.freethetampons.org/.

20. "Talking About Periods: An International Investigation," HelloClue.com, accessed April 8, 2017, http://www.helloclue.com/survey.html.

Chapter Seven: Parting the Red Sea

1. Jasmine Tucker and Caitlin Lowell, *National Snapshot: Poverty Among Women & Families, 2015* (Washington, DC: National Women's Law Center, 2015), http://nwlc.org/resources/national-snapshot-poverty-among-women-families-2015/.

2. "70% of the Nation's Poor are Women and Children," *Legal Momentum*, accessed March 25, 2017, https://www.legalmomentum.org/women-and-poverty-america.

3. Shriver, *A Woman's Nation Pushes Back from the Brink*.

4. Rich Morin, "The Politics and Demographics of Food Stamp Recipients," Pew Research Center, July 12, 2013, http://

www.pewresearch.org/fact-tank/2013/07/12/the-politics-and-demographics-of-food-stamp-recipients/.

5. "A Quick Guide to SNAP Eligibility and Benefits," Center on Budget and Policy Priorities, September 30, 2016, accessed March 25, 2017, http://www.cbpp.org/research/a-quick-guide-to-snap-eligibility-and-benefits.

6. M. V. Badgett, Laura E. Durso, and Alyssa Schneebaum, *New Patterns of Poverty in the Lesbian, Gay and Bisexual Community* (Los Angeles: The Williams Institute, UCLA School of Law, June 2013), https://williamsinstitute.law.ucla.edu/research/census-lgbt-demographics-studies/lgbt-poverty-update-june-2013/.

7. Megan V. Smith, Anna Kruse, Alison Weir, and Joanne Goldblum, "Diaper Need and Impact on Child Health," *Pediatrics* 132, 2 (2013), http://pediatrics.aappublications.org/content/pediatrics/early/2013/07/23/peds.2013-0597.full.pdf.

8. "Tampons: FSA Eligibility," FSAStore.com, accessed March 26, 2017, https://fsastore.com/FSA-Eligibility-List/T/Tampons-E693.aspx.

9. "Catalyst: Women CEOs of the S&P 500," Catalyst.org, March 14, 2017, accessed March 26, 2017, http://www.catalyst.org/knowledge/women-ceos-sp-500.

10. Julie Vogtman and Katherine Gallagher Robbins, *Fair Pay for Women Requires a Fair Minimum Wage* (Washington, DC: National Women's Law Center, May 2015), http://nwlc.org/resources/fair-pay-women-requires-fair-minimum-wage/.

11. "U.S. Bureau of Labor Statistics Report 1054, Characteristics of Minimum Wage Workers, 2014," accessed April 23, 2017, https://www.bls.gov/opub/reports/minimum-wage/archive/characteristics-of-minimum-wage-workers-2014.pdf.

12. "America's Women and the Wage Gap," National Partnership for Women & Families, October 2016, http://www.nationalpartnership.org/research-library/workplace-fairness/fair-pay/americas-women-and-the-wage-gap.pdf.

13. "2012 Workforce Diversity," Walmart, accessed March 26, 2017, http://cdn.corporate.walmart.com/d5/34/df2a49394a7797f-5399beeb67f9d/2012-workforce-diversity-report.pdf.

14. "Walmart on Tax Day: How Taxpayers Subsidize America's Biggest Employer and Richest Family," Americans For Tax Fairness,

April 2014, https://americansfortaxfairness.org/files/Walmart-on-Tax-Day-Americans-for-Tax-Fairness-11.pdf.

15. Paul Ziobro, "Wal-Mart to End One-Day Wait for Sick Pay," *Wall Street Journal*, February 201, 2015, https://www.wsj.com/articles/wal-mart-to-end-one-day-wait-for-sick-pay-1424466584.

16. Annual Financials for "Wal-Mart Stores Inc." MarketWatch, accessed March 26, 2017, http://www.marketwatch.com/investing/stock/wmt/financials.

17. Alyssa Mastromonaco, *Who Thought This Was a Good Idea?: And Other Questions You Should Have Answers to When You Work in the White House* (New York: Twelve, 2017), 13-16.

18. Jessica Goldstein, "Thank Alyssa Mastromonaco for the White House Tampon Dispenser," ThinkProgress, March 29, 2017, https://thinkprogress.org/thank-alyssa-mastromonaco-for-that-white-house-tampon-dispenser-6e34a2059f8f.

19. United States Department of Labor, "Restroom and Sanitation Requirements," OSHA.gov, accessed March 26, 2017, https://www.osha.gov/SLTC/restrooms_sanitation/.

20. "United States Department of Labor, Standard Interpretation 1910.1030," OSHA.gov, accessed April 23, 2017, https://www.osha.gov/pls/oshaweb/owadisp.show_document?p_table=INTERPRETATIONS&p_id=20877.

21. "United States Department of Labor, Most Frequently Asked Questions Concerning the Bloodborne Pathogens Section," OSHA.gov, accessed April 23, 2017, https://www.osha.gov/pls/oshaweb/owadisp.show_document?p_table=INTERPRETATIONS&p_id=21010.

22. Emily Matchar, "Should Paid 'Menstrual Leave' Be a Thing?" *The Atlantic*, May 16, 2014, https://www.theatlantic.com/health/archive/2014/05/should-women-get-paid-menstrual-leave-days/370789/.

23. Kennedy Gondwe, "Zambia Women's 'Day Off for Periods' Sparks Debate," BBC, January 4, 2017, http://www.bbc.com/news/world-africa-38490513.

24. Anna Momigliano, "Giving Italian Women 'Menstrual Leave' May Backfire on Their Job Prospects," *Washington Post*, March 24, 2017, https://www.washingtonpost.com/news/worldviews/

wp/2017/03/24/giving-italian-women-menstrual-leave-may-backfire-on-their-job-prospects/?utm_term=.9852c247171a.

25. "Johns Hopkins Medicine, Endometriosis," hopkinsmedicine.org, Accessed April 23, 2017, http://www.hopkinsmedicine.org/healthlibrary/conditions/gynecological_health/endometriosis_85,P00573/.

26. "Red School," accessed March 12, 2017, http://www.redschool.net/.

27. Ricki Lake, Abby Epstein, and Holly Grigg-Spall, "From Birth Control to Body Literacy: The Power of the Pro-Period Movement," *Alanis Morissette Blog*, March 4, 2016, http://alanis.com/contributors/birth-control-body-literacy-power-pro-period-movement/.

28. "Fact Sheet: Incarcerated Women and Girls," The Sentencing Project, November 2015, http://www.sentencingproject.org/wp-content/uploads/2016/02/Incarcerated-Women-and-Girls.pdf.

29. United Nations General Assembly, "United Nations Rules for the Treatment of Women Prisoners and Non-custodial Measures for Women Offenders (the Bangkok Rules)," July 22, 2010, accessed March 26, 2017, http://www.ohchr.org/Documents/Professional Interest/BangkokRules.pdf.

30. Goodman et al., *Reproductive Health Behind Bars in California*.

31. Tim Loc, "County Supervisors Vote to Ensure Tampon Access for Juvenile Detainees," LAist.com, January 24, 2017, http://laist.com/2017/01/24/supervisors_vote_for_tampons.php.

32. Florence v. Board of Chosen Freeholders of County of Burlington, slip-op, 566 U.S. ___ (2012), https://www.supremecourt.gov/opinions/11pdf/10-945.pdf.

33. Jonathan Mattise, "Private Reach Deal with Women Forced to Show Tampons," *U.S. News and World Report*, March 7, 2017, https://www.usnews.com/news/best-states/tennessee/articles/2017-03-07/agreement-reached-in-strip-search-suit-against-prison-firm.

34. Kristina Marusic, "The Sickening Truth about What It's Like to Get Your Period In Prison," *Women's Health*, July 7, 2016, http://www.womenshealthmag.com/life/women-jail-periods.

35. Chandra Bozelko, email message to author, January 23, 2017.

36. *The State of Homelessness in America 2016* (Washington, DC: National Alliance to End Homelessness, 2016), http://www. endhomelessness.org/library/entry/SOH2016#ChapterOne.

37. Mimi Kirk, "How Sacramento Rolled Out a Mobile Restroom for the Homeless," *The Atlantic* CityLab, December 2, 2016, http://www.citylab.com/cityfixer/2016/12/why-sacramentos-toilets-for-the-homeless-succeeded/509375/.

38. "#Pink Box Period Pack Dispenser," Share the Dignity, accessed March 26, 2017, http://www.sharethedignity.com.au/dignity-vending-machine.html.

39. Brooks, "Boots to Support Campaign to End 'Period Poverty.'"

40. Ann C. Herbert, Ana Maria Ramirez, Grace Lee, Savannah J. North, Melanie S. Askari, Rebecca L. West, Marni, Sommer, "Puberty Experiences of Low-Income Girls in the United States: A Systematic Review of Qualitative Literature from 2000-2014," *Journal of Adolescent Health* 60, 4 (2017), 363-379.

41. "State Laws and Policies: Sex and HIV Education," Guttmacher Institute, April 1, 2017, accessed April 3, 2017, https://www. guttmacher.org/state-policy/explore/sex-and-hiv-education.

42. "Toni the Tampon," TonitheTampon.com, accessed March 26, 2017, https://www.tonithetampon.com/thecoloringbook.

43. Leonardo Blair, "'Toni the Tampon' Coloring Book That Teaches Men Get Periods Amounts to Child Abuse, Says Expert," *Christian Post*, March 9, 2017, http://www.christianpost.com/news/toni-the-tampon-coloring-book-that-teaches-men-get-periods-amounts-to-child-abuse-says-expert-177040/.

44. "School's Out! Not Before One Last Lesson on Menstruation," *The Green Feminine Hygiene Queen Blog*, June 26, 2014, http://www.maximhy.com/blog/2014/06/26/schools-out-not-before-one-last-lesson-on-menstruation/.

45. Rebecca Alvandi, email message to author, December 10, 2015.

46. Andrew R. Flores, Jody L. Herman, Gary J. Gates, and Taylor N. T. Brown, *How Many Adults Identify as Transgender in the United States?* (Los Angeles: Williams Institute, UCLA School of Law, June 2016), https://williamsinstitute.law.ucla.edu/wp-content/uploads/How-Many-Adults-Identify-as-Transgender-in-the-United-States.pdf.

47. Crosby Burns, "The Gay and Transgender Wage Gap," Center for American Progress, April 16, 2012, https://www.americanprogress.org/issues/lgbt/news/2012/04/16/11494/the-gay-and-transgender-wage-gap/.
48. Brad Sears and Lee Badgett, "Beyond Stereotypes: Poverty in the LGBT Community," *Tides-Momentum* 4 (June 2012), https://williamsinstitute.law.ucla.edu/headlines/beyond-stereotypes-poverty-in-the-lgbt-community/.
49. "Housing & Homelessness," National Center for Transgender Equality, accessed March 26, 2017, http://www.transequality.org/issues/housing-homelessness.
50. Jaime M. Grant, Lisa Mottet, Justin Tanis, *Injustice at Every Turn: A Report of the National Transgender Discrimination Survey*, (Washington, DC: The National Gay and Lesbian Task Force and the National Center for Transgender Equality, 2011), http://www.thetaskforce.org/static_html/downloads/reports/reports/ntds_summary.pdf.
51. Ibid.
52. Zoyander Street, "Yes, Men Can Have Periods and We Need to Talk About Them," *The Daily Beast*, September 21, 2016, http://www.thedailybeast.com/articles/2016/09/21/yes-men-can-have-periods-and-we-need-to-talk-about-them.html.
53. Parker Molly, "A Gynecologist Tweeted about Periods, and a Great Discussion about Gender Happened," *Upworthy*, September 6, 2016, http://www.upworthy.com/a-gynecologist-tweeted-about-periods-and-a-great-discussion-about-gender-happened.
54. Jody Herman, *Gendered Restrooms and Minority Stress: The Public Regulation of Gender and its Impact on Transgender People's Lives*, (Los Angeles: The Williams Institute, UCLA School of Law, 2013), https://williamsinstitute.law.ucla.edu/wp-content/uploads/Herman-Gendered-Restrooms-and-Minority-Stress-June-2013.pdf.
55. S. E. James, J. L. Herman, S. Rankin, M. Keisling, L. Mottet, M. Anafi, *The Report of the 2015 U.S. Transgender Survey* (National Center for Transgender Equality, 2016), http://www.ustranssurvey.org/.
56. Corinne Jurney, "North Carolina's 'Bathroom Bill' Has Flushed Away $600 Million in Business," *Forbes*, November 3, 2016,

https://www.forbes.com/sites/corinnejurney/2016/11/03/north-carolinas-bathroom-bill-flushes-away-nearly-1-billion-in-busi-ness-and-governor-mccrorys-re-election-hopes/#1ab3cdd5682a.

57. Emery P. Dalesio and Jonathan Drew, "Price tag of North Carolina's LGBT Law: $3.76B," Associated Press, March 27, 2017, http://bigstory.ap.org/article/fa4528580f3e4a01bb68bcb272f1f0f8/ap-exclusive-bathroom-bill-cost-north-carolina-376b.

58. Jones, "Free Tampons and Pads are Making their Way to U.S. Colleges, High Schools and Middle Schools."

59. Jaime M. Grant, Lisa A. Mottet, and Justin Tanis, *National Trans-gender Discrimination Survey Report on Health and Health Care*, (Washington, DC: National Center for Transgender Equality and the National Gay and Lesbian Task Force, October 2010), http://www.thetaskforce.org/static_html/downloads/resources_and_tools/ntds_report_on_health.pdf.

60. Jeff Green, "LGBT Purchasing Power Near $1 Trillion Rivals Other Minorities," *Bloomberg*, July 20, 2016, https://www.bloomberg.com/news/articles/2016-07-20/lgbt-purchasing-power-near-1-trillion-rivals-other-minorities.

61. "Underwear for People With Periods," accessed March 26, 2017, https://www.shethinx.com/pages/people-with-periods.

62. "Classify Your Medical Device," U.S. Food & Drug Administra-tion, updated July 29, 2014, accessed March 26, 2017, https://www.fda.gov/MedicalDevices/DeviceRegulationandGuidance/Overview/ClassifyYourDevice/.

63. Fetters, "The Tampon: A History."

64. "Cosmetic Labeling Guide," U.S. Food & Drug Administration, updated December 23, 2016, accessed March 26, 2017, https://www.fda.gov/Cosmetics/Labeling/Regulations/ucm126444.htm.

65. *The Deadly Chemicals in Cotton*, (London: Environmental Jus-tice Foundation, 2007), http://ejfoundation.org/sites/default/files/public/the_deadly_chemicals_in_cotton.pdf.

66. Robin Danielson Feminine Hygiene Product Safety Act of 2017, H.R. 2379, 115th Cong. (2017-2018), accessed June 17, 2017. https://www.congress.gov/bill/115th-congress/house-bill/2379/text.

67. Elizabeth Nash, Rachel Benson Gold, Zohra Ansari-Thomas, Olivia Cappello, and Lizamarie Mohammed, "Policy Trends in

the States: 2016," Guttmacher Institute, January 3, 2017, https://www.guttmacher.org/article/2017/01/policy-trends-states-2016.

68. Elizabeth Nash, Rachel Benson Gold, Zohra Ansari-Thomas, Olivia Cappello, and Lizamarie Mohammed, "Laws Affecting Reproductive Health and Rights: State Policy Trends in the First Quarter of 2017," Guttmacher Institute, April 12, 2017, https://www.guttmacher.org/article/2017/04/laws-affecting-reproductive-health-and-rights-state-policy-trends-first-quarter-2017.

69. Elena Mejia Lutz, "Texas Lawmakers Push Bipartisan Effort for Tax-Free Tampons," *The Texas Tribune*, December 6, 2016, https://www.texastribune.org/2016/12/06/texas-lawmakers-push-bipartisan-effort-tax-free-ta/.

70. Hannah Smothers, "Women are Urging Each Other to Send Bloody Tampons to the Texas Governor," *Cosmopolitan*, December 9, 2016, http://www.cosmopolitan.com/sex-love/a8480433/texas-women-protest-used-tampons/.

71. "Ashley Judd FULL Speech at 'Women's March' in Washington, DC. 'I am a Nasty Woman,'" YouTube, accessed March 25, 2017, https://www.youtube.com/watch?v=VNXMOxBbt6g.

72. "Giving USA: 2015 Was America's Most-Generous Year Ever," Giving USA, June 13, 2016, accessed March 26, 2017, https://givingusa.org/giving-usa-2016/.

73. "All In For Her: A Call to Action," Women Moving Millions, 2014, http://allinforher.org/sites/default/files/ALL_IN_FOR_HER-A_Call_To_Action.pdf.

74. Tom Watson, "A Gender Lens for Giving: Women in Philanthropy Urged to Invest More in Women and Girls," *Forbes*, September 18, 2014, https://www.forbes.com/sites/tomwatson/2014/09/18/a-gender-lens-for-giving-women-in-philanthropy-urged-to-invest-more-in-women-and-girls/#1032f3cd38fe.

75. "Girls and Women," Clinton Global Foundation, accessed March 26, 2017, https://www.clintonfoundation.org/our-work/by-topic/girls-and-women.

76. Chelsea Clinton, "Why We Need To Talk About Menstruation and Breastfeeding," *Well + Good*, April 14, 2017, https://www.wellandgood.com/good-advice/chelsea-clinton-menstruation-breastfeeding-taboo-hurts-women/slide/4/.

77. Sue-Lynn Moses, "Menstruation Holds Back Millions of Poor Women. Does This Outfit Have a Solution?" *Inside Philanthropy*, August 10, 2015, https://www.insidephilanthropy.com/home/2015/8/10/menstruation-holds-back-millions-of-poor-women-does-this-out.html.

78. Sue-Lynn Moses, "Menstruation Frustration: Why Don't More Funders Care About This Key Global Issue?" *Inside Philanthropy*, June 3, 2016, https://www.insidephilanthropy.com/home/2016/6/3/menstruation-frustration-why-dont-more-funders-care-about-th.html.

79. Lisa Schechtman, "Menstruation Matters: Why Menstrual Hygiene Management is Core to our Contract with the Future," *Impatient Optimists*, The Bill & Melinda Gates Foundation, May 28, 2015, http://www.impatientoptimists.org/Posts/2015/05/Menstruation-Matters-Why-Menstrual-Hygiene-Management-is-Core-to-Our-Contract-with-the-Future.

80. Moses, "Menstruation Frustration: Why Don't More Funders Care About This Key Global Issue?"

81. Watson, "A Gender Lens for Giving."

Final Thoughts

1. Kiran Gandhi, "Fight Period Stigma," *Motto*, June 9, 2016, http://motto.time.com/4362473/fight-period-stigma/.

INDEX

INDEX